An English graduate of Aberdeen University, Eric Linklater has been intermittently a soldier and for longer periods a most prolific writer. He was assistant editor of *The Times of India* from 1925–7 and Lord Rector of Aberdeen University from 1945–8. His previous publications include: *Poet's Pub, Juan in America, Magnus Merriman* and *Private Angelo*.

The Voyage
of the Challenger

Eric Linklater

CARDINAL

This book was produced by George Rainbird Ltd,
Marble Arch House, 44 Edgware Road, London w2
and edited and designed by Tony Birks

First published 1972 by John Murray (Publishers) Ltd
CARDINAL edition first published in 1974
by Sphere Books Ltd, 30/32 Gray's Inn Road,
London wc1x 8jl

Filmset by Jolly & Barber Ltd, Rugby
Colour plates printed by Westerham Press Ltd, Westerham, Kent
Text printed by Jarrold and Sons Ltd, Norwich

ISBN 0 351 17223 8

Contents

List of colour plates

Acknowledgments

Invaluable in the preparation of this book has been the help of the Royal Society of Edinburgh.

In collecting and compiling the illustrations, Tony Birks would like to acknowledge the assistance of Sir Alister Hardy, the Department of Zoology, University of Oxford; Dr John Wiseman of the Department of Mineralogy, British Museum, Mr E. H. H. Archibald and Commander George Naish of the National Maritime Museum, Greenwich, Mr Arnold Madgwick of the National Institute of Oceanography, Sir Maurice Yonge, President of the Royal Society of Edinburgh, and in particular, Dr John Tait of the Challenger Expedition Centenary.

ROBERT JAMESON, ESQ. F. R. S. L & E.

REGIUS PROFESSOR OF NATURAL HISTORY IN THE UNIVERSITY OF EDINBURGH.

1 Edinburgh and the Navy

In the long century from the mournful triumph of Trafalgar to the German challenge in 1914 the Royal Navy maintained, over the oceans of the world, an authority that assured the peaceful traffic of all nations, no matter how deeply disturbed they were behind their own frontiers; but who remembers the ships that had fought – in the years before an oceanic peace was won – to create it in such strength that there came into being a tradition of peace?

The *Golden Hind* and Grenville's *Revenge* are not quite forgotten, but what of Rodney's *Formidable*, Hood's *Barfleur*, old Black Dick Howe's *Queen Charlotte*, and forty others whose names would fill a chorus of victory if anyone could recall them?

There were, too, ships that won no glory in loud fleet action but worked against the enmity of arctic weather, the violence of hurricanes and tropic storms, to gather a little knowledge of those tempestuous parts of the earth that cover its crust, not with mountains, cities, and savannahs, but with lunar tides and the ever changing, unpredictable seas that lie between the Roaring Forties and the fog-haunted Bering Straits. Ships of this sort, serving a duty to science, have rarely been much regarded. Cook and his *Resolution* may have a limited immortality; Anson and his *Centurion* – though their interests were not specifically scientific – deserve it; as do the unfortunate Sir John Franklin and the lost *Erebus* and *Terror*.

But there were many more: little, unnoticed ships that sailed under the White Ensign on voyages of the most arduous sort, for unspectacular rewards and the tedious investigation of unknown depths and unsuspected reefs from the Persian

Gulf to tortuous channels beyond Batavia, from Baffin Bay to the farthest atolls of the Pacific. Their history and their achievements are recorded only in scientific journals or, by inference, in the Admiralty's Pilot Books.

To be brief about it, the Royal Navy's daily work and constant toil have not consisted only of dislodging or disappointing the attempts which, from time to time, have been made to contest its authority; but have been much occupied by mapping, charting, sounding and exploring the oceans that carried until quite recently all the far-ranging traffic of the world. For many years ships had been commissioned to pursue knowledge only, and in 1872 the corvette *Challenger* set out on a voyage that made oceanography a science in its own right.

Where praise is due – and praise is due in plenty – it may be that priority should be given to the Royal Navy, but close behind – as close as the trigger that fires the cartridge in a loaded gun – was the University of Edinburgh which, since the second half of the eighteenth century, had been expanding in virtue and increasing its influence. Its reputation for scholarship was generously based on its Medical School and Moral Philosophy, and in the earlier years of its progress towards a continental fame its teaching was acclaimed far beyond that of Oxford or Cambridge; largely, perhaps, because professors drew no salary but depended on the fees their students paid. Physics and chemistry were taught by men of recognized authority, students were encouraged to explore the opportunities offered by applied science, and in the last third of the nineteenth century there was a revival of interest in a vast, unfathomed mystery – literally unfathomed – that recurrently had exercised some of the liveliest minds in Edinburgh since that century's earliest years, when a student possessed of uncommon experience became friendly with a professor of rare sympathy and understanding.

The student was William Scoresby, who at the age of eleven had gone to sea with his father, the master of a whaling ship, and a few years later sat down in the classroom of Robert Jameson, Professor of Natural History in Edinburgh from 1804 till 1854. Scoresby, by immediate experience, had learnt a great deal about whales and the Arctic and, in the happy fashion of genius, acquired other knowledge and later surveyed, with scrupulous care, much of East Greenland. In a reversal of the usual habit of a university he had so much influence on his professor that for forty or fifty years scarcely a ship, chartered for research, left Britain without a biologist who had been taught by Robert Jameson.

Charles Darwin was one of his students, and so was Edward Forbes, who succeeded to his Chair and died a few months later. But Forbes, before the age of forty, had made his contribution to marine science – a rash, opinionated contribution that stimulated further investigation and was soon disproved – by his assertion that, in all probability, animal life in the sea did not exist at a greater depth than three hundred fathoms. Forbes had entered the university as a medical student, but lost sight of his original purpose as he listened to Jameson's lectures and learnt of a new sort of dredge designed for naturalists interested in the life of the sea's depth or on its

Edward Forbes, 1815–54, pupil of Robert Jameson, and later Professor of Natural History at Edinburgh. His theory about the limits of life in the oceans was wrong.

unknown bottom. He went dredging in the Aegean, he plumbed the record depth of two hundred and thirty fathoms, and to lower depths gave the name of the Azoic Zone: the zone, that is, where life could not exist.

It was entirely appropriate that he who demolished this theory was a subsequent Professor of Natural History in his own university: Charles Wyville Thomson, like Forbes before him, had entered as a medical student, but found more compelling attractions in botany, geology, zoology – and dredging. He went to Norway, and saw living specimens of animal life that had been brought up out of dark Norwegian fjords from depths below Forbes's azoic frontier. From Fleeming Jenkin, Edinburgh's first Professor of Engineering, he learnt that on a broken telegraph cable, sunk a thousand fathoms deep in the Mediterranean and hauled up for repair, animals – in the zoologist's category of animals – had been found clinging to its frayed wires. Wyville Thomson was a man capable, not only of deduction, but of decision and action. He had a useful friend in Dr W. B. Carpenter of the Royal Society, and with the help of the Royal Society and the Admiralty's goodwill, Carpenter and Wyville Thomson borrowed HMS *Lightning* for a short period in the summer of 1868, and went dredging in the difficult waters between Shetland and the Faeroes. Not much was accomplished – the ship was crank, the weather savage – but they found abundant and varied life at more than six hundred fathoms, and discovered that the sea's temperature, beyond a certain depth, did not vary according to latitude, as had

The partnership between Charles Wyville Thomson LEFT *and William B. Carpenter* RIGHT *was a fruitful one for marine biology. In the ships* Lightning *and* Porcupine *they disproved Forbes' Azoic theory. When Wyville Thomson went to sea in* Challenger, *his captain was George Nares* FAR RIGHT.

been thought, but that great masses of water were in movement, each of them keeping its own temperature and its own course.

A year later the Admiralty let them have the use of a better vessel, HMS *Porcupine*, and persistent, enthusiastic dredging, some two or three hundred miles west of Ushant, discovered animal life from protozoa to molluscs at a depth of two thousand fathoms. A second cruise confirmed and enlarged what had been learnt aboard *Lightning* about the curiosities of oceanic circulation and temperature.

In 1870 Wyville Thomson became Professor of Natural History in Edinburgh, and – as a scholar with a taste for action – persuaded the Royal Society of London to ask the Government to lend and furnish one of Her Majesty's ships for a prolonged and arduous voyage of exploration across the oceans of the world. He and the Royal Society got a generous response. Mr Gladstone's Government agreed to subsidize the voyage, and HMS *Challenger* was manned and equipped for that other traditional service of the Royal Navy: not war, but the advancement of science. And in December, 1872, an expedition conceived and partly organized in the University of Edinburgh put to sea under the White Ensign.

14

2 Ship's Company

Challenger was a three-masted, square-rigged, wooden ship of 2,300 tons displacement and some 200 feet over all. Officially described as a steam corvette, she had an engine of rather more than 1,200 horse-power, but was still essentially a sailing-ship; for on a voyage designed for searching the depths of the sea she could not order her course from coaling station to coaling station, but used wind and canvas to make her passages, and kept her steam-engine for dredging, for harbour work, and emergencies that had to be anticipated though they could not be foreseen. All but two of her seventeen guns were removed, and in the space that they and their ammunition had occupied, laboratories and workrooms were built, storage found for trawls and dredges and the specimens they would collect. The ship became, in effect, a many-celled, seaworthy and sea-faring department of the Royal Society in which accommodation was provided for a staff of able-bodied scientists, the officers customary in a ship of that sort and size, a numerous crew, and the victuals required for them.

Her commanding officer was Captain George Nares, born in Aberdeen, in later years Sir George and an Arctic explorer of distinction. Under him were about twenty naval officers, including surgeons and engineers; while the civilian staff, whose Director was Professor Charles Wyville Thomson, numbered six, of whom he who subsequently became the most famous – who did more than anyone else to ensure recognition by the whole world of science of the *Challenger*'s unique achievement, her magisterial accumulation of oceanic knowledge – had been enlisted almost by chance, because he was available at the last moment. One of those originally invited by

15

Wyville Thomson to join his team had suddenly found it impossible to sustain his acceptance of that offer, and Professor Peter Guthrie Tait, physicist and another of those great Edinburgh teachers, recommended as a substitute John Murray, a young man, Canadian by birth but of Scottish parentage, who had been working in his laboratory.

Here, before the voyage begins, it seems proper to say something of Murray in his relative youth – he was thirty-one when *Challenger* put to sea – because it was he who raised the edifice that finally became a memorial to all his *compagnons de bord*: it was he who became identified with the voyage and whose wealth finally made possible the publication, in fifty ponderous volumes, of its momentous discoveries. For students of the present day it may be advisable to add that his habits, as a student, should not be regarded as a model of undergraduate behaviour unless the contemporary student, who reads of him, possesses that sort of genius which is instinctive, devoted to an issue that is the confluence of several related issues, and has inherited physical robustitude, an exceptional self-assurance, and an uncommon aptitude for getting his own way and reaping, from science and his own shrewdness, a large profit.

John Murray, born in Ontario, pursued his education in Scotland and on the continent, and found a dominating interest in natural history. At the University of Edinburgh he showed no respect for the tedious discipline of examinations, no wish to acquire the decoration of degrees, but worked at any subject which interested him: 'At literature with Masson, at anatomy with Goodsir and Turner, at chemistry

'Chemicals in drawers and jars in racks, all secured from accident from the rolling of the ship by many ingenious devices.' Space, too, was ingeniously devised, and the chemical laboratory LEFT *was installed in a gun bay.* RIGHT: *John Murray, pictured at the beginning of the voyage.*

with Crum Brown, at natural history with Allman, and he was, at least occasionally, to be seen at lectures in law and in theology; but the teacher who most powerfully interested him was undoubtedly Professor Tait, in whose laboratory he worked for more than one session.'[1]

In that laboratory Murray's director of studies was William Robertson Smith, temporarily a physicist, but later more widely known and deeply respected as theologian and orientalist; while in a helpful but more distant relationship were James Clerk Maxwell, the leading theoretical physicist of his century, and William Thomson – mathematician, natural philosopher, engineer – who became Lord Kelvin and from Glasgow exercised an inspiring influence for some fifty years.

As an intellectual John Murray was largely the product of Scottish scholarship and teaching; but to meet that scholarship and teaching his own genius came eagerly and with a brusque impatience. At Edinburgh he first enrolled as a medical student, but quickly tired of the lectures to which he had to listen, and boldly made use of a minimum of knowledge by offering himself as surgeon in the whaler *Jan Mayen*. The whaler left Peterhead in February, 1868, and Murray, during seven months in the Arctic, went ashore on Jan Mayen, that dreadful, cloud-girt, volcanic little island, nearly 8,000 feet high, in the Greenland Sea; explored some parts of Spitzbergen; collected marine organisms and dabbled in oceanography. In subsequent years he found friends whom he persuaded that summer holidays could profitably be spent in dredging the shallow seas of Scotland's Atlantic coast; and

[1]A. E. Shipley; *Sir John Murray, A Great Oceanographer*, in the Cornhill magazine, May 1914.

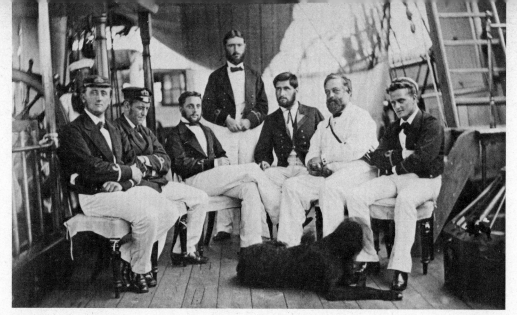

Wyville Thomson, all in white, sits among the sub-lieutenants. On his left is Lord George Campbell; on his right, Herbert Swire. All pose stiffly for the camera except for the Newfoundland dog, who never learned the meaning of a time-exposure.

in Skye met Professor William Thomson of Glasgow with whom he discussed the phenomenon of phosphorescence at sea. More remarkably, perhaps, he earned the rebuke of Robert Louis Stevenson – himself a somewhat undisciplined student – for his failure to pursue his studies in an orderly, purposive, and profitable fashion.[1]

Later in life Murray acquired the authoritarian voice and habit – the rough geniality, the dominating manner – that one associates with admirals of the eighteenth century, and in his latter years became rich enough to pay for the publication of the long shelf of volumes that record the *Challenger*'s findings in the oceans of the world. Something will be said of that in the concluding chapter of this narrative, but of Murray at the age of thirty-one enough has been told to suggest his uncommon quality, and there are others, who made the long voyage and wrote about it, who deserve formal introduction.

There were two young Naval officers who took sufficient interest in what they were doing – and had sufficient talent and ingenuity – to keep private journals in circumstances that gave them neither comfort nor privacy, for junior officers did not enjoy the luxury of cabins, and these were Sub-Lieutenant Lord George Campbell, youngest son of the eighth Duke of Argyll, and the Navigating Sub-Lieutenant, Herbert Swire. Their youth must be emphasized, for some of Swire's comments on the voyage, and his opinion of the grave scientists who were the most important persons aboard, are not over-burdened by respect. He was an unusually able and efficient young man; he could draw a little, paint a little, and some of the illustrations to his journal are vividly evocative; but with youthful insouciance he labelled all the learned representatives of the Royal Society 'the philosophers', he poked fun at their clothes both afloat and ashore, and even Wyville Thomson – rotund as befitted his

[1]W. N. Boog Watson; *Sir John Murray: A Chronic Student.*

years and inclined to a vanity that his eminence excused – did not escape his mockery. Swire, however, was not a frivolous youth; he found a vast pleasure in the beauty of sunset and the morning sky, he worked hard and well, and both he and Campbell are useful witnesses to some of the simple accidents and realities of the voyage which escaped the notice of their elders and betters.

Perhaps the most indefatigable of the scientists was H. N. Moseley, subsequently a Fellow of the Royal Society and Linacre Professor of Human and Comparative Anatomy in the University of Oxford. A man of sturdy build and kindly temper, his portrait shows searching, dedicated eyes and a moustache that obscures his mouth like a dark waterfall. It might be an exaggeration to say that his eyes missed nothing, but there is evidence of something very like panoptic vision in his book, called *Notes by a Naturalist*, that fills more than five hundred close-packed pages with precise and tireless recollection of the fauna and foreign people, of the flowers and fishes and intricately fashioned marine animals he had seen. It is a book that stands in curious contrast with the ornate volume published by J. J. Wild, an artist of Swiss nationality. To the official report[1] he contributed a great number of drawings, reproduced as woodcuts, of scenery and the minute creatures brought up in dredge or trawl; and with considerable charm he painted romantic pictures of tropical harbours. On the evidence of his book, however, he seems to have lived almost unaware of his ship-board companions, for he never mentions them. W. J. J. Spry, a Sub-Lieutenant in the engine-room, also composed a narrative, flat in tone but full of information, which went into many editions.

LEFT: *J. J. Wild. A self-portrait of the official artist of the expedition.* RIGHT: *Sub-Lt W. J. J. Spry.*

[1] *Report of the Scientific Results of the Exploring Voyage of HMS Challenger, 1873–76.* Subsequent reference will be, without addition, to 'the Report'.

20

Of minor interest, but perhaps worth noting, is the fact that none of the enlisted scientists was going to be extravagantly rewarded for his work and talent. Wyville Thomson would have the respectable salary of £1,000 a year, and Wild, who was his Secretary as well as official Artist, £400. But Henry Nottidge Moseley, curtly labelled Naturalist, and John Murray with the same designation, had only £200 apiece, as had John Young Buchanan, Chemist and Physicist.

Second-in-command to Captain Nares – already mentioned – was Commander J. L. P. Maclear, and the Navigating Lieutenant was T. H. Tizard who subsequently – in collaboration with Murray, Moseley, and Buchanan – was part-author of the Report. The seamanship and navigation of these senior officers were impeccable, and their discipline seems to have been quite unlike the iron-hard brutality that still dominated some ships of Her Majesty's Navy. Their discipline, indeed, may have been libertarian – there is no record of drastic punishment to mar the story – but they knew how to handle a ship in all conditions of weather, and from Antarctic ice, or the reefs and atolls of the ravelled Pacific, to the shrieking Straits of Magellan no navigational problem defeated, and may not even have perplexed them.

The ship's whole complement numbered about 240 of whom little can be told except that their quarters must have been cramped, and a good many, unimpressed

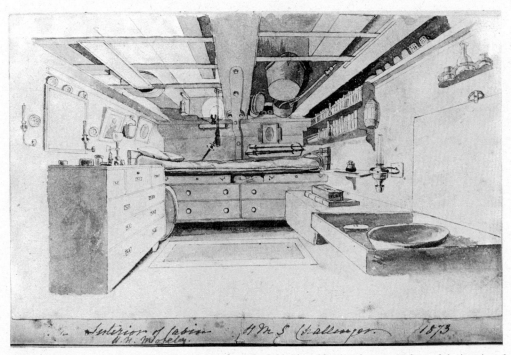

Henry Moseley, portrayed LEFT *after his return to Oxford, himself painted a watercolour of the interior of his cabin* ABOVE. *More spacious than most, it had room for his books, and his bathtub, but his pottery plates cannot have lasted long above the mirror in a heavy sea.*

by the importance of the voyage – and weary of the constant labour of dredging that was added to their normal duties – took advantage of the liberties they were allowed, and deserted. In the special circumstances of the voyage, and because of its unusual duration, they were granted generous shore-leave, and in South Africa and Australia there were obvious, and probably vocal, temptations to desert. Ratings were not highly paid, and sailors in the 1870's were not notably subject to domestic bonds.

H.M.S. CHALLENGER.

3 Atlantic isles, Atlantic depths

'We always kept in view,' wrote Wyville Thomson, 'that to explore the conditions of the deep sea was the primary object of our mission, and throughout the voyage we took every possible opportunity of making a deep-sea observation.'

At the outset of the voyage, however, it was the tumultuous surface of the sea that engaged their interest, and for ten unhappy days compelled them to observe its violent response to the unfettered wrath of the sky. The *Challenger* left Portsmouth on December 21st, 1872, and immediately ran into heavy weather. She lay rolling and plunging in the chops of the Channel, and hove-to in a south-westerly gale. Gale followed gale, and their Christmas dinner, says Swire philosophically, was 'very rough-going'. Secure in his possession of a well-mannered stomach and proven sea-legs, Swire is a little complacent and happily records that Wyville Thomson was sick and Wild seldom to be seen. John Murray was 'sailor-like', however, and Moseley, with whom Swire became very friendly, showed himself 'chock-full of science' even in those comfortless, early days when others rarely remained chock-full of anything.

Not until they had crossed the Bay of Biscay and were past Finisterre did the weather moderate, and then, in calmer seas, they began to practise the strange, arduous, and monotonous exercise that would so often occupy them, test their energy and try their temper, for three and a half years as they traversed and traversed again the endless waters that enclose humanity's smaller moiety of the world. They encountered difficulties, as doubtless they expected; and in surmounting their difficulties they improved their technique or found some better way of working.

In those experimental days, between Finisterre and Lisbon, they sounded five times, and three times dredged in depths down to almost two thousand fathoms; and three times the sounding line parted, the dredge rope once, and another time the dredge came up foul. Inexperience and ill luck were, perhaps, equally to blame, but the exercise would always be tedious. For sounding they used a hemp rope, one inch in circumference, because piano-wire could not be trusted to carry such instruments as thermometers and density-gauges, and stranded-wire rope was not yet made. Friction was considerable and, as they later found, it took forty-five minutes to reach three thousand fathoms. To sink a dredge to two and a half thousand fathoms took three hours and – as recorded in the Introduction to Swire's narrative – 'it used to take us all day to dredge and trawl in any considerable depth, and the net was usually got in only at nightfall', hauled up by a twelve horse-power donkey-engine.

The dredge was an iron frame – the jaws that held its mouth open – which crawled along the surface of the bottom, and behind the frame was a bag to hold what it scoured; the largest dredge had jaws five feet long. The dredge, however, was soon replaced by 'an ordinary beam-trawl'; that was Captain Nares' idea. The beam-trawl which superseded the dredge consisted of a beam of wood, with an iron bracket at either end, to which was attached a big V-shaped net lead-weighted to keep it down. The beam varied in length between ten and seventeen feet, the smallest being used for the greatest depths; and the trawl, being more flexible and capacious, proved more efficient than the dredge. The end of both trawl-net and dredge-net was commonly lined with what was called 'bread-bag stuff', to prevent small animals from being washed out; and despite the greater efficiency of the trawl, the tedium of the operation was not much diminished. Here, at the very start of that long, immensely useful, and uncommonly entertaining voyage, there became evident its essential paradox: a great adventure and a vast reward of knowledge would be paid for by many months of industrious boredom.

Their voyage would take them far to the south, to the uncharted ice of the Antarctic; to New Zealand and the Friendly Isles; Fiji and the Philippines; New Guinea, Hong Kong, the Admiralty Islands and Tahiti; and down to the wild butt-end of South America before turning for home again. But, to begin with, their route lay in familiar, almost domestic waters. They sailed up the Tagus to Lisbon; then came Gibraltar and Madeira, and before reaching Madeira the trawl brought up, from a depth greater than two thousand fathoms, the first of their marine prizes: a bunch

RIGHT: *the first page of Pelham Aldrich's journal of the voyage. With accuracy and humour he kept this record in good weather and bad, and he had the patience and skill to include watercolours of the most exciting events.*
OVERLEAF: *the original charts of HMS* Challenger *after her conversion for scientific duties at Sheerness. Most of the accommodation on the deck was given over to the scientists, and the captain's apartment in the stern was reduced in size to make room for the Professor next door.*

...30 a.m. cast off from the Jetty in Portsmouth Harbor, and with Steam commenced our voyage of Scientific exploration and Circumnavigation. by a wonder the sun shone out just as we started and remained out as we discharged our Pilot and a few friends to the Tug which had accompanied us out as far as Spithead. These good people did their best to enliven our departure - and we were greeted with three cheers as they shoved off - and immediately afterwards we proceeded for the Needles. The lively propensities of the ship were soon to be developed, for even before we reached the Needles - signs of motion were observable, and made me anxious to get everything secured as quickly as possible - precautions which were soon to be found necessary - as a falling Barometer and awkward looking sunset were very indication of a gale from the Sea. In the first watch it became thick - and plenty of drizzle - at 2.30 a.m. we got a glimpse of the Start Light abeam - and lost

sight of him 2 hours afterwards.

The 22nd opened with a fine bright sunshine - the wind having hauled gradually from West round to the Southward

a moderate breeze. to which we made all Plain Sail except Royals and F. Jib.

steering course to W'S. to keep

a good Westing in case of falling in with the expected SW gale. — At midnight the wind and sea began to increase - and necessitated a gradual shortening of sail until 4 a.m. found us under Topsails on the Cap and Courses - There was a nasty confused sea - and the Ship was uncommonly uneasy rolling 22° to Starboard and 4° to Port, with a few hints that she could and would ultimately do more - The Barometer still fell steadily and the ship was kept rap full on the Port Tack to make Westing in case of a shift to the NW. — A lively day promised - under close reefed Topsails and Gaff sails with heads hauled in - a fresh gale from the SSW.

the ship rolling 35° to leeward - During the day the Bar. fell and the wind rose. Now in the hope of getting wind from NW - but Boreas wouldn't "the wind never getting farther round than from SW. SW to WSW. a heavy Sea running and ship knocking about a great deal. The first night in a gale of wind always produces a few mishaps intimately ours were confined to those at which one could well afford to laugh - nothing more serious happening than the "guttering" of

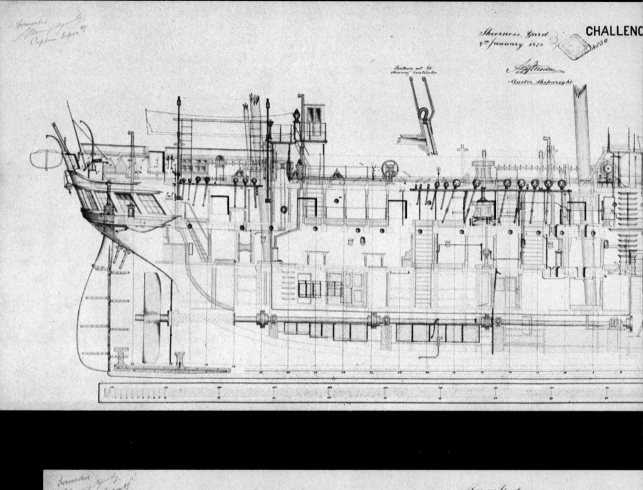

Sheerness Yard
5th January 1872

Master Shipwright

Section at tt
shewing ventilator

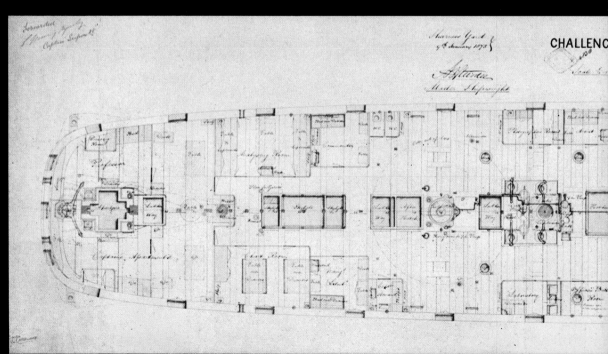

Sheerness Yard
5th January 1872

Master Shipwright

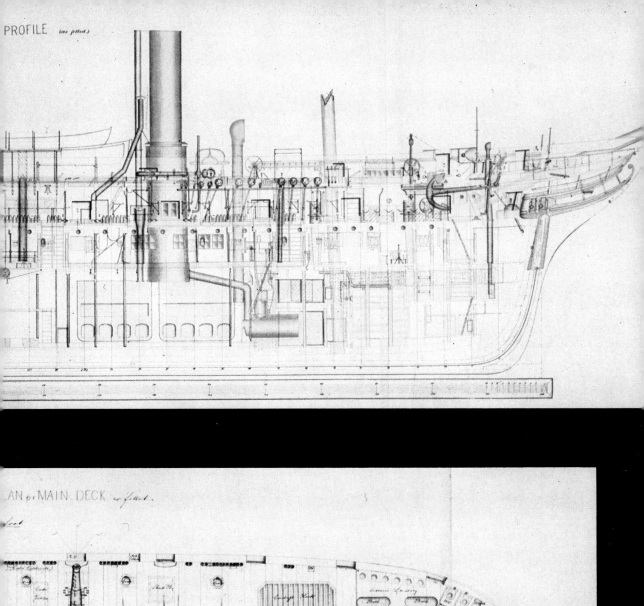

PROFILE (as fitted)

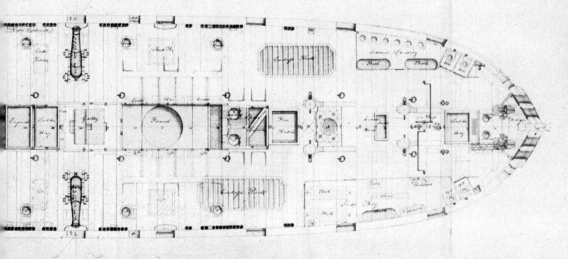

PLAN of MAIN DECK as fitted

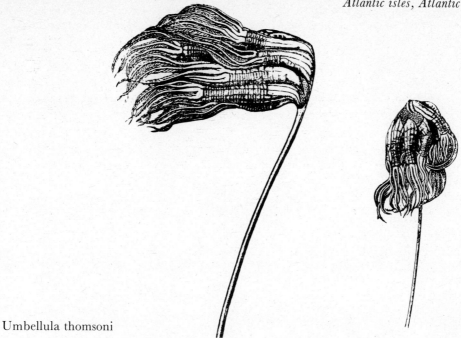

Umbellula thomsoni

of phosphorescent polyps on a long stem, an *Umbellula* 'of the remarkable Alcyonarian genus', to which was given the name *Umbellula thomsoni*.

Santa Cruz was their next port-of-call, and three days later they sailed round Tenerife, sounding all the way, and in fine clear weather its high Peak, capped with snow, was clearly visible at the centre of the circle they drew. A small party that included Murray and Moseley had been left ashore to climb the Peak, to exercise their legs and power of observation, and Moseley noted the cactus-like *Euphorbia canariensis*: the broad-lobed cactus that had been introduced as pasture for the cochineal insect which the islanders cultivated; the black trousers and dirty white blankets that mule-drivers wore; the fine figures of their handsome wives and daughters; some relics in a small, decayed museum of the Guanches, the original inhabitants of the Canaries – 'Man', he wrote, 'appears to be almost the only mammal that collects and stores uneatable objects' – and, as they climbed up towards the snow at 9,000 feet, the tree-like heath, the broom, and the little violets that grew on the upper slopes. Moseley was much happier ashore than afloat. He found the sea voyages tedious, and dredging dull and monotonous; but in Tenerife he discovered a gecko hibernating at 6,000 feet, a luxuriant vegetation, snails and beetles of many sorts, a rare finch, a male spider with bright silver patches on its abdomen, and a flag that the Spaniards had taken from Nelson. In Moseley's opinion islands were incomparably more attractive than the surrounding sea.

LEFT: *Captain George Nares, painted by Stephen Pearle in 1877, after the Arctic expedition of 1875.*

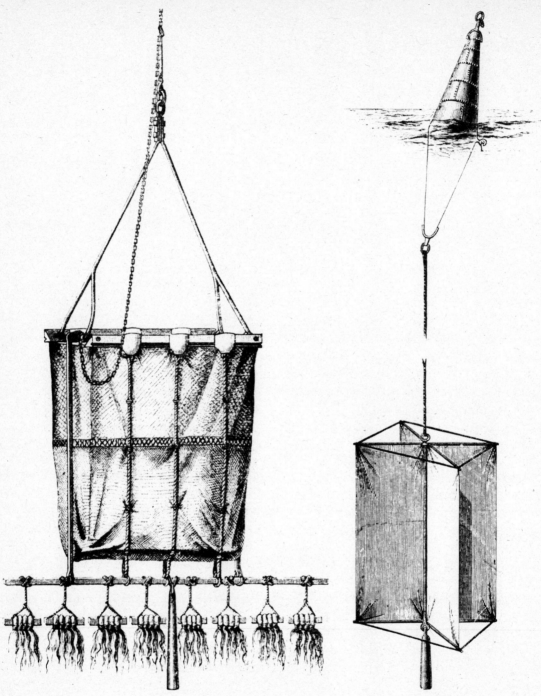

ABOVE LEFT: *the dredge, like a lady's purse with its mouth braced open. It was replaced by Captain Nares' beam trawl, which was more efficient and is shown on the facing page, being repaired.* ABOVE RIGHT: *the current drag and marker buoy. The drag was lowered to a pre-determined depth, and the rate of movement of the buoy on the surface noted.*

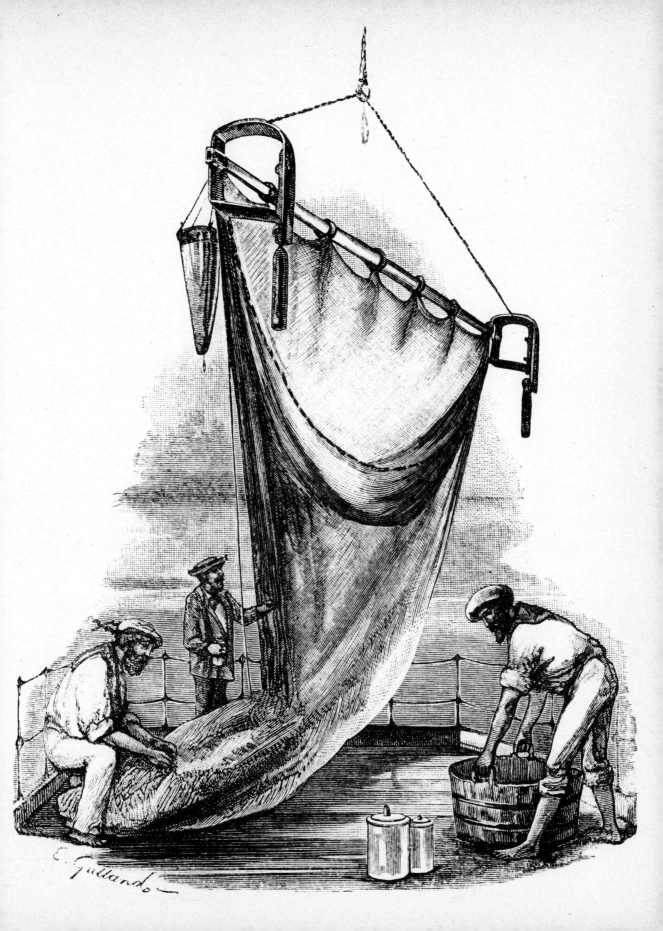

Challenger *at anchor in the outer harbour, St Thomas. All the journals remark on the idleness of the negroes of St Thomas, and Lt Channer contrasts their happy lot in the cartoon* RIGHT *with that of the poor English sailor.*

From Tenerife the *Challenger* crossed the Atlantic to St Thomas in the Danish West Indies. The passage lasted from February 14th till March 16th, though the ship under full sail, with a wind of force five a little abaft the beam, could make eight knots or better; but the service of the good Trade Wind had to be interrupted to permit investigation of the sea's bottom. Every two hundred miles sails were furled, the screw unlocked and steam brought up, the ship turned head to wind, and dredge or trawl or sounding gear launched overside. When sounding the ship had to be kept directly over the spot where the sinkers went down; when dredging – if the dredge had not fouled – the ship was allowed to drift broadside to the wind for half an hour or longer; then the rope was brought to the donkey-engine that was housed beside the mainmast on the upper deck, and slowly the dredge was hove up.[1] Then sails were loosed, the screw locked, and to the great relief of Sub-Lieutenant Swire – who could never detect anything but mud in the dredge – *Challenger* resumed her voyage.

Sharks, frigate birds, and brown pelicans welcomed her at St Thomas. Once a resort of buccaneers – and during the Napoleonic wars a favoured rendezvous for merchant ships waiting for convoy – St Thomas later acquired importance as a coaling station. It was to coal and refit that the *Challenger* put in, but for a week her busy naturalists found much to interest them. Until emancipation of the slaves it had been planted with sugar cane, but since then most of the land had been allowed to run wild; all but one of the planters had been ruined – they were given only fifty dollars a head compensation for their lost slaves – but the negroes appeared to enjoy their freedom and to live in contented idleness. Young Swire admired their merry faces, their musical voices, and the company of black girls who enjoyed being chaffed, but

[1]Though a beam-trawl had been found more efficient than the original dredge, the operation was usually called dredging.

'despite provocation' retained their good manners, while his graver companions took note of calcareous seaweeds and the island's lesser fauna.

There was only one sort of humming bird on St Thomas, but it was common – constantly seen poised before a flower – and Moseley remarked on the resemblance of its flight to that of Sphinx moths. There was a bird, familiarly called Black Witch, that behaved like a magpie but structurally resembled a cuckoo. On a neighbouring islet there were puffins, and Moseley shot brown pelicans for the German overseer of a farm. Their flesh, he thought, could hardly have been less unpleasant than that of a vulture, but the German assured him it was very good.

There were spiders – 'great, heavy, venomous-looking brutes, about three inches across' – that lived in holes in the ground, at the bottom of which they excavated a little room. There were white ants that made globular nests, as much as two feet in diameter, high in the fork of a tree, and to reach them constructed small covered galleries up the bark of the tree. There was a sort of rodent called an Agouti, and among the plants was one that bore a prickly pod which contained spherical beans that floated out to sea and were sometimes carried as far as Tristan da Cunha and the Azores. The naturalists found occupation wherever they went.

From St Thomas *Challenger* sailed to the coral islands of Bermuda, and the first tragedy of the voyage occurred soon after leaving. When dredging over broken ground the dredge stuck, the dredge rope broke, and the heavy block to which it led flew loose. It hit a boy called Stokes, and injured him so badly that later in the day he died. On the following day, when barely a hundred miles from land, they sounded to 3,875 fathoms, and when poor young Stokes was buried, in a hammock weighted with round shot, his body was truly committed to the deep.

Much work was done in Bermudan waters, but in these pages there is no room for the scrupulously recorded contents of trawl or dredge. 'At a depth of 200 fathoms the deposit was composed of large fragments of coral, foraminifera, echinoderms, polyzoa, molluscs, algae, and concretionary lumps. At 380 fathoms the fragments

33

On Bermuda the scientists spent much time ashore. Professor Wyville Thomson and Dr Suhm are seen LEFT *out shooting with an unidentified companion.* RIGHT: *Dr Moseley, botanizing.*

were smaller, and there were many Pteropod and Heteropod shells.' That is a fairly typical entry in the scientific log, and there are thousands of such entries which, to the lay mind, may convey little more than the indubitable fact that the ocean's bottom was being subjected to such a scrutiny as had never before been attempted. A careful collection of Bermudan plants was also made – they included far more vegetable forms peculiar to the island than had hitherto been realized – and it was a reasonable deduction that the presence of many North American plants was due to migratory birds such as the American Golden Plover and various gallinules, rails, and snipe. But the bird which the naturalists found most interesting was the pretty little white 'Bo'sun Bird', which looked like a tern or sea-swallow.

Before he wrote *The Tempest* Shakespeare had heard a good deal about 'the still-vext Bermoothes', but his knowledge was imprecise and Caliban could not have shown Prospero 'fresh springs', for there is none, nor pond nor stream : no fresh water, indeed, except rain. But in 1873 Bermuda may have looked more like Prospero's island than today's crowded tourist-trap. The Bermudans grew excellent potatoes, onions, and tomatoes which, very early in the season, they sold at a high price in North America. It had not occurred to them, however, that they could grow enough for their own use, and in April the ships that carried new potatoes to Manhattan were returning with large quantities of the previous year's American crop. Except for this happy note on the island's economy there is, in the *Challenger*'s records, no mention of human activity in Bermuda other than a cricket match played against another of Her Majesty's ships. There were many species of ferns, there were crabs

34

that could climb mangrove trees with the greatest ease, and a terrestrial Nemertine worm – almost a unique discovery – was found living in moist earth. But human life seems to have been inconspicuous.

On passage to Sandy Hook and Nova Scotia there was rough weather as the ship crossed the Gulf Stream, and sailors charting the length of a reef, in the ship's boats, were sea-sick and had to be brought aboard again. They tied-up in Halifax on May 9th, saw a fine display of aurora borealis, but nearer at hand only a little, smoky, wooden town with great piles of timber on its wharves. It seemed to offer no attraction, but two men and three boys deserted there, weary, perhaps, of 'drudging' – so the sailors named their deep-sea exercise – or hopeful of finding their way to the United States where, it was commonly believed, any man could make an easy living.

After ten days in Halifax *Challenger* headed south to Bermuda again; another energetic fortnight followed, and then they re-crossed the Atlantic to the Azores. The trawl was busily used, a host of small, fantastically shaped creatures was captured – many of them previously unknown – and when all sail was set again the ship sometimes made as much as nine and a half knots. But her speed brought no immediate reward, for there was smallpox in Horta and healthier surroundings were sought at Ponta Delgada on the island of San Miguel. Moseley was one of the few who went ashore in Horta – he took passage in a boat selling fruit – and had time to observe that, although the charming little town was thoroughly Portuguese in appearance, the women were better-looking than in Lisbon, and many wore dark blue cloaks with enormous hoods, like a coal-scuttle, that permitted only a distant

view, as if through a tunnel, of the pretty face within. Moseley was a naturalist of the catholic sort, and learnt that such a cloak cost about six pounds and a girl had to work for two and a half years before she could afford to buy one.

On San Miguel were hot springs, and those who went to look at them rode in carriages drawn by four mules: fine flower-gardens, Australian blue gums and araucarias diversified a countryside still so primitive in its economy that oxen trod the corn on open threshing-floors, and old women ground it in heavy querns. For botanists there were some of the forty flowers that grow in the Azores and nowhere else, and the boiling springs spurted from grey mud with a memorable stink of sulphuretted hydrogen.

Then Madeira, where fish almost unknown to the naturalist might be found in the market, and great tunnies, their flesh as red as beef, were cut up and sold like butcher's meat. A profusion of flowers and fruit – bananas and pineapples, prickly pears and guavas, mangos and oranges – but, as Moseley sadly writes, 'the island being resorted to by so many invalids, the cemetery forms a conspicuous feature in the scenery'. South or south-east from there to the Cape Verde Islands, and 'more barren and desolate-looking spots than San Antonio and St Vincent appear, as approached from seawards, after they have been suffering from their usual prolonged droughts, it is impossible to conceive. Their general aspect recalls Aden or some of the volcanic islands in the Red Sea. At the time of our visit no rain had fallen for a year at St Vincent. Sometimes it does not rain for three years.'

Porto Grande, on St Vincent, was a coaling station inhabited only – according to Swire – 'by negroes, vultures, and English merchants'. Much more agreeable was Porto Praya on the nearby island of St Iago, where good beef and vegetables could be bought, and there was sport for both afterguard and lower deck. Shooting parties brought back a few quail, pigeon, and guinea fowl, and in one of the cutters about thirty men went ashore to enjoy some fishing, with Mr Cox the bo'sun close behind with a seine net in a dinghy. The long net was paid out, waist-deep the sailors lay on the lines at either wing, and Mr Cox in his dinghy watched the cod-end. Great excitement attended one haul, when a big shark was captured. It was fourteen feet long, and but for the bo'sun would have broken the net. He, however, repeatedly hit it on the head with a boat-hook, it was dragged ashore, and while Mr Cox thrust the boat-hook down its gullet the others attacked it with sticks and knives. 'The sailor', writes Moseley, 'has absolutely no pity upon a shark'; and when all ships were small, or relatively small, there was some excuse for their cruelty. Sharks are inclined to follow small craft, they have a curiously menacing appearance, and their voracity is notorious. 'Ah, thou beggar' – so Moseley heard a sailor say, but decently bowdlerised the epithet – 'thou'd hurt I if I was in the water, and now I'll hurt thee'.

Moseley, that observant man, had lately seen a baobab tree forty-two feet in circumference; he had watched kites, wheeling like gulls round the stern and catching scraps of food, not in the beak but neatly in the claws of one foot; and among the fish taken with the shark he had identified grey and red mullet, a garfish, and

37

'curious fish with deformed-looking heads (*Argyreiosus setipinnis, Galeoides polydactylus*)'.
He was genial as well as observant, and when a fire was lighted on the shore he joined
the sailors in a good supper of fried fish and bread and beer. Darkness fell, but again
they put out the net, and when at last they tired of fishing they had hot tea and grog
before going aboard.

It was a pleasant little holiday from 'drudging', and when *Challenger* left the Cape
Verde Islands she headed south and west for more distant and lesser known lands.

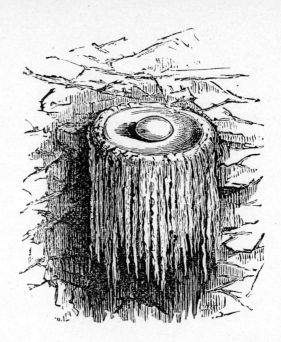

4 *Noddies, Boobies, and Brazil*

In overcast and squally weather they sailed on August 9th and found the south-easterly Trades about 160 miles from Sierra Leone. Some of 'the philosophers', says Swire with youthful irreverence, were alarmed by their approach to what was then known as the White Man's Grave because they had taken out life insurance policies 'for sums payable only on condition of their not going to the West Coast of Africa'. The Trade Wind saved them from danger, however, and with all sail set they pointed west for St Paul's Rocks, a thousand miles away and some 500 miles from the north-eastern shoulder of Brazil. The passage was rewarded by dredging, from a great depth, several fragments of the worm *Balanoglossus*, an animal, says the Report, of an importance 'which has rendered it familiar to all students of animal morphology'.

The Rocks lie just north of the Equator, and are small: five little peaks, black at sea-level, white-capped with dung, and their only inhabitants except various insects, spiders, and crabs are Noddies and Boobies – small black terns and a sort of gannet – but the terns are to be counted in thousands. Captain Nares and Tizard, the Navigating Lieutenant, climbed to the fore-top to con the ship in, and found the Rocks so steep-to that they could moor in a hundred fathoms and lie a hundred yards off, held there by the rushing Equatorial current.

The Noddies, if they could, nested on green sea-weed cemented by dung. Such nests, on the leeward side of the Rocks, had become solid, permanent structures, and only strong and lively birds could keep possession of them; the others had to lay

'On August the 27th we sighted St Paul's Rocks, steamed to leeward of them and as there is no anchorage, sent boats with ropes and hawsers to the rocks, bound a rope round and round a rock, made a hawser fast to that rock . . . and there we lay comfortably for a day and two nights, made fast to a pinnacle of rock in the middle of the Atlantic. Something no other ship has ever done here before!' Lord George Campbell.

their eggs on bare rock. The Boobies – fully grown, they were almost as big as geese – appeared to nest on only one of the peaks. Pugnacious birds, they frightened the ship's dogs – there were two spaniels aboard – of which even the young, Noddies and Boobies alike, showed no fear. Natural selection, says Moseley, had bred bravery in them as a necessary defence against their constant enemies, the crabs. He acquired a great admiration for the crabs of St Paul's Rocks, which were quick in movement, alert, and uncommonly intelligent.

The whole crew were landed on the Rocks, 'to run about and fish', but under strict orders to do no harm to the birds. Fish were abundant in the deep, fast-running sea, and a sort of mackerel called *cavalli* gave excellent sport on a salmon-rod; they were surface fish, a weighted line caught nothing, and no line was strong enough to hold a really big shark. Cavalli were a welcome addition to the ship's rations, for there was little fresh food left except melons bought in St Iago; even the ward-room was almost down to salt-horse.

Small but menacing, remote and of disputed origin, St Paul's Rocks presented

'the philosophers' with an engaging puzzle. Their situation, 'far removed from any continent, together with their aspect and lithological character, caused them to be considered as the last trace of some vast district lost by submergence'. So says the Report, and adds that Darwin declared the olivine rock of the rough islets to be unlike any other he had seen. He denied its volcanic origin, but not all petrologists agreed with him. Among the Boobies and the Noddies Captain Nares left a sealed glass tube containing a page of the Navy List, the names of the *Challenger*'s officers, and a notification on parchment that 'near this spot the officers of HBMS *Challenger* took magnetic observations, August 29th, 1873. Caught plenty of fish'. To that statement none could take exception, and the ship made sail for Fernando Noronha, in a group of small islands about two hundred miles from the shoulder of Brazil, where there was a population, not of Boobies, but of convicts.

Wyville Thomson's intention had been to survey and explore Fernando Noronha, but neither he nor anyone else had thought it necessary to obtain permission from the Brazilian Government, and the Commandant of the small garrison – a Major who had a hundred and sixty soldiers to look after fourteen hundred convicted criminals – refused to allow a party of unknown scientists the freedom they required. Their sojourn on the island was short, but long enough to discover its unpleasant character. It was difficult and even dangerous to walk about on its savagely cracked and broken rocky soil; there was a stinging plant, *Jatropha urens*, that grew in sinister abundance and was 'a horrible pest' like a nettle of extraordinary malignancy whose poison remained active for a couple of days; and there were vast numbers of mice and large black crickets. There were no large butterflies, but the woods were full of flocks of reddish-brown doves. In that forbidding and forbidden environment the convicts lived in small huts, which they built for themselves; worked for ten hours a day on plantations of one sort or another; but enjoyed – or, more probably, a favoured few enjoyed – the privilege of fishing from small rafts that simply consisted of three or four logs, lashed together and topped with a stool. They were too small to be used as vessels of escape, and no boats were permitted on the island.

The indefatigable Moseley gathered most of the information acquired in a very short time, and showed a scientific scepticism when reporting the conversation of a socially superior convict who was allowed to act as interpreter. Most of the convicts – many of them murderers – had 'a horribly ruffianly appearance, especially the blacks', but the interpreter was 'a most gentlemanly-looking fellow, and well-dressed'. According to his own story he 'had had a misfortune', and been awarded a sentence of sixty-four years. During the last seven months, he told Moseley, two-thirds of the convicts had been flogged for minor or major misdemeanours, the usual punishment being fifty lashes, but troublesome prisoners might be sentenced to five hundred. No one, he said, had ever stood to receive more than two hundred and fifty; after that they had to be supported by crutches, were taken to hospital, and never seen again. 'His statements', says Moseley, 'must be taken for what they are likely to be worth.'

Sugar cane, maize, cassava, sweet potatoes, bananas, pumpkins, and melons grew on the island, and a great store of melons – 'remarkably fine, both in size and flavour' – was bought for threepence apiece before *Challenger* up-anchored and sailed, on September 3rd, for Bahia in Brazil. The scientists' last view of Fernando Noronha was dominated by the bare, columnar rock, the Peak, that rises from its rich but treacherous soil to a height of 1,000 feet.

Convict Fisherman
Fernando Noronha
Catamaran

RIGHT: *The peak of Fernando Noronha. Most of what* Challenger's *people saw of the island was from the sea, and when they left after two days, Campbell was 'mighty glad, as it was a stupid little place'.*

Tall ships in harbour at Bahia; Challenger *is somewhere among them.*

They had a busy little passage. They were sounding, dredging, and taking temperature readings all the way; in a sea teeming with life they found many species of minute and delicately patterned *Radiolaria*; they caught a fish like a smelt, but of a previously unknown genus, called *Bathypterois*; and with almost empty bunkers – the last of the coal had to be saved for harbour-work – they entered the Bahia de Todos os Santos dressed overall by a swarm of butterflies (*Heliconia narcea*) that had descended on the ship. It was September 14th, and as soon as they could, the scientists went ashore as eager as tourists but more observant.

The domestic architecture of Bahia was Portuguese in appearance; palms and banana plants were tropically green. From the flat lands about the harbour to the plateau of the main town indolent inhabitants were carried in old-fashioned sedan chairs, but Moseley preferred to walk up stinking little streets where passers-by were constantly threatened – as in Edinburgh long ago – by the discharge of slops from upper windows. Church bells were loudly ringing – they reminded him of Swiss cow-bells – and he met a long, elaborate procession in which was borne, on a silver-coated platform, the image of a saint 'with a Van dyck-like countenance, black hair, moustache, and beard'. Behind the saint came soldiers with fixed bayonets, a valiantly playing military band, and a great crowd of negro women, 'strapping females' stout of body. From the windows and balconies above they were pelted with flowers, and then came a display of fireworks.

44

But Moseley was a scientist as well as a tourist. He watched with lively interest the behaviour of human beings, but with dedicated zeal searched the suburbs of Bahia for 'land planarian worms' which he found 'resting beneath the sheathing leaf-stalks of the banana plants' just as he had previously found them in Ceylon, 'and accompanied, curiously enough, as in Ceylon, by a peculiar slug (*Vaginulus*)'. He also found butterflies that uttered a clicking sound while flying: Darwin had previously taken note of them, and Moseley discovered they were common near Bahia. The more one reads his *Notes by a Naturalist* the more one enjoys the company of Mr Moseley; who sadly killed himself by constant over-work some ten or twelve years later.

Britain's association with Brazil had had a beginning in Cromwell's time, and in 1703 it was amplified by a treaty that gave port wine a preferred market in England in exchange for a declared preference for English woollen goods in both Portugal and Brazil. In later years there had been recurrent unhappiness in relations with Britain, but in 1873 an ambitious railway – based upon Bahia and hopefully extending into the interior – was still managed by British officials who gave a hearty welcome to the *Challenger*'s scientists, and provided them with free passes. The scientists took full advantage of their privilege, and Moseley scrupulously recorded all they had seen while Swire, and others of his sort, played cricket matches – one of them in pouring rain, the other enthusiastically attended – against local clubs.

The prime purpose of the voyage – the exploration of the depths of the sea – was not advanced by a few days of holiday-making in Brazil, but the scientists' catholic curiosity, their constant impulse to search and see and classify what they had seen, are made evident in memoranda of excursions undertaken for pleasure and rewarded by discoveries minutely and most engagingly described.

The scenery, some thought, was reminiscent of the Rhine – though there were no castles – but small trees and large shrubs growing in a thick net of creepers, and plants allied to the pineapple with blue and scarlet flowers, proclaimed their tropic latitude. Then they entered a forest so tall and thick that the bright sky was hidden, but despite the gloom they identified an Oven Bird 'gathering mud for its curious nest'. They slept at a railway station where fireflies lit the darkness, and, 'thanks to

Bathypterois longipes

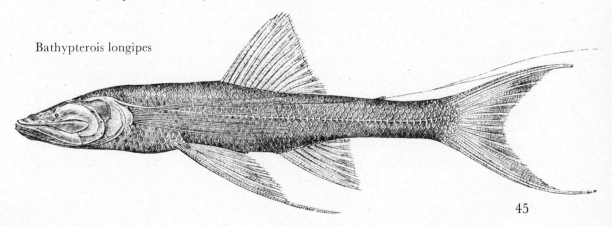

45

Cricket on the Campo Grande. A team from Challenger *played against the Bahia Cricket Club, and Wild sketched the match from long-off.*

the energy of the English railway officials', there was Bass's ale for two shillings and twopence a bottle. In the morning they set off to look for toucans, and on the way shot a few humming-birds. Toucans were more difficult to find, but eventually they heard 'a short shrieking sort of noise ending in a hiss', and Moseley hit a big bird which fell, but retained strength enough to bite him severely with its huge bill. He recorded the several brilliant colours of its plumage, and took advantage of another free pass on a river steamer that carried him to the town of Caxoeira. Among his fellow-passengers – the boat was crowded – he noted 'several German Jews going to buy diamonds'.

He and his companions slept in an hotel where they were discomforted by the droppings of bats in the rafters, the snoring of less inhibited guests, and the deafening noise 'like a very loud harsh cat's mew' emitted by small toads in a pond: 'a bull-frog (*Rana pipiens*) shouting the loudest with a deep bass voice'. Then, mounted on large mules, they set off to Feira St Anna, a ride of twenty-eight miles. They enjoyed a cock-fight on the way, and some good Lisbon wine, and in a primitive inn settled down for the night. A cattle fair was the attraction, and Moseley was much taken by the skill of the cowboys, or *vaqueiros*, who drove their wild herds into town, and did not fail to note that they were 'of all shades of colour from black to white', and dressed 'from head to foot in undyed red-brown leather'.

He spent a night with a German farmer who had recently bought a slave. Slaves had been emancipated, in Brazil as elsewhere, but apparently 'all foreigners except

English' (whose discretion could not be trusted?) were allowed to own one or two. The German's slave, worth perhaps £120, was married to a freed negress, and their child 'was a great pet in the house'. Moseley proceeds from a little enquiry into social conditions to description of the preparation of tapioca from the plant *cassava*, his capture of a curious bat, some notes on the activities of soldier-ants, and his purchase – having returned to Bahia – of a 'living full-grown three-toed sloth' for two shillings. The sloth – 'the most inane-looking animal I ever saw' – lived for a few days only: it would not eat and had to be killed.

Their departure from Brazil was hastened by fear. Yellow Fever – 'Yellow Jack' to the sailors – was still a recurrent menace there, and when one of the crew fell ill with threatening symptoms there was appropriate alarm and it was decided to put to sea and seek healthier conditions in colder latitudes. Their next destination was Tristan da Cunha, and the passage, as usual, was repeatedly interrupted by dredging or trawling. There was much disappointment when dredge-ropes broke as a difficult and heavy load was slowly brought to the surface, but great satisfaction when two specimens of a fish of a genus new to science were captured from a depth of nineteen hundred fathoms. *Ipnops murrayi* – so it was named – was not a handsome fish, and the ordinary, untaught observer might have described it as a long, thin, tubular creature with butterfly fins and a prognathous snout of uncommon ugliness. But the scientists saw more than that, and wrote:

'This genus belongs to the Scopeloid family; the shape of the body is elongate, subcylindrical, the caudal portion much exceeding the abdominal in length. The scales are large, but deciduous. Fins normally developed. The head is depressed, with a long, broad, spatulate snout; the mouth wide, with the lower jaw projecting, and armed with rows of minute teeth.

'The structure of the eyes is quite unique. Externally they appear as a continuous flat cornea-like organ, longitudinally divided into two halves, which covers the whole of the upper surface of the snout and partly overlies the bone. The functions of the organ are difficult to determine. It seems at present probable that it is an organ of modified vision.'

For microscopic examination of the eyes John Murray cut sections, and he was the first to discover their peculiarity. From nineteen hundred fathoms to the microscope – from the dark unknown to the bright light of scientific investigation – the *Challenger* was dredging its discoveries, and *Ipnops murrayi* was one of a myriad rewards.

Ipnops murrayi, *with a plan of the head to show its 'organ of vision'.*

Peter Green, head-man of Tristan da Cunha, 1873.

5 The Penguins of Tristan da Cunha

Lying 1,550 miles west of the Cape of Good Hope, Tristan da Cunha is the largest of a group of three small islands, the others being Nightingale and Inaccessible Islands. First discovered by the Portuguese, in or about the year 1506, their history was scanty, their position uncertainly known, until 1816 when the Emperor Napoleon was removed, for public safety, to the island of St Helena, about 1,300 miles to the north, and to prevent sympathizers from making it a base of operations, from which to attempt his rescue, Britain took possession of Tristan and from HMS *Falmouth* put ashore a tiny garrison consisting of Lieutenant Rich, RN, a Lieutenant of Marines, four midshipmen, and thirteen men. A few months later Rich was relieved by Captain Cloete of the 21st Dragoons, who brought a few soldiers from the Cape, and remained on the island until November, 1817. By then the British Government had decided that Tristan – which offered no shelter to ships, was a long way from South Africa and almost as far from St Helena – was not a useful or probable base from which to attempt Napoleon's liberation, and made preparation to evacuate it.

That was not done without difficulty and loss. The sloop *Julia* was wrecked on the north shore and out of her whole crew of ninety-five, fifty-five were drowned. The frigate *Eurydice* was more successful, though Captain Wauchope had to stand off for thirteen days, in very dirty weather, before he was able to anchor and embark the troops and their baggage. Wauchope has left a memorable description of the island, its occasional beauty, and its perilous climate:

'In fine weather nothing can be more beautiful or picturesque than Tristan, with

49

Tristan da Cunha, 7,640 ft. 'I was called on deck to look at a snow-clad pyramid which rose out of the sea', writes Wild. 'Whilst admiring this landmark . . . I became aware of a sudden change in the climate.'

its lofty peak covered with snow, the sea as smooth as the stillest lake, just rippling against the fine volcanic black sand on the beach, and a cascade of the purest water falling over the cliff directly into the sea; but it must not be forgotten that in the course of an hour this calm and placid scene may be rendered one of the most terrific in nature, and prove in an unmistakable way the power of the ocean, for in that short time the beach, so lately covered with fine sand, has had forced up on it immense stones, which, tossed against each other by the surf, create a noise resembling thunder, and so quickly are these large stones cast up that a fortnight after the wreck of the *Julia* she was almost entirely buried beneath them.'

Not all the little garrison went aboard *Eurydice*. Corporal William Glass of the Royal Artillery, a married man with a family, asked permission to remain on the island, and persuaded John Nankivall and Samuel Burnell, natives of Plymouth and said to have been stone-masons, to stay with them. With Captain Cloete's detachment from the Cape had come cattle, sheep, poultry and pigs, and the colonists, well provided for, seem to have lived happily enough. On two or three occasions their numbers were increased by shipwrecked sailors, and in 1827 a kindly ship's captain brought five women from St Helena to comfort five men in need of wives. Then American whalers began to visit the island, and the colonists were able to barter fresh meat and vegetables for flour, coffee, tea and sugar. Sometimes the whalers also took off a restless young woman, but slowly the colony grew, and in 1873 Tristan had a population of eighty-four human beings who jointly owned six hundred cattle and six hundred sheep, as well as fowls, geese, and pigs. They grew apples and potatoes, they sold beef at fourpence a pound, potatoes at four shillings a bushel, and had acquired a reputation for strict morality, industry, hospitality to strangers, and longevity.

To the scientists their island, as round as a penny, presented a cold, dark, almost uninhabitable appearance. It had a circumference of tall black cliffs, a plateau two thousand feet above the sea, and over the plateau loomed a volcanic cone, half-hidden by cloud and capped with snow, nearly 8,000 feet high. The islanders, moreover – despite their reputation for industry and morality – appear to have made on their visitors an impression no better than the land they lived in. They were curt in speech, except when begging for matches or copybooks for their children. They saw, perhaps, a dozen ships a year, so they had experience in bargaining and were sharp at a bargain. Some who came aboard *Challenger* stayed too long and drank too much: it was said that they never kept any store of whisky, rum, or gin, because when any spirits are landed 'the liquor is cleared out at once in a single bout'.

It must be added, however, that the visitors had little opportunity to become friendly with the natives. Such was the wild uncertainty of the weather that the scientists were warned, when they went ashore, to stay no more than half an hour out of sight of the ship, and to watch for the recall flag that was instantly hoisted if the sky darkened. Moseley, after botanizing under the cliffs, was climbing the steep hill-side when a fierce squall came racing over the sea and chilled him to the bone. He had a guide with him, a small boy born on the island, who immediately crouched down into the tall grass and fern – drew up his legs, tucked in his head – and made himself as comfortable as a hare in her form. Moseley, and others with him, followed the boy's example and found almost perfect shelter. That the boy was weatherwise could not be denied, but Moseley found him perculiarly taciturn and complained that he had constant difficulty 'in understanding what I said to him in ordinary English'. It may be, of course, that an Oxford accent was too seldom heard on Tristan.

The islanders' houses – there were fifteen in the village called Edinburgh – were solidly built of huge rectangular blocks of a soft red stone, fitted without mortar, and

Housebuilding at Edinburgh. Lava blocks are lighter than they look.

such a style of building may have been the legacy of Nankivall and Burnell, the Plymouth masons who stayed behind with Corporal Glass. Timber retrieved from wrecks, or begged from American whalers, made rafters for them, and they were thickly thatched with tussock grass. Walled gardens surrounded the cottages, and potato fields were also walled against the wind. There, in the village, Moseley made a very injudicious offer, and quickly regretted it. He had heard there were penguins on the island – he was keenly interested in penguins – and he offered a reward of £1 for a pair of them, with their eggs. In one of the cottages he was given his pair, and paid for them; and a day or two later he found himself surrounded by so dense a multitude of penguins that he could hardly escape from them.

Inaccessible Island, only half the size of Tristan, lies west by south about twenty miles distant, with a safe channel between. The ship anchored on the north-east side, and on the night of October 16th lay close under high cliffs. All night penguins were to be heard screaming on the shore and round the ship, and diving into calm water left vivid phosphorescent tracks behind them. Then, in the morning, a cutter took the naturalists ashore, and first they crossed a broad belt of water 'covered with the floating leaves of the wonderful seaweed *Macrocystis pirifera*', beyond which was a scene that enthralled and bewildered them. They saw what looked like a shoal of very active, very small porpoises or dolphins. Moseley could not imagine what the creatures could be unless 'they were indeed some marvellously small Cetaceans'. They were black above and white beneath, they came from seaward in a shoal of fifty or more, they leapt from the water and splashed into it again. A leap and a curve and another header into the sea – splash, splash, went this marvellous shoal of animals – till they went splash through the surf on to the black stony beach, and there struggled and jumped up amongst the boulders, and revealed themselves as wet and dripping penguins.

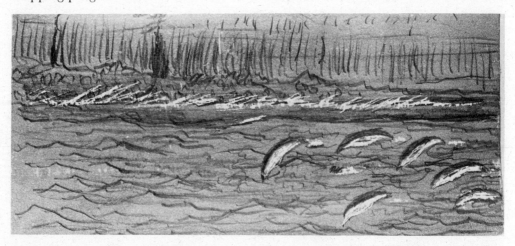

Moseley's sketch of the Rock Hoppers leaping through the water. The penguin, Eudyptes chrysocome, *is seen* RIGHT *with a youngster.*

There was only one species of penguin in the Tristan group: Rock Hoppers or *Eudyptes chrysocome*, the 'diving jumper', and Moseley, perhaps with unscientific enthusiasm, calculated their population in millions and discovered, with evident triumph, a kind of symbiosis uniting them and the singularly coarse tussock grass that covers much of the two lesser islands. The penguins saturate the soil with a very strong manure, and the responsive grass grows tall and thick to shelter the birds which feed it so lavishly. Slate-grey on back and head, snow-white in front, whiskered with sulphur-yellow plumes, the Rock Hoppers had bright red bills and remarkable eyes in which the iris was also red. So sensitive were their eyes to light that when a captive bird, aboard the ship, stood with one side of its head towards a port, the other away from the light, the pupil on the one side was contracted to a pin-point, the other was widely dilated.

The rookeries on Inaccessible Island were evil-smelling, deafeningly noisy, blind and crowded labyrinths. A beaten path led into the filthy jungle where the birds nested side by side in their dung – minor roads, leading off the main street, penetrated the grass that grew taller than a man's head – red-eyed and red of beak, the penguins yelled their savage defiance and fiercely attacked the intruders' unarmoured legs. The appalling din, the stench, the sense of being lost in an endless maze, and the pain of being stabbed, again and again, in calf or ankle, drove even gentle scientists to frantic violence, and careless of where they set their feet – it was, indeed, impossible to avoid eggs and young, so close they lay – stampeded through the slimy dirt, crushing or tripping over the anguished, ferocious birds, while attendant sailors, burdened

ABOVE LEFT: *Admiralty House, at the entrance to Simon's Town; an early nineteenth century lithograph. When* Challenger *visited Simon's Bay, it was still 'a small town of one street, stretching along the shore, and a few houses scattered on either side.'*
BELOW LEFT: Challenger *at sea.*

RIGHT: *a scientist kicks out at penguins on Inaccessible Island.*

with vasculum and luncheon-basket, took open pleasure in kicking as many as they could reach of the fierce things whose voices frightened, whose slum-like jungle horrified them. But to cross the island, to gather plants and explore the cliffs and look for smaller birds, it was necessary to force a way through the rookeries; and naturalists in pursuit of knowledge had perforce to tread an invader's bloody path. How much more agreeable it had been to watch the Rock Hoppers leaping like miniature dolphins through a shallow sea and the surf on a black beach!

The smaller birds included thrushes of a sort peculiar to Tristan and its neighbouring islands, finches like Greenfinches, and both, unafraid of human beings, paid no attention to their visitors. There were, too, Noddies of the sort seen on St Paul's Rocks; petrels and puffins, predatory skuas, and – on Inaccessible – wild pigs that fed on sea-birds and their eggs. On Nightingale, smallest of the group, the big Yellow-billed Albatross nested, but Rock Hoppers still dominated the scene and the tussock grass grew immensely tall.

From the deck of the ship there appeared to be a smooth, green coating of inoffensive herbage that covered easy slopes on the upward path to a peak hardly more than a thousand feet tall. No difficulty there, it seemed, and not until the visitors had gone ashore did they see a dark and sinuous path that divided the grass, and recognize the penguins' high street through another dark and stinking jungle. In places the street was eight or ten feet broad, and as on Inaccessible alleys led off at right angles to rows of nests on either side. Moseley, followed by three sailors carrying

Nightingale Island from the south, ' . . . . one vast Penguin rookery'. LEFT: *the penguins' high street.*

his botanical cases, lost them all in the jungle, but in a state of exhaustion reached the summit of the slope, where he found the rest of his party looking like beaten men.

The Yellow-billed Albatrosses sometimes made their nests in the middle of the penguins' high street, but the birds lived happily together. A handsome bird, as big as a goose – pure white below, wings grey, black-billed with a yellow streak – the Albatross was called Mollymauk by the Tristan people. Mollymauk, more truly, was the old popular name of the Arctic Fulmar; and Moseley obligingly adds that 'albatross' is in fact a corruption of the Spanish *alcatraz*, which means a Gannet. He ventures a little farther into etymology and tells us that 'penguin' was not, as often supposed, coined by early Dutch navigators from the Latin word *pinguis*, meaning either fat or stupid, but comes from Welsh or Breton words, *pen gwyn*, meaning white head, and originally applied, perhaps, to puffins. As an English word it may be as old as Sir Francis Drake, who is said, on somewhat doubtful authority, to have called an island in the Straits of Magellan Penguin Island.

On Tristan, where beef and mutton had been bought, Mollymauk's eggs were also purchased, at four shillings a dozen. Who ate them is not precisely stated, but they appear to have been edible, and were certainly less unpleasant than the flesh of the penguin-eating pigs on Inaccessible, which the sailors could not stomach. As

57

well as wild pigs Inaccessible had had, for nearly two years, a small human population: a pair of brothers, German by origin and Stoltenkoff by name, who had landed
there from a whaling ship. Both spoke English, one had been a sailor, the other an
officer in the German army. They had hoped to kill fur seals and become rich; but
they had been sadly disappointed. They had also failed – or so it seems – to establish
friendly relations with the people of Tristan, and were devoutly thankful to be
rescued by *Challenger*.

The ship sailed for the Cape of Good Hope on October 18th, and reached Simon's
Bay ten days later. The passage was interrupted, in overcast and squally weather, by
five soundings, five temperature readings, and two dredgings: five hundred miles
west of the Cape there was a depth of 2,600 fathoms. Between noon on the 26th and
6 a.m. on the 27th the ship, under sail, showed her quality by covering 214 miles at
an average speed of almost twelve knots. The zig-zag Atlantic voyage, lasting nearly
ten months, had been completed, and both sailors and scientists had now to contemplate adventure into less familiar waters and – as a prelude to tropical islands
on the farther side of the world – some cold and dangerous navigation among
Antarctic icebergs. But for rest and refreshment before that chilling exploration, and
a long passage to Australia, there were to be about seven weeks of relative ease, with
liberal shore-leave, in Simon's Bay and Table Bay. Half the ship's company were
immediately given four days' holiday, and not all returned.

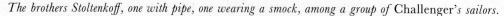

The brothers Stoltenkoff, one with pipe, one wearing a smock, among a group of Challenger's *sailors.*

6 Shore-leave at Cape Town

Cape Colony, as it was known in 1873 – officially the Province of the Cape of Good Hope – had been a British possession since 1806. Against a background of natural magnificence Cape Town, the capital, presented a dull, undistinguished appearance, for the original Dutch design of broad, tree-lined streets had been ruined by the blind, commercial instincts of British incomers, who filled open spaces and reduced the amplitude of the streets by putting up buildings which, for a generation or two, may have been profitable. The Colony, however, was in the most interesting stage of its development, for the discovery of diamonds on the Orange River in 1867 had quickly been followed by their excavation elsewhere, out of unprofitable soil, and in 1871 the great mines at Kimberley had been opened. The Boers were an unimaginative people, their agriculture was primitive, but a glittering wealth below the surface of an ill-ploughed land had begun to give it a new importance. By far the greater part of South Africa, however, still retained an aspect which nowadays would be labelled 'unspoilt'.

It was not the practice of the *Challenger*'s naturalists 'to make any extensive collections' at places, such as the Cape, where botany and zoology had already been studied, and the Report has no detailed or extensive description of its flora and fauna. But such natural enthusiasts as Sub-Lieutenant Swire and Mr Moseley gossiped agreeably about what they saw, and Swire, that ingenuous young man, proclaimed his lively appreciation of the scenery about Cape Town, and the generous hospitality of its people. He walked to Wynberg, and admired the heavy wagons

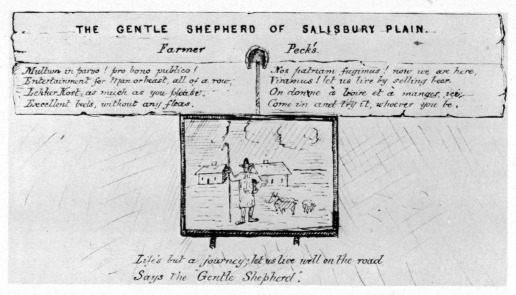

Farmer Peck had a taste for international relations, as the signboard outside his inn shows.

pulled slowly by a whip-taught span of five, six, or seven pairs of oxen. After long weeks at sea he went into 'raptures of delight' to find himself surrounded by woods, and when he went up-country as far as Stellenbosch he was gratified to hear that 'nothing could be more cordial and friendly' than the existing relations between the Dutch and 'their English fellow-subjects'. There was, admittedly, some speculation as to who would win control of the newly found diamond fields, but they had not, as yet, become an open exacerbating problem. At the Cape, Swire found nothing but friendliness: there was dancing ashore to which the scientists and the ship's officers were invited, there were dinners and return dinners, there was a ball for their Cape Town hosts aboard *Challenger*, and eager parties of the townspeople were taken – not always with undiluted pleasure – for a sail round the Bay.

There were, however, some unanticipated problems. Wyville Thomson had to go ashore to try to enlist a photographer, willing to join the expedition in place of its original photographer, a Corporal of the Royal Engineers, who had taken advantage of shore-leave to desert, presumably because the enticement of the diamond mines was more than he could resist. And there were others, similarly weak-minded or capable of rebellious initiative, who took the road to Kimberley.

Moseley, on the other hand, begins by rebuking himself for a false assumption: the Cape of Good Hope is not, as he had thought, the southernmost point of Africa, for Cape Agulhas to the eastward is far south of it. He takes careful note of rock formation – 'a hard metamorphic sandstone passing in many places into a white quartz disposed in perfectly horizontal strata' – and observes the striking difference between the soft and delicate outlines, lighted with Italianate pink and violet, of the eastern shore of False Bay, and the hills about the Cape which look like Scotch moorland. Like young Swire he is greatly impressed by the beauty of Wynberg – but notes that its trees were imported, not indigenous – and then typically offers a glimpse of the humanist who slept so lightly in a scientist's skin. He finds time to observe that midway between Simon's Bay and Wynberg there was a wayside inn called Farmer Peck's, where it was 'the custom to stop and take stimulants'. For anyone returning with a bad head 'after dissipation in Cape Town' there was a highly recommended and peculiar drink of milk, eggs, and brandy.

Moseley preferred Simon's Bay to Cape Town because, while the officers liked dancing and gaiety, he, given his choice, would rather contemplate wild nature and troops of baboons, as big as full-grown Newfoundland dogs, that lived in clans up to seventy strong, posted sentries while they fed, and though they were monkeys, were independent of trees and roamed open moors. There were, too, rock-rabbits, whose young played as if they were kittens, a sort of pheasant, a large shrike with a yellow breast, and honey-birds splendidly feathered in gold and green. Rodent moles and true moles presented interesting problems, and in shell mounds, or 'kitchen middens', he found stone implements, flat but grooved, that Bushmen or Hottentots had used for an uncertain purpose. Somewhere he uncovered a complete skeleton, either Hottentot or Bushman, and not far away made friends with an old

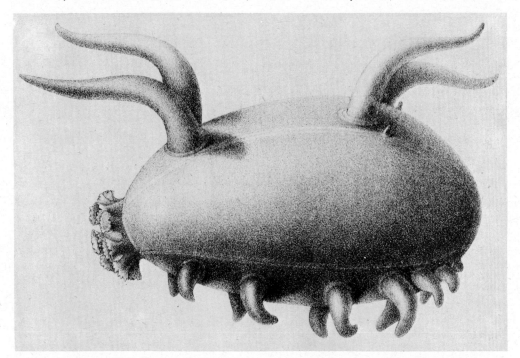

The holothurian Scotoplanes globosa. *The seven pairs of pedicels on its 'belly' help it to move along the ocean's bottom, with its mouth open, taking in a constant supply of ooze, very little of which it can digest.*

Boer who had married a young wife, and gave him milk, coffee, and Cape brandy. The old man had 'a huge old Dutch Bible, a hundred and fifty years old with pictures, maps, and commentary. He prided himself very much on his knowledge of it, and got it down, put on his spectacles, and showed me the map of the Garden of Eden.'

From the house of the old Boer, who 'terribly disliked modern innovations', Moseley moved to the Cape peninsula where he tried to shoot antelope – there were two local species called by the Dutch roebuck and grey goat – and met Mr McKellar who had an ostrich farm. McKellar owned the Cape of Good Hope, the whole length of it, and among his birds was an old hen ostrich, a household pet, that used 'to do sad damage in the farm-yard, eating the young goslings, swallowing them like oysters'. Beyond the terminal rocky mass of the Cape were cormorants, dazzling white sands, very pretty small tortoises, and tracks across the sand of cobras and 'the terrible puff-adder (*Clotho arietans*)'. Ichneumon and musk-cat, porcupine and a clawless otter, he saw them all, or found their tracks, and to his great pleasure the flora of the Cape was bewildering in its variety. To go walking, in imagination, with Mr Moseley is to become sadly aware of one's fearful insufficiencies: he attracts people who will be useful to him, he sees forty times as much as the ordinary tourist and describes what he sees without pomposity – unless it is pompous to claim possession of an educated eye – and with a charming precision. Moseley aboard the *Challenger* is like a seafaring Pepys, while Wyville Thomson, one imagines, was always aware of his responsibilities, and, it may be, a little overburdened by them.

John Murray played his part with tireless energy, but not until the voyage was over did he reveal his major share in it and emerge, not only as a robust and pertinacious naturalist, as its dedicated historian, but eventually as its patron too. And while each of them went about his business, Captain Nares was compiling his report to the Hydrographer of the Navy, and informing him 'that our observations indicate that the broad and comparatively sluggish South Atlantic drift current, running to the eastward before the continuous westerly winds, accumulates its water against the west coast of Africa, raising the level of the sea sufficiently to prevent the Agulhas current continuing its course, and swallows or diverts nearly the whole of it'. A statement which amply explains the well-known fact that the waves in Table Bay are colder than the kindly water of Simon's Bay.

Colder water lay ahead of them – seas glacially cold under the breaking cliffs of Antarctic ice – and vast quantities of heavy clothing were taken aboard to give the sailors some protection against freezing wind and flying spume. Woollen comforters, mittens, jerseys, thick drawers, sea-boots and sou'westers and iron-stiff pea-jackets were issued; and Swire thought it monstrously unfair that, while seamen got them free, officers had to pay for them. A lot of work had been done in South Africa: the ship had been fitted out again, and a new deck-house built for the greater convenience of the naturalists. They, moreover, before leaving Simon's Bay, had the satisfaction of recording 'one of the most important of the zoological discoveries of the voyage'.

The discovery was made by Moseley, and to the layman may, at first sight, seem

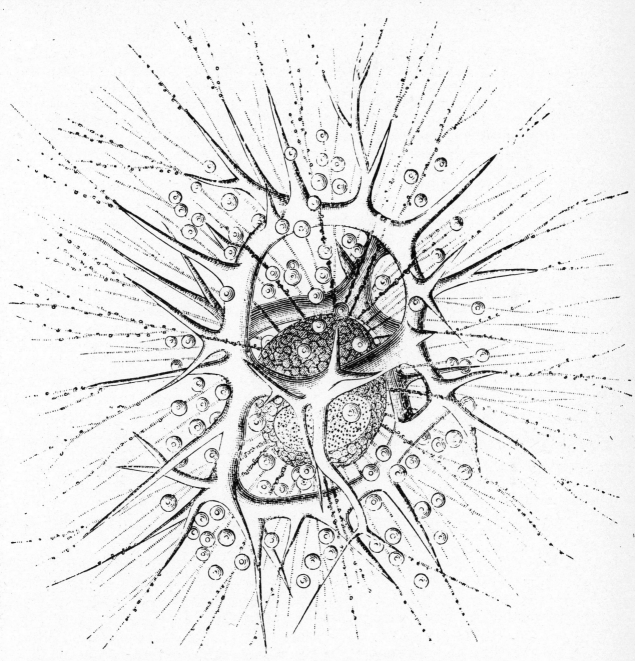

Lithocoronis challengeri, *one of the protozoa called radiolaria, so thoroughly investigated during the* Challenger's *voyage. Their characteristic division into two parts is clearly shown* ABOVE. *The central capsule is a highly organized structure surrounded by a skeleton made, in this instance, of a loose framework of siliceous rods. The whole protozoan might be the size of a pin head.*

insignificant. But to the naturalist, or anyone who, like a naturalist, is susceptible to the wonder that must attend revelation of yet another genus in the still uncounted diversity of life, the finding of 'a black caterpillar', *Peripatus*, may be as rewarding as, to the mountaineer, the sight of another snow-headed peak, bright and high in the Karakoram, that no geographer had yet mapped and named.

Peripatus – it might measure as much as three inches – had been seen before, but no naturalist had ever examined a freshly taken specimen. Previously thought to be 'a peculiar and aberrant form of earthworm', Moseley opened his capture – he had found it under an old cart-wheel at Wynberg – and immediately saw its tracheae and fully formed young within it: it breathed air and was viviparous. Moseley's educated eye also discerned horn-like antennae projecting from the head, which had a single pair of small and simple eyes; two muscles supported horny jaws, behind which was a mouth; further aft were seventeen pairs of short, conical feet; the skin was soft and flexible, and males were smaller than the females. The little creature belonged to an ancient genus that had colonized parts of the world so remote from each other as South Africa and New Zealand, the West Indies and Chile; and its success must have been due, in part, to its possession of a pair of glands, one on either side of its mouth, which were able, in emergency, to project with great force and rapidity a sticky fluid that discomfited its enemies.

Peripatus capensis and Moseley's discovery of it were both applauded, and after seven weeks in harbour the *Challenger* and her complement were ready for sea again.

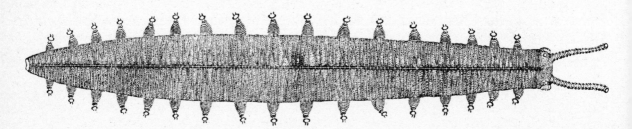

Peripatus capensis

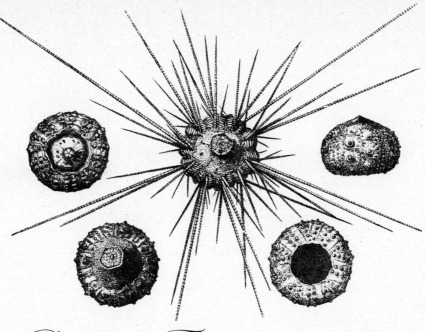

7 In the Roaring Forties

At 6.30 a.m. on December 17th *Challenger* left Simon's Bay under steam, and seven hours later sounding line and dredge were down in just under 100 fathoms. At 6 p.m. sail was made and a course shaped for the south. Sounding and dredging were resumed twelve hours later, and as on the previous day the dredge brought up green glauconitic sand, abundant on the Agulhas Bank that reaches south and east from the edge of the continent. On the 21st there was a moderate gale that raised waves twenty feet from hollow to crest, and the curious behaviour of the Agulhas Current was observed: on the 20th it had been running fast towards the west, on the 21st it was running equally fast to the east.

The air grew colder, the barometer fell. On the 23rd the wind backed into the north, and grew very squally. On the following day the weather was gloomy, the wind freshened to another moderate gale, and before dusk on Christmas Day Marion Island and Prince Edward Island were sighted. These were the nearest, and the first to be visited, of a chain of inhospitable islands – Edward and Marion, the Crozets, Kerguelen, and Heard – that stretches east and south from longitude 37° east to longitude 73° or thereabout, and from latitude 46° down to 53° south. Marion is about a thousand miles south of Cape Town.

It is pleasant to record that Christmas in the Roaring Forties was celebrated with an appropriate robustitude. On Christmas Eve, says Swire, 'one of the philosophers produced a large Scotch Bun, also some shortbread, and some dozens of bottles of fine old Mountain Dew'. The shortbread and the Mountain Dew were a suitable reminder of Edinburgh University's imaginative conception of the voyage, but one cannot help feeling that young Swire was in an excited mood when he counted 'some dozens' of bottles. He, however, who was not unduly given to adulation of the philosophers, offers a genial picture of them on Christmas Day when, he says, they drank and sang on the main deck after dinner; and Captain Nares was a generous commanding officer who saw that his sailors had their share of entertainment. The labour of dredging and sounding was always rewarded, it seems, by a tot of madeira wine, and on Christmas Eve and Christmas Day madeira was served to all hands. On Christmas Day the sailors had ham and plum duff, rum as well as madeira, and after the bo'sun's mates had piped all hands to dinner, the ship's band played *The Roast Beef of Old England*, a cheerful noise in those grim latitudes.

Marion Island was named in 1772 by Marion du Fresne, a French sailor looking for the Antarctic continent; Prince Edward, four years later, by Captain Cook; and in later years both whaling and sealing ships had made use of them in their rough and lonely trade. Marion rose to cloudy, snow-ridged peaks of over 4,000 feet; Prince Edward, much smaller, to rather more than half that height. As to their climate, the Report says glumly: 'The weather in the vicinity of the islands is seldom favourable, for owing to their height, their position in the open ocean far away from any larger tract of land, and the general prevalence of strong winds in their latitudes, they are seldom free from fog or mist, and their summits are but rarely visible, whilst days may elapse before a landing can be effected on either of them. . . . It is advisable to avoid their neighbourhood unless some considerable object is to be gained by visiting them.'

It was, however, in uncommonly fine, sunny weather that exploring parties landed on Marion on the 26th. Everyone carried a heavy stick, in the expectation of finding fur seals, and on the shore an elephant seal suffered from mistaken identification and was unhappily killed. Both fur and elephant seals had, indeed, been almost exterminated by the ruthless crews of the sealing ships that used the islands, but birds were still numerous. The Giant Petrel or 'Break-bones'; the large White Albatross, or 'Goney'; bold, savage skuas; and three kinds of penguin – Gentoo, Crested, and King – were all abundant. On an acre of hard, black mud, stamped smooth, there was a splendid rookery of King Penguins, many of the adults in fine plumage – white-shirted with a flash of bright orange-yellow on either side – and the young, who stood three feet high like their parents, looked as though they had been tightly inflated within their thick coats of chocolate-coloured down. All stood with head high, beak aloft, or ran upright at considerable speed, except a group that moved off at a clumsy hop, as if their feet were tied together: these were hen-birds who carried an egg in the brooding-patch between their legs.

This was the only King Penguin rookery that the naturalists saw, as a fully active community, throughout their voyage. They studied it with an absorbed interest, they laughed outright at the clownish gaiety of the birds, and someone observed that in the farther south the Giant Penguins who lived on perpetual ice must have

66

developed a brooding-patch as the only way of keeping their eggs alive until they hatched. Admiration grew when it was seen that the King Penguins were attended by a flock of Sheathbills (*Chionis minor*) that served as scavengers on the rookery. White Albatrosses, Sooty Albatrosses, and petrels (*Prion banksi*) that snarled like a puppy were also numerous, but for variety the birds could not compete with Marion's extraordinary vegetation: the botanists collected thirty-one different species of moss.

A volcanic island whose foundation of old lavas had been broken and covered by recent eruption, it had been covered again by an almost indecently riotous vegetable growth. *Azorella selago*, a characteristic plant of the southern islands – one of the Umbelliferae – grew in large convex masses, often several feet in diameter, so firm and compact that they scarcely yielded under foot. The Kerguelen cabbage grew there, though less abundantly than farther south, and there were great expanses of a persistent anonymous dull green broken only by the snowy plumage of nesting albatrosses. An attempt was made to find and reach the upper limit of vegetation, but failed because the fine weather before noon had changed for the worse and the sky was darkening. The explorers had enjoyed a few hours of bright visibility, but when thick cloud came down across the snow-line they returned to the ship; and when morning showed darker clouds and a rising sea it was realized that there would be no landing on Prince Edward; so *Challenger* made sail for the Crozets.

It was 6 p.m. on December 27th when she left Marion Island, and the following day – as if to advertise the inconstancy of the world's weather in its wilder parts – was again bright and sunny, with a smooth sea, barometer high, and a light northerly wind. It was misty but still calm on the 29th and 30th, and on those two days the trawling and dredging at depths of 1,375 and 1,600 fathoms were probably the most rewarding exercises, in deep sea exploration, of the whole voyage. It has already been made clear that in a narrative of this sort – designed for general reading and as a description of the manner in which the voyage was ordered and controlled – there is no room for a detailed account of the scientific discoveries that justified its labours and its cost; but occasionally there are statements in the Report which are of the utmost value – to the general reader as well as the specialist – because they exhibit and make clear, in much of its variety, the continuous work of the scientists, and throw light on the wide range of their interests, the limitless extent of what they might hope to find.

On the 29th and 30th, for example, 'between one and two hundred animals, belonging to nearly all the marine groups, were taken at each of the hauls, and with few exceptions they belonged to genera and species discovered for the first time by the Expedition. In the memoirs already published, seven new genera and thirty-five new species are described from the trawling in 1,375 fathoms, and nine new genera and twenty-nine new species from 1,600 fathoms; among these, twelve species are common to both stations. It is probable that these new species do not represent more than one-third of the whole number discovered, but this cannot be said with certainty till all the specialists have completed their reports.

67

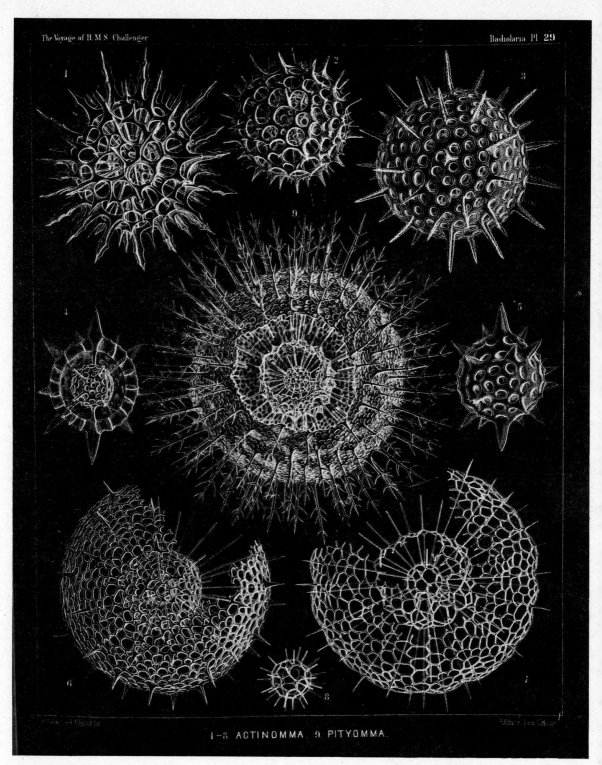

1–8 ACTINOMMA. 9 PITYOMMA.

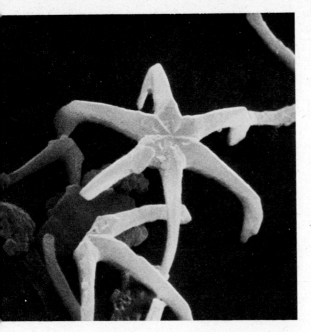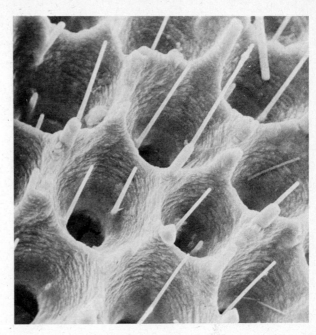

The delicate architecture of the radiolaria is shown LEFT *in one of the original plates from* the Report. *The technique of stereoscan photography, only recently developed, makes it possible to display similar animals convincingly in three dimensions at high magnifications.* ABOVE LEFT: Discoaster brouweri *(× 4,680), calcareous organisms, now extinct, related to coccoliths.* ABOVE RIGHT: Globigerinoides sacculifera *(× 1,000), a common foraminifera showing primary and secondary spines. Details: p282.*

'The deposit at 1,375 fathoms was a Globigerina ooze, containing eighty-one per cent of carbonate of lime, the residue being almost wholly remains of diatoms and radiolarians. At 1,600 fathoms there was only thirty-five per cent of carbonate of lime, forty per cent of diatom and radiolarian remains, and twenty-five per cent of minerals and argillaceous matter. There were a few rounded quartz particles in each of the deposits, but the great majority of the mineral particles were of volcanic origin. The carbonate of lime in these deposits consisted chiefly of Globigerinas and Coccoliths. Neither Orbulinas nor Rhabdoliths were observed in the deposits, nor at the surface, so that these stations are probably beyond the southern limit of these organisms.'

It would be a pity to reduce such words as Coccolith and Orbulina to the common tongue, and explain, in terms immediately comprehensible, what it was that trawl and dredge had brought to the surface or failed to find. The language of the biologist does something to symbolize, or even preserve, the secrecy of the ocean-floor; and the mere statement that, within a couple of days, fifty-two new species of marine 'animals' – minute but living creatures – had been captured, reveals the bewildering variety of life, hitherto unknown, that animated those profound and icy seas. The scientist can find elsewhere the animals' identifying names; the layman will be satisfied with the thought of so much that was new being gathered up in so short a time by gravely academic gentlemen working far from their familiar desks and laboratories in alien waters – very stormy waters under skies of monstrous enmity – with a devotion that obliterated all memory of the distance between the Old Quadrangle in Edinburgh and latitude 46° south.

At 1.30 a.m. on the last day of the year Hog Island in the Crozets was sighted, and *Challenger* tacked and stood off until daylight; which, in those latitudes and at that time of year, filled the sky at 3 a.m. Or, to be accurate, would banish the darkness of night but might be defeated by fog. On that morning, indeed, fog followed the dawn and *Challenger*, under topsails and jib, again had to stand off. At 3 p.m. the island was sighted once more – that is to say, its shore-line was made visible by breakers – and the ship ran southwards in deep water until, at 5 p.m., Penguin Island was seen through the mist, when sail was shortened to double-reefed topsails and in anticipation of darkness the ship hauled to the wind on the starboard tack. By 7 p.m. she was sailing slowly in a fog so dense that no one could see ahead for more than a few yards.

At midnight the New Year was brought in with sixteen bells – eight for the Old and eight for the New – and daylight came with low-lying fog, though overhead the sky was clear. The wind freshened, fog continued, and rain fell. The ship stood to the south, away from land, and morning came with a moderate gale. The wind grew less, however; the ship bore up for Possession Island, largest of the Crozets; and by midday the weather was fine, though still misty. From time to time the tall peaks of the island hills were visible, free from snow, and were thought to be as high as 5,000 feet; and while fog, still thick in patches, obscured the weather side of Possession, the lee side was sunlit. A course was laid along the south side of the island, and though there was fog ahead and fog behind the shore was visible, scored and gashed by waterfalls. On the south-east side there was a little sheltered cove, used by sealers, and at the head of the beach a deserted hut could be seen. The hill-slopes were covered with a vegetation like that on Marion, and with nesting albatrosses. An awkward swell, however, made it impossible either to land or anchor, and again the ship stood off under double-reefed topsails. On the morning of the 3rd there was a short, sharp gale, and from a distance of about fifteen miles the weather was still so thick that nothing could be seen of Possession Island or of the precipitous high cliffs of East Island, its smaller neighbour.

Hope was abandoned of landing anywhere on the Crozets; invisibly they receded into the inhospitable distance of their sad and treacherous climate; and *Challenger* headed eastwards to Kerguelen.

'King Penguins, standing bolt upright, side by side, as thick as they could pack, and jostling one another as one disturbed them', wrote Moseley of the King penguin rookery on Marion Island. RIGHT: *King penguins, adults, colourful, and juveniles, chocolate brown.*

70

On approaching them, they clapped their beaks, but were easily approached and are very far from graceful in their movements on shore — Their nests are composed of a round mass of clay — or rather earth. about 8 or 10 ins in height, and a foot in diameter, Under some we found an egg. which was quite white and about 6 inches in length. Several of these birds were slaughtered for their fur, and wing bones. the former from which to manufacture tobacco pouches; and the latter for pipe stems — It seems a pity almost to kill these beautiful birds for such purposes, but there are

of them, and the
few that we
compunction
a few of

such great quantities
visitors were &
felt such
in killing
their

Prince Edward's Island   from Marion Isd

We found the walking rather hard, the ground being composed of a soft clumpy grass and moss, which from constant snow and rain is quite sodden, and sometimes lets you through above one's knees Not a tree of any description is to be seen, and were it not for the Albatross. the Island would be very un-interesting indeed — We did not find any other of these birds, which measured more than 12 feet across the wings. but 11 to 12 feet was a common size for them — I was much astonished at their weight, and found it to be only 19½ lbs. this one was about 11 feet across the wings — Penguins again are remarkably heavy — and a much smaller bird — indeed he did not look more than a third as large weighed a good 14lbs. Albatross have a certain amount of difficulty in getting on the wing from the ground — being obliged to first run, then gradually

open out their
by attaining
they are
to
themselves
get the
under
when

wings, when
greater speed
enabled
lift
up
air
their
they

All we saw of
East Island   Crozt Group

sail away in of
manner — They sometimes miscalculate their speed in alighting too — for we saw them touch the ground, and turn a complete somersault before finally stopping — The Island abounded in beautiful fresh water, which fell in little rivulets on all sides — and under the lee and close by them, we found plenty of the Kerguelen cabbage which Cook mentions in his voyages to the Southward — It is a very curious

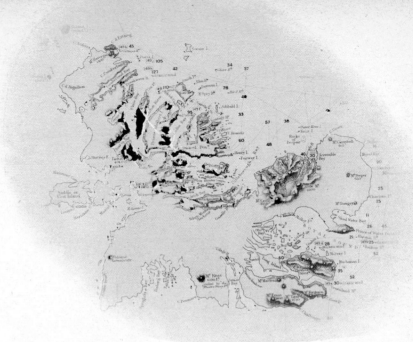

8 *Elephant Seals and Kerguelen Cabbage*

South-east by almost 3,000 miles of Cape Town, and south-west by rather more than that, of Australia, Kerguelen's Land lies just north of latitude 50° south, is between eighty and ninety miles long, and is also known as Desolation Island. It is mountainous, rising to 6,000 feet, of volcanic origin, and so deeply indented by long fjords that on a map or chart it appears to have been torn apart in naked anger. Beaten by the prevailing north-westerly winds of the Roaring Forties, it is subject to a considerable rainfall throughout the year, and in the centre of the island are permanent snowfields. Despite these climatic disadvantages, its scenery is said to be magnificent. It was discovered in 1772 by the Breton sailor, Yves Joseph de Kerguelen-Trémarec, one of those hopeful explorers who believed in the existence of a rich southern continent; and it was Yves Joseph, sadly disappointed, who re-christened it Desolation.

Challenger had a rough voyage from the Crozets, rolling violently in high seas, and there were a good many men on the sick list. It was not *mal de mer* from which they suffered, but coughs and colds and rheumatism; and Herbert Swire thought it unfortunate that discipline still required decks to be scrubbed every morning, for in that cold, wet climate they had no chance to dry again, and despite hot stoves and their warm clothing the sailors suffered.

The ship reached Christmas Harbour, near the northern corner of the island, on

LEFT: *Watercolours by Pelham Aldrich from his journal. Tantalizing views for the sailors and scientists, as the weather was bad and there was no landing on either Prince Edward's Island or East Island.*

January 7th, and anchored between high hills in vividly coloured scenery. Coal-black cliffs rose above a shore clothed with the bright, yellowish green of its rank vegetation, and at the head of the fjord was a sandy beach where a large party went ashore, all eager to kill a fur seal. Four sea elephants roared angrily when they were disturbed, and while they still held the attention of his companions, Moseley went farther and found an old male fur seal; or sea bear, as he calls it. Its gait was nimble – unlike that of other seals – and it was, he decided, a connecting link between true seals and sea otters. It was, moreover, difficult to kill: 'Fur seals are easily knocked over with a blow on the nose, but are very tenacious of life, and require to have their throats cut directly they are stunned, or they escape after all.' Moseley himself, however, killed two, though he deplored the indiscriminate slaughter of which the crews of some whaling schooners had lately been guilty: at Howes Foreland, not far away, over seventy sea bears had been killed in one day.

Teal were abundant, and many were killed. The Kerguelen Teal – brown with a metallic blue streak, and larger than the Common Teal – were remarkably tame. Moseley watched a flock rise from the bed of a river, and thought they were flying wildly because they had recently been shot at: 'but no, they got up merely to come and look at me. They pitched about forty yards off, and then set off running towards me in line, like farm-yard ducks, seven of them in a row, headed by a drake. As a sportsman, I hesitate to describe the termination of the scene. Only those who have been long at sea know what an intense craving for fresh meat is developed.' He

74

A vast assembly of wild birds forms a reception committee as Challenger *arrives in Christmas Harbour, Kerguelen,* LEFT: *Once ashore, the scientists and sailors were soon attacking seals, as Lt Channer's drawing shows.*

was, after all, shooting for the pot; 'the teal were excellent eating, and there were many mouths to feed'.

The succulence and flavour of the little brown duck were due to the abundance of the so-called Kerguelen cabbage, the fruit of which was their favourite food. The cabbage *(Pringlea antiscorbutica)* has some resemblance to the common or garden cabbage, but is perennial, peculiar to the Prince Edward, Crozet, Kerguelen and Heard islands, and belongs to a genus with no near ally. Its leaf-heads carry a pale yellow, highly pungent oil which gives the plant a peculiar flavour and a wholesome essence. It was discovered by Captain Cook, but first described by the botanist Joseph Hooker who in 1839 sailed with Sir James Ross on a voyage of Antarctic exploration. Ross commanded the ships *Erebus* and *Terror*, which later Sir John Franklin led to near-discovery of the North-West Passage. The sailors of these ships, during their stay on Kerguelen, had to eat its curious cabbage every day, boiled with salt beef or salt pork from the ships' harness casks. What the sailors thought of it, no one knows; but it added a fine flavour to Kerguelen Teal.

The *Challenger's* company enjoyed some unexpectedly fine weather, but though at times the sun shone brightly, it never shone for long. On the 8th the ship left Christmas Harbour in a snow-storm, and sailed under a bleak and cloudy sky for Accessible Bay – its shallow waters thick with kelp – at the eastern end of the island. A sheltered anchorage was found in a narrow inlet called Betsy Cove, and surveying and exploring parties left the ship. Sunday, the 11th, was as fine as a good day in May in England, and the whole ship's company went ashore to stretch their legs, while the officers and the naturalists shot enough teal to satisfy all hands. On the

75

Mr Wild, seated on a rock at Kerguelen, makes a drawing of Royal Sound RIGHT.

following day, however, a sudden violent squall from the north-east sent *Challenger* swinging across the narrow cove till her stern came within a few feet of the farther shore, and if her anchor had dragged she would have gone aground. The 13th was bright and cold – too cold for comfort – but surveying parties went about their work, and on the 14th there was so much swell outside the cove that the steam pinnace, which set out to carry an exploring party westward, had to return to harbour.

Then, on the 16th, began a very stormy passage from Accessible Bay to the north-eastern corner of the island, to double Cape Digby and sail south along the coast to the great islet-studded, sheltered expanse of Royal Sound. Under sail and steam the ship cleared the land, but the wind freshened to a gale – by 9 p.m. it was blowing at force ten – and she lay hove-to under triple-reefed fore and main topsails till some time after midnight when the wind moderated. At daylight she wore round, made more sail to double-reefed topsails and courses, and continued the passage in better conditions. The wind fell, and as soon as the weather permitted dredging began again, and surveying parties were put ashore.

It was Captain Cook who had given Royal Sound its noble name, and it was indeed a handsome sheet of water that another fine day – not a cloud in the sky – allowed all to appreciate. Twenty miles from its broad sea-door to its brightly coloured western beaches, the Sound in its inner parts bore a covey of flat-topped islands sloping gently to the east and divided by deep-water channels, which may have been shaped by a huge glacier that once covered them all, then gradually

76

shrank and carved channels between the masses of rock which survived erosion. Islands, bays, and shore-line were carefully and busily surveyed, and then *Challenger* left Royal Sound for Cape George at the south-eastern corner of Kerguelen, but the weather was brutally unkind, with a great swell under the Cape and – as the Report says – 'the willywaughs coming down from the hills with much force and raising a quantity of spoondrift'. ('Spoondrift' is merely a variant of spindrift, and 'willy-waugh', usually spelt williewaw, is the whalers' word for the fierce squalls that race down such forbidding slopes as those which dominate Kerguelen, or rise above the dismal Straits of Magellan, and, as they open out across the sea, make a melancholy, daunting noise above its blackened water.) To avoid the swell and the williewaws the ship stood north again, and found shelter in the steep-sided fjord called Green-land Harbour.

Another attempt was made, and defeated, to sail westward round Cape George, and from the 22nd till the end of January *Challenger* was on passage – often hindered by adverse, violent, or foggy weather – to the north again, round Cape Digby to Betsy Cove, and back to Christmas Harbour. On Howe Island, and other salient points, surveying parties took station to relate, or connect, the little known southern parts of Kerguelen with its more familiar north shore; and all admitted that to stand by a theodolite for three or four hours on the top of a hill, with a wind that blew coldly through reefer jackets and heavy drawers, was wretched work. But a vast amount of surveying had been done before they left, and the naturalists had

Kerguelen cabbage, Pringlea antiscorbutica.

been well pleased to find more penguin rookeries, to look at the curious wingless flies *(Calycopterix moseleyi)* that infested Kerguelen cabbage, and conjecture the age of fossilized tree-trunks.

There was a sort of coal on Kerguelen – but a coal that would not burn unaided – and there were sea elephants (or elephant seals) of so large a size that a bull, twelve feet long and enormously heavy, defeated all attempts by Mr Moseley and Lieutenant Channer to kill it with a weighted club; its skull, as Moseley explains, 'is protected above by a high intermuscular ridge or crest, and the bones around its nostrils are very strong.' Moseley needed its bones to build a skeleton, however, so he shot it, and as they rolled it down to the water they were attended by great flocks of birds, in hope of carrion, chief among them the Giant Petrel or 'Break-bones'. Mutton-birds, skuas and sheathbills – a multitude of birds, a jungle density of vegetation in the low-lying parts of the island – these were the dominating features of that high-rearing Antarctic outpost, and when they sailed away Moseley was sorry to leave it. With something less than his usually objective judgement he says that they had had 'wonderfully good weather' – a statement not wholly substantiated by the Report – and one can only infer that he had richly enjoyed himself.

Herbert Swire, on the other hand, was unfeignedly glad to leave. He had, indeed, been captivated by the occasional splendour of a green and golden sky, but he remembered the outrageous gales of wind that alternated with spells of fair weather and he was very tired of standing by a theodolite on the top of some dismal, barren hill while a piercing wind sought the very marrow in his bones.

Kerguelen, again abandoned to the whalers, still bore lasting memories of the *Challenger*'s visit, for some of its ragged heights, some of its many islands, hitherto anonymous, now had distinguished names. Mount Wyville Thomson, on the south side of Royal Sound, rose to 3,160 feet; Mount Moseley, near Betsy Cove, to 2,400; west of Cape George were Mounts Ferguson and Tizard, named after the Chief Engineer and the Navigating Lieutenant; and near the entrance to Royal Sound were Buchanan and Murray Islands.

From Kerguelen to Heard Island – farther to the east and lying below latitude 53° south – was only about three hundred miles, but for four days the ship beat about in fog, lay becalmed one day, and did not sight the small inaccessible Macdonald Islands, some sixty miles west of Heard, until February 6th. Between Kerguelen and Heard the sea varied greatly in depth, from less than 100 fathoms to 425, and from its surface the towing net took great masses of diatoms, which are unicellular algae with the power of locomotion and cell-walls of silica. In the afternoon of the 6th *Challenger* anchored in Whisky Bay on the north shore of Heard, and Captain Nares, Moseley, and Buchanan promptly went ashore.

Six glaciers, coming right down to a beach of black, volcanic sand were visible, but cloud enveloped Big Ben, the peak that towered, 6,000 feet high, above the backbone of the island. Deep blue crevasses split the glaciers, and above and beyond their fantastically sculptured ridges lay deep snow. The whole coastline seemed to consist of ice-cliffs and headlands of ice, but at the head of Whisky Bay was half a mile of flat black sand and there, to help the *Challenger*'s boat through the surf, were half a dozen sealers, of wild appearance and rifle in hand, who had come down to question their unexpected visitors. They could not imagine why anyone should land on Heard Island for any purpose other than their own. On the dismal sandy plain beyond the beach was evidence of what the sealers came for: on the lanes of their slaughter lay the bones of thousands of skeletons of sea elephants. The climate of Heard Island, said the sealers, was a great deal worse than that of Kerguelen; and to prove it the black sand blew fiercely against the visitors' faces, and great rocks, tumbled from the heights above, had been cut by sand-blast as smoothly as if they had been dressed by a mason's chisel. But the sealers' voyages to an inhospitable shore had not been unprofitable.

In Kerguelen the glaciers had retreated into the interior, leaving most of the land free from ice; but Heard Island, only three hundred miles away, was still in its glacial period, and for that the tall height of Big Ben, and the large area where snow lay and never melted, were responsible. Plant life did exist: beyond the dismal plain were patches of green on muddy hummocks, there was a grass called *Poa cookii*, and the Kerguelen cabbage grew. But Heard Island, says Moseley, has 'a miserably poor flora, even for the higher latitudes of the southern hemisphere', and the greater part of its land surface, that was free from ice, was without vegetation. The sea was more productive, for seaweed lay in masses on the beach – Moseley discovered eight species, two of them previously unknown – but no kelp grew though it had grown abundantly at Kerguelen.

On that glacial, barren, storm-beaten land there lived about forty men whose job was to kill sea elephants, remove their blubber, and boil it down. They were visited once a year by the American barque *Roman* and her tenders, the schooners that the *Challenger*'s people had encountered at Kerguelen; and the majority of the sealers were, presumably, citizens of the United States, though two of the six who met Captain Nares and his party were Portuguese from the Cape Verde Islands. They had engaged to remain three years on the island, during which time a man might make as much as 500 dollars. They appeared to be reasonably contented, they had good clothing, and 'did not look particularly dirty'. They lived in wooden huts sunk deep into the ground – a roof over a hole was what they resembled – and their rations were biscuit, pork and beans, flour and molasses; but their principal food was penguins, and penguin skins, with fat adhering to them, gave them fuel on which to cook the birds. Their lives were hazardous, for to establish or maintain communication with other groups they had to walk along the beach under the overhanging eaves of the glaciers – from which a small iceberg might fall, and often did – or across the glaciers and the crevasses that split them; and sometimes a man might despair of such employment, succumb to an Antarctic *cafard*, and run amok.

Their employment was, indeed, both brutal and squalid. In the breeding season the sea elephants gathered in thousands on a long beach on the weather side of the island, but boats could not land on that beach, and heavy loads of blubber could not be carried across the glaciers that separated it from the leeward beaches. The sea elephants had therefore to be driven off the weather beach, where men were stationed and armed with long whips made of elephant hide. The bulls fought back, and old males, called 'beach-masters' by the sealers, were enormously strong and marvellously pugnacious. When the weather was really bad, however, and by ferocious attack the whole herd had been driven into the sea, the animals swam obediently round to a leeward beach where another party of sealers waited to club them to death.

The females give birth to their young soon after coming ashore, and suckle them. Then the young – almost black at birth – are left to themselves, and the sealers ignore them until they have put on weight. The sealers thought they grew fat without further feeding, and Moseley, though he did not share that curious belief, could not explain the rapid growth of the calves.

He and the others spent only three hours on the beach, for the wind was increasing, the sea rising, and they left in a hurry. On the following morning there was snow on the ship's deck, two inches deep, and worsening weather prevented them from going ashore again. *Challenger* put to sea, and for six days sailed almost due south.

RIGHT, ABOVE: *adult Weddell seal with her pup.* BELOW: *a harem of Elephant seals with an old male beach-master in the centre, his proboscis raised. These were the creatures the sealers killed in their thousands.*

OVERLEAF: *tabular icebergs on the edge of the Antarctic.*

first Iceberg Wednesday Feb 11. 1874
Lat 61°S Long 80°E after H. Swire.

9 An archipelago of glittering ice

At the very start of her passage to the Antarctic ice she was warned – as it may seem – of the danger she invited, for at 1 a.m. on February 8th a heavy sea struck her and stove in the two foremost ports on the starboard side of the main deck, flooding the sick-bay; which, by good fortune, was unoccupied. Then the gale began to subside, and by 8 a.m. *Challenger* was under all plain sail, the day was fine and clear, and a fine night followed. A sharp look-out was kept for icebergs, but none was seen.

On the 9th, despite occasional snow-squalls, the weather continued clear, but in a squall the temperature fell, for the first time, below freezing point. Position at noon on the 10th was latitude 60° south, longitude 77° east; and still no ice to be seen. Then, in the early morning of the 11th, a long pale rectangle showed above a calm sea; soundings were taken and showed a depth of 1,260 fathoms over diatom ooze. The table-topped berg was 2,100 feet long and 220 feet high; if a cube, its depth under water would be about 1,800 feet. But despite its size it was unstable, and before noon – making a great commotion in the water – it calved.

More bergs were seen on the 12th, one of them a bright cobalt blue in colour, but now the weather was overcast, with a drizzle of rain, and before midnight the ship was hove-to, just in time to avoid a collision. At daylight sail was again made to the south, and icebergs became numerous. No albatrosses were seen but there were many Cape Pigeon and petrels, and a few whales. At 3 a.m. on the 14th pack-ice was

LEFT: *two watercolours by Moseley. The upper picture shows Corinthian Harbour, Heard Island.*

85

in sight to the south-east, the ship's position being latitude 65° south, longitude 79°
east, and the curious discovery was made that the temperature of the sea, 33 °F at
the surface, remained constant at 29 °F to a depth of 200 fathoms, and below that
began to rise. At 3.30 p.m. sail was made, and *Challenger* stood to the west along the
edge of the pack-ice.

For the next fifteen days – from February 15th till March 1st – the ship went
sailing through a strange and beautiful archipelago of many-coloured islands:
islands that gave the archipelago a fascinating but perilous character, because they
were all in movement. On the 16th, after passing a pyramid of ice the hue of a turquoise – the sea calm, visibility perfect – it appeared, to an observer at the mast-head,
that icebergs ahead formed a solid cliff; but always, as the ship drew closer, the cliff
broke into tabular islands, some at least four miles long, but all about 200 feet high
with steep, inaccessible sides. It had been hoped to land on one of them, but vertical
walls and a constant swell made that impossible, and *Challenger*, still heading south,
crossed the Antarctic Circle, stood on for another ten miles, and then tacked and
turned to the north. Her purpose was not to go as far south as possible, but only to
ascertain the temperature and depth of the sea on which a galaxy of icebergs drifted;
and Captain Nares may have remembered that American officer, aboard the ship
which discovered some parts of Wilkes Land, who when asked for his written
opinion as to the expediency of going farther into the Antarctic, replied that 'he
failed to see the utility of proceeding when there was so great a probability of no one
living to carry home the tale'.

Much interest was taken in the architecture of icebergs – in the uniformity of so many, in their table-tops above steep sides and a submarine foundation as much as nine times their visible height – but it was their colouring that gave most pleasure. White with a bluish tint – often capped with the absolute white of newly fallen snow – was the general hue, the mass effect; but closer inspection might show parallel streaks of cobalt blue, or a marbling of blue. The caves and crevasses of a large berg seemed to reflect a pure, deep azure light, of marvellous intensity; occasionally a small berg resembled a huge crystal of copper sulphate; and the grey sky beyond would redden to a complementary rose. At their foot the sea was dark as indigo, and rising surf froze into pendant icicles. The sea would fill their caves with a resounding roar, and roar out again pursued by thundrous echoes. The southern ocean and its dazzling archipelago were full of a tumultuous noise, and in their beauty was recurrent danger.

When, in a clear sky, the sun set round and red, the bergs immediately in front of it showed a menacing outline, hard and dark, but on the horizon, on either side, they turned bright red, and against the scarlet of distant ice there were nearer islands of salmon-pink. There was, says Moseley, one exceptionally brilliant sunset when the sun, before it touched the horizon, was a golden incandescence that lighted *Challenger*'s spars and shrouds with a lambent flush; then, when the sun went down, the horizon became very dark, and above it was a streak of gold topped by a band of green, and dark clouds with crimson edges. And icebergs, with gem-like clarity, reflected both crimson and gold.

The danger of such beauty came disconcertingly near on the 24th, when the dredge was put over in 1,300 fathoms, but had to be hauled as a south-easterly wind increased to a gale. Snow was falling, and visibility poor. With steam up, and close-reefed topsails, the ship at slow speed sought shelter under the lee of a berg. But in a momentary lull – as the opposing wind fell and briefly the sky was calm – she gathered way, and before the engines could be stopped rammed the berg, carrying away the jib-boom and its securing stay, or martingale. She went astern, topsails were furled, and she lay-to under staysails while the wreckage of the jib-boom was brought in. The weather worsened, and snow fell heavily. Steam was got up in all four boilers, and main-deck ports were barred. Then, in the thick of a heavy squall, a berg loomed up under the lee bow. There was no room to steam ahead, so with engines full stern the main yards were backed, the weather half of the main topsail shaken out, and the ship gathered stern-way. She lay broadside to the wind until the drifting berg was cleared, and then an attempt was made to steam up under its lee. But even under full power, and with stay-sails set, she refused to face the wind, and drifted again. Providentially another large berg appeared to leeward, the weather moderated a little, and under its lee she was able to come about. But an anxious night followed, and *Challenger* could do no better than tack to and fro in the dubious shelter of the slowly drifting bergs.

That résumé of mischance and evasive or remedial action does not tell the whole story. It contains the dry, official bones of the story, but does nothing to illustrate its violence or expose the emotions, inseparable from violence, of actors in the story. In the next chapter, however, there will be a brief description of the working parts of a sailing-ship – of masts and rigging, yards and the sails roped to them – and there, in its appropriate place, against that background, will be another, much more vigorous rendering of the story by an officer on duty at the time. Here the narrative must keep in step with events.

On the 26th, at 4.30 p.m., there were forty bergs in sight, and the Edinburgh naturalists may have anticipated the lively emotion – if not the actual words – of that memorable couplet in *McAndrew's Hymn:*

> 'Hail, Snow and Ice that praise the Lord! I've met them at their work,
> An' wished we had anither route or they anither kirk.'

Snow threatened, and another gale was blowing up. At 6.30 p.m. a very large iceberg was seen to windward, and under steam and sail the ship worked up towards it. Having found shelter, as if behind a vast breakwater, sails were furled and with steam in all four boilers she was able to hold her position. But the night was not without its dangers, for the wind rose to force nine, blew in fierce gusts over the top of the berg, and then for a little while would fall away, before howling again in the fullness

RIGHT: *Pelham Aldrich gives a close description of the events of February 24th in his journal, and illustrates the action himself.*

at about 9 am. but the wind had in the meantime freshened to a gale and he found it had not been to the bottom — As the Barometer is in its way down, and the weather looked very threatening. the ship was steamed under the lee of a Berg, and orders given to take reef the topsails. Unfortunately the ship just forged ahead into the Berg — an

one or two slight heaves of the swell alongside deprived us of a Jib-boom Dolphin Striker & Starboard Whisker gaff! — We immediately got clear — and it came on fearfully thick with heavy wind and sleet — and I spent a very lively forenoon watch on the Bowsprit clearing away the wreck from under the bows — as the Boom dropped immediately the Jib Stay was let go! — notwithstanding a good Jib whip was put on the Boomwork! — By noon the wreck was got in — and the ship hove to under steam and some small fire of Canvass — During the afternoon it came on still thicker — and it was

very anxious work — about 3pm. a large Berg loomed out in the mist under the lee of the ship — and it became a question of whether or no we could clear it — the gale was too strong to beach the ship up — and there was no room to wear — our hands were turned up, and by dint of loosing the Main Topsail, hoisting the Staysail and reversing the engines at full speed we escaped and of its fury; and that kept the engineers awake and anxious, for in 1873 steam-power was less instantly responsive, and needed more nursing, than in later years.

At daylight on the 27th the ship left the shelter of her breakwater, sail was made though the wind still blew at force nine, and she headed northward. The wind moderated, the glass was rising, and though on the following day icebergs were still numerous, the greatest number visible at any one time was only twenty-four. *Challenger* was emerging from the archipelago, and on Sunday, March 1st, though four bergs were seen in the early morning, at noon and midnight no ice was visible; and a course was set for Melbourne.

An iceberg photographed from the deck of Challenger.

10 *A starfish and a storm*

At noon on March 1st the ship's position was latitude 58° south, longitude 101° east. She was still two or three hundred miles south of the latitude of Cape Horn, that is, and approximately in the longitude of the Gulf of Siam. She was more than 3,000 miles from Melbourne.

The first part of the voyage that was renewed in Cape Town – the exploration of Marion Island, the attempt on the Crozets – gave the voyagers a rough introduction to the vagaries of weather in sub-Antarctic latitudes; it rewarded them with the enthralling and hilarious spectacle of a full community of King Penguins, and on December 29th and 30th the deep sea yielded to the dredge an astonishing number, in remarkable variety, of 'animals' hitherto unknown. The second part, from Christmas Harbour in Kerguelen's Land to the black beach on Heard Island, was made memorable by fur seals and elephant seals, Kerguelen Teal and Kerguelen cabbage; and a great deal of hard work was done by surveying parties. The third part, in the icy archipelago, was an historic occasion, for only five previous expeditions had been sent out, from Britain and other countries, to explore Antarctic regions; though many ships, for purposes of their own, had gone far beyond the Antarctic Circle. On that third part, moreover, the naturalists had observed the difficulties of ship-handling in confined waters and rough weather.

Before leaving the Antarctic, however, it seems proper to mention an uncovenanted benefit of seeking life in the depths of the sea. Among the discoveries made in the mixed cargoes of dredge or trawl there were often creatures which, apart from

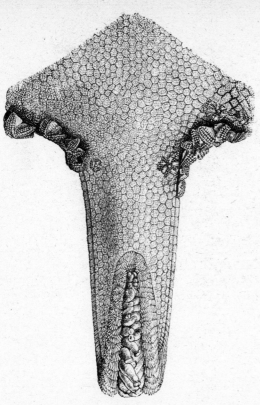

LEFT: Leptychaster kerguelensis
RIGHT: Cladodactyla crocea

their scientific interest, were so intricately made, so fantastically designed – so beautiful, to be brief and absolute – that in comparison with them the confections of a master-jeweller are no better than laboured, unimaginative 'prentice work. Laboratory specimens of the choicest sort, a biologist's delight, they were also works of art – of consummate, living art – and the language of the scientist who describes them, difficult though it may be, is often worth a little study because at its best – its curious best – it may achieve an elegance not unworthy of what it describes.

Consider, for example, a starfish found some distance from the south-east coast of Kerguelen's Land that acquired the unwieldy name of *Leptychaster kerguelensis*. It was quite a large animal – the woodcut is a little larger than its actual size – and at first sight it looks very like a creation by Fabergé, designed for the Czarina of Russia; but, of course, better than anything Fabergé made because it was living, as its description – or some part of its description – amply proves:

'The dorsal surface of the body is covered with a tessellated pavement composed of capitate paxilli.[1] The heads of the paxilli in close apposition combine to form a mosaic with rudely hexagonal facets; and as they are raised upon somewhat slender shafts, whose bases, like the plinths of columns, rest upon the soft perisome,[2] arcade-like spaces are left between the skin and the upper calcareous pavement. The eggs pass into these spaces from ovarial openings: on bending the perisome and separating the facets, they may be seen in numbers among the shafts of the paxilli. There is a

[1] Latin *paxillus* is a small stake or peg; capitate paxilli are pegs with knobs on.
[2] Perisome is the body-wall of an echinoderm.

92

continual discharge of ova into the passages, so that eggs and young in different stages of development occupy the spaces at one time. The young do not escape until at least six ambulacral[1] suckers are formed on each arm; they may then be seen pushing their way out by forcing the paxilli to the side, and squeezing through the chink between them.'

For another, very different example of the *objets d'art* retrieved in the interests of science regard the sea-slug called *Cladodactyla crocea*. In other than scientific terms it might be labelled 'zoological baroque'; and it may be remembered that according to Bernini the baroque architects – of whom he knew more than most – regarded themselves as vessels of divine grace. The sea-slug was captured in 75 fathoms north of Heard Island, its colour was a bright saffron-yellow, its length between eighty and a hundred millimetres, and Wyville Thomson describes it:

'The mouth and excretory opening are terminal; ten long, delicate, branched tentacles surround the mouth; the perisome is thin and semi-transparent, and the muscular bands, the radial vessels, and even the internal viscera can be plainly seen through it. The three anterior ambulacral vessels are approximated, and on these the tentacular feet are numerous and well developed, with a sucking-disk supported by a round cribriform calcareous plate, or more frequently by several wedge-shaped radiating plates arranged in the form of a rosette; and these three ambulacra form together, at all events in the female, a special ambulatory surface.

[1]From Latin *ambulare* to walk: ambulacral suckers are a sort of feet.

'In a very large proportion of the females which I examined, young were closely packed in two continuous fringes adhering to the water-feet of the dorsal ambulacra. The young were in all the later stages of growth, and of all sizes from five up to forty mm. in length; but all the young attached to one female appeared to be nearly of the same age and size. Some of the mothers with older families had a most grotesque appearance – their bodies entirely hidden by the couple of rows, of a dozen or so each, of yellow vesicles like ripe yellow plums ranged along their backs, each surmounted by its expanded crown or oral tentacles. All the young I examined were miniatures of their parents.'

That the scientists, for their successes, depended on the sailors is clear enough – in that respect visibility is excellent – and something more should be said of those days and nights in the sea of icebergs when, it is evident, mishap was avoided only by the exercise of sound seamanship. At no time was the ship in danger of becoming a total loss, but in less skilful hands she might, on more than one occasion, have suffered serious damage; and a few notes on marine engines of the 1870s, and the handling of a square-rigged ship under sail, may be a useful guide to appreciation of what Captain Nares, his officers, petty officers and men had to do in all circumstances, and with great speed and dexterity in difficult circumstances.

The nominal horse-power by which engines used to be rated was an arbitrary term of no special significance, and 'the indicated power of 1,234 horses' that *Challenger* was said to possess cannot be accepted as a measure of her engine's actual efficiency. A reciprocating compound engine, it depended on steam raised, to a pressure of between forty-five and sixty lb. to the square inch, in four cylindrical or 'Scotch' boilers; and can only be described as post-primitive. It lacked flexibility, it required a great deal of attention, it depended on the quality of the coal in the ship's bunkers, and its consumption of coal was heavy in comparison with what was later expected of an engine. Only sixty years had passed since Henry Bell's *Comet* first moved under steam-power on the Clyde, and not for another thirty years would turbines be in common use. *Challenger* made history as the first vessel, depending in part on steam-power, to enter the Antarctic Circle, but she could not have gone so far, and come safely out again, without her sail-power.

As a three-masted, square-rigged ship she carried on her foremast – from the deck upwards – a fore-sail or fore course; a large topsail, a much smaller topgallant sail; and above that a little royal. On her mainmast a main-sail or main course, main topsail, topgallant, and royal, and on her mizen another topsail, topgallant, and royal. All these hung square from the yards, and she had in addition eight or nine fore-and-aft sails: flying, outer, and inner jibs, fore-topmast staysail, two staysails between fore and mainmast, two more between main and mizen, and, farthest aft, spanker and gaff-topsail. Each of these sails can justifiably be regarded as a wind-engine, and to use their power to the full they all had to be set – the yards trimmed according to the direction of the wind – in such a way that each was full and drawing. In changeable weather constant attention was needed to their set, which was

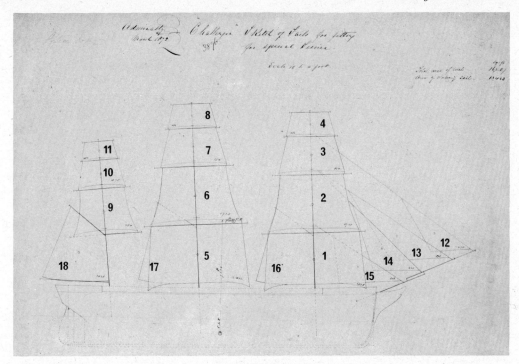

When Challenger *was fitted out for special service in 1872, she carried over 16,000 square feet of sails. On the original sail plan* ABOVE *is a superimposed key. 1 fore-sail. 2 fore topsail. 3 fore topgallant. 4 fore royal. 5 main-sail. 6 main topsail. 7 main topgallant. 8 main royal. 9 mizen topsail. 10 mizen topgallant. 11 mizen royal. 12 flying jib. 13 outer jib. 14 inner jib. 15 fore topmast staysail. 16 main topmast staysail. 17 mizen staysail. 18 spanker. Not all the fore and aft sails are shown.*

governed by braces, halyards, tacks and sheets – clew-lines, bunt-lines, and other purposive strings – and the officer on watch needed an artist's eye as well as the robustitude without which sailors did not long continue to be sailors.

Life was easy, indeed, when reaching before a steady Trade Wind, with the wind on the quarter, and day after day in brisk, warm weather the ship sailed on without a hand touching brace or tack; but to go about – to change direction when facing the wind, that is – was a major exercise in any weather. Unlike a steamship, that turns to port or starboard in obedience to her rudder and the man at the wheel, a sailing-ship had to be coaxed and driven – had to dress her yards and trim her sails to overcome the opposition of the wind before, on the other tack, she could again use the wind to send her forward – and to understand the complexity of the operation, if not the operation itself, a description of it, in some detail, is necessary.

Richard Henry Dana, an American lawyer who became famous for his description of a seaman's life in a book called *Two Years Before the Mast*, wrote also, and published in 1815, *The Seaman's Friend, A Treatise on Practical Seamanship;* and here are his directions for going about:

95

'Have the ship so suited with sails that she may steer herself as nearly as possible, and come to with a small helm. Keep her a good full, so that she may have plenty of headway. *Ready, About!* Send all hands to their stations. . . .

'Ease the helm down gradually; *Helm's alee!* and let go the jib sheets and fore sheets. As soon as the wind is parallel with the yards, blowing directly upon the leeches of the square sails, so that all is shaking, *Raise tacks and sheets!* and let go the fore and main tacks and main sheet, keeping the fore and main bowline fast. As soon as her head is within a point or a point and a half of the wind, *Mainsail haul!* let go the lee main and weather cross-jack braces, and swing the after yards round. While she is head to the wind, and the after sails are becalmed by the head sails, get the main tack down and sheet aft, and right your helm, using it afterwards as her coming to or falling off requires. As soon as she passes the direction of the wind, shift your jib sheets over the stays, and when the after sails take full, or when she brings the wind four points on the other bow, and you are sure of paying off sufficiently, *Let go and haul!* brace round the head yards briskly, down fore tack and aft the sheet, brace sharp up and haul your bowlines out, and trim down your head sheets.'

Dana, of course, assumes good weather and ideal conditions for the operation. But conditions were never ideal throughout a voyage, and in *Log Letters from the Challenger*, by Sub-Lieutenant Lord George Campbell, there is a good, lively description of the circumstances in which the ship had to beat-about among the icebergs on the night of February 24th and the following day. *Challenger* was fortunate in having an engine that helped her to go about, or go astern, but Campbell's account makes it clear that she was primarily a sailing-ship, dependent on the power of her sails.

'Hitherto we have had tolerably fine weather,' he writes, 'nothing much to disturb our peace of mind except darkness, snow-squalls, and thick weather among icebergs. But now we are going to have a disagreeable change. During the night we hove to, and at four o'clock put the dredge over; but the wind suddenly coming on to blow fresh from the southward, the dredge was hove up in a hurry, by which time it was blowing a gale, with heavy snow-squalls and very thick weather. Having steam up we went under the lee of a sloping-sided berg, and treble-reefed the top-sails. During this operation the eddy current carried the ship too near. Bump, bump! smash, crash! as the ship rose and fell with the swell, spearing the ice with the dolphin-striker which, as well as one whisker and the jib-boom, carried away, left all the head-gear in a state of wreck, while the men aloft, thinking they would have the topgallant mast about their ears, scurried down with marvellous activity. We then sheered off, hove to under storm trysails, got steam up ready in four boilers, laid the yards ready for making a stern-board, and so drifted along; the gale increasing fast, weather thick as pea-soup, and small, very hard snow pinging into one's face like a shower of peas blown through a steam blast. Temperature 22°F (the coldest we experienced, but 22°F with a whole gale blowing over the pack feels very much colder than it sounds). We drifted on all fore-noon, seeing no bergs through the fog and blinding showers of snow, though we knew that they were close around somewhere. In the meantime we were hard at work getting in the wreck of the head-gear – no easy work in the intense cold and violent wind – when suddenly, at three o'clock, in the middle of a tremendous thick squall, comes the hail from the forecastle, "Iceberg close to under the lee bow, Sir!" There is no room to steam ahead, so "Full speed astern!" Rattle, rattle, goes the screw, sixty revolutions a minute; "Clear lower deck, make sail!" shriek the boatswain's mates; on deck flies everybody; "Maintopmen aloft, loose the maintopsail!" "Fore part, take in the fore-trysail!" The captain and commander howling out orders from the bridge, hardly heard in the roaring of the wind; officers repeating the howls. The weather-clew of the maintopsail is set back, the headsails taken in, slowly she gathers sternway, keeping her head turning slightly towards the berg, a towering, dim white mass looming grimly through the driving snow, and then she clears it – a narrow shave! The violence of the wind prevented us then from making a friend of our enemy by keeping under its lee, so the ship was again allowed to drift on, amid dense fog and snow, till five o'clock, when another iceberg was seen at a little distance ahead, to leeward of which we drifted, where, the wind being broken, the ship's head was turned by means of steam and sail, and all night long we kept dodging backwards and forwards between these two bergs, where we knew the sea to be clear of dangers. In the evening the weather became clearer, though it still blew hard; deck covered with slush ice. Anxious work enough for the officers of watches and the captain, who was on deck for I don't know how many continuous hours.'

For the sixteen days of her passage from the icebergs to Melbourne, *Challenger* relied on her sails except when sounding or dredging, and in tolerably fine weather encountered no trouble. She had left Cape Town on December 17th, and it was on March 17th that she anchored off Sandridge, the seaport suburb of Melbourne; when, says Campbell, 'there was joy among us'. They had been three months at sea, except for a few days ashore on Marion and Kerguelen, and 'of gales, snow, icebergs, and discomfort generally we had had enough, and the memory of a dinner I ate at the club the first evening, followed by the opera, yet lingers in my memory as one of the pleasantest experiences of a poorly paid and laborious career'. But then – he is writing home – honesty compels him to admit that 'the Southern cruise was well worth the discomfort', and already, in retrospect, those desolate southern islands seem delightful; the weather, on the whole, had been very fine; and 'there are few people now alive who have seen such superb Antarctic iceberg scenery as we have'.

Australia gave the explorers a very warm welcome; there were formal receptions, excursions were arranged, and hospitality opened a hundred doors. The visitors reciprocated, and showed their admiration of Melbourne's busy harbour, of the crowded city whose solid buildings and broad streets were evidence of rapid growth and a stable prosperity that none could view without a surprised respect; for Melbourne, founded in 1837, was not yet fifty years old. In the history of the cruise, however, the Australian interlude was of small importance: the ship was refitted

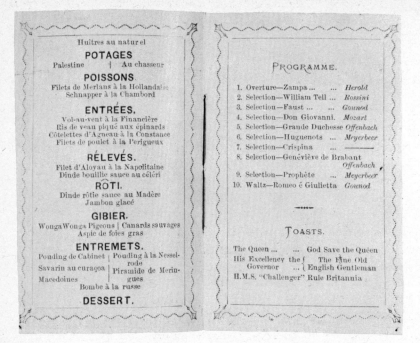

Huîtres au naturel

POTAGES

Palestine | Au chasseur

POISSONS

Filets de Merlans à la Hollandaise
Schnapper à la Chambord

ENTRÉES.

Vol-au-vent à la Financière
Ris de veau piqué aux épinards
Côtelettes d'Agneau à la Constance
Filets de poulet à la Périgueux

RELEVÉS.

Filet d'Aloyau à la Napolitaine
Dinde bouillie sauce au céléri

RÔTI.

Dinde rôtie sauce au Madère
Jambon glacé

GIBIER.

Wonga Wonga Pigeons | Canards sauvages
Aspic de foies gras

ENTREMETS.

Pouding de Cabinet | Pouding à la Nessel-
Savarin au curaçoa | rode
Macedoines | Piramide de Merin-
Bombe à la russe | gues

DESSERT.

PROGRAMME.

1. Overture—Zampa ...	...	*Herold*
2. Selection—William Tell	...	*Rossini*
3. Selection—Faust ...	...	*Gounod*
4. Selection—Don Giovanni.		*Mozart*
5. Selection—Grande Duchesse		*Offenbach*
6. Selection—Huguenots	...	*Meyerbeer*
7. Selection—Crispina	...	
8. Selection—Genéviève de Brabant		
		Offenbach
9. Selection—Prophète	...	*Meyerbeer*
10. Waltz—Romeo é Giulietta		*Gounod*

TOASTS.

The Queen ...   ... God Save the Queen
His Excellency the {   The Fine Old
    Governor   ... { English Gentleman
H.M.S. "Challenger" Rule Britannia

The menu of the Australian Club Dinner, held to honour the officers and scientists of HMS Challenger.

and re-provisioned, Moseley and Wyville Thomson and John Murray reconnoitred, and that was all – except for the inevitable desertion of a few more sailors. If South Africa could tempt them with its diamond mines, Australia could lure them with goldfields and the prospect of an easier way of life than 'drudging' and sending down topgallant sails in a gale of wind.

Moseley, going inland, found that urban civilization was strictly limited. A few miles from Melbourne the road became 'a sort of slough through which our horses could hardly drag the wagon'; but in a tent in the bush he had the satisfaction of hearing opossums 'caterwauling in the gum trees, and in the early morning the Laughing Jackasses and Piping Crows kept up a curiously contrasted concert'. He saw too, and marvelled at, the footsteps carved by Aborigines on the bare, smooth trunks of tall eucalyptus trees: little notches, each made by three blows of an axe – a stone axe before the colonists brought steel – were enough to make toe-holds and a ladder, reaching to an astonishing height, for hunters in pursuit of opossums, or hungry for wild honey. The gum trees, so elegant and slender, he thought far more impressive than the *Sequoia gigantea* of California, and confidently he asserts that *Eucalyptus amygdalina* is the tallest tree in the world.

His opinion of the Aborigines suffered a curious change. Their ability to climb a gum tree by cutting small holes for their big toes was remarkable indeed, but when he went to a Government reserve, where he found them playing cricket while white men were working, he denounced them as incorrigibly lazy; and the women – not even playing cricket – were worse than the men. Then, a little while later, he made an excursion from Sydney to hunt bandicoots, and found an old settlement on a

RIGHT: Eucalyptus amygdalina, *drawn by Mr Wild.* OVERLEAF: *a page from Moseley's albums.*

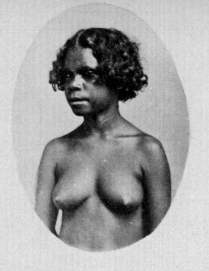

Group of Australian Natives

the Richmond River N S Wales
near the boundry of Queen's Land.

LEFT: *Aborigine with a government class ticket around his neck, showing him officially recognized as a king.*

RIGHT: Challenger *at anchor at Farm Cove, Sydney, with a French man-of-war astern.*

creek where a huge shell mound, or kitchen midden, was a memorial to the good appetite, and good taste, of the long dead Aborigines who had feasted there on oysters and mussels. Nearby, moreover, were caves whose walls were covered with charcoal drawings by which Moseley was completely fascinated; and before leaving Sydney he made a devastating comparison between the white colonists and the race they had ousted. He had found delightful friends in Sydney, and was grateful for their hospitality; but still he wished that, instead of them, he had been able to meet the people they had destroyed, who were 'far more interesting and original from an anthropological point of view'.

Moseley in Australia had less than his usual good luck. He failed to find a Platypus in the Yarra river, he failed to see a kangaroo; and two Duck-bills that someone shot for him were spoiled, for microscopic examination, by the jolting and heat of the coach on the journey down to the coast. He admired, with some reservation, Sydney Harbour, and saw the Blue Mountains. Though he liked to think of himself as a sportsman, it was with the ruthlessness of the scientist that he and his companions shot opossums – 'about 20 opossums in a couple of hours on each occasion on which I went out' – and in nearly all the females found a single young one in the pouch. But he wanted young ones in a much earlier stage of growth, and again was disappointed.

The ship left Melbourne on April 1st, and sailed round to Sydney. From there Wyville Thomson set out on an expedition that threatened to be as unrewarded as

Moseley's hope of securing a living Platypus. His purpose was to examine the fauna of some Queensland rivers, and with him went Lieutenant Aldrich and John Murray, with a couple of bluejackets in attendance. They took ship to Brisbane, stayed there for a few days, and went on to Maryburgh. They borrowed a boat and spent ten days beside the river Mary in the hope of catching the fish called Barramunda. As well as rods and nets they had thoughtfully provided themselves with a box of

Duck-billed Platypus

dynamite cartridges; but even they failed to bring up a Barramunda. They caught other fish in abundance, they shot cockatoos, wallaby, and duck for the pot, but until the very end of their stay they saw no Barramunda. Then three were taken: one by Aldrich on a rod, one in a clumsy trammel net, and one – in a manner not disclosed – by some Aborigines who had joined them.

The steam pinnace dredging in Sydney harbour.

11 From Tonga to Fiji

The Tasman Sea is not the most pacific of waters, and *Challenger* had a rough voyage from Sydney to Wellington. She left on June 8th, lay to outside the Heads to sound and dredge, but in a confused and stormy sea it was impossible to do anything, and she returned to Watson's Bay. On the 12th she again put out, and on the 15th there was a wind of force ten; in a heavy swell the waves were at least twenty feet from trough to crest. The weather improved, but on the 16th, in 2,550 fathoms, the sounding line parted, and from 2,600 fathoms on the 17th the dredge came up empty. Work and dirty weather alternated until the 26th, when shelter was sought under the lee of D'Urville Island at the top end of the South Island. In Cook Strait, on the last leg to Wellington, there was a short, heavy sea that washed the leadsman out of the chains: the ship was stopped, and search made for him, but he must have sunk immediately.

Wellington, in 1874, made a poor appearance in comparison with Sydney. In a long street following the shore all the buildings were of wood – as was Government House – and in poulterers' shops, as if to advertise a primitive economy, the native parrot, or Kaka, was hung up for sale. Maoris, closely tattooed, walked about and disappointingly wore English dress. More surprising – to those who know New Zealand as it is to-day – is Moseley's statement that 'all the valleys and inland slopes are covered with a dense forest and almost impenetrable bush'. Year by year that bush – very dark in hue – would be burnt and eradicated to let New Zealand clothe itself with bright green pasture; and then, when hardly anything was left of

A shooting party ashore, a cartoon by Lt Channer. From left to right: Professor Wyville Thomson, Commander Maclear, John Murray, Lord George Campbell (with monocle), Lt Pelham Aldrich, Lt Hynes, Captain Nares. The next man is unidentified, but leading the field is Channer himself.

its ancient covering, there would emerge a sentimental regard for what remained, and the rare surviving fragments of its old complexion would be zealously preserved.

Challenger stayed in Wellington for a few days only, and putting to sea on July 7th rounded Cape Palliser and headed north – past Hawke Bay and East Cape – towards the Little Kermadec Islands where a good deal of dredging was done and large pieces of pumice and a strange new sponge were brought up; but to Moseley's vexation there was no opportunity to go ashore. 'Further information concerning the flora of the islands is very much wanted,' he complains.

The ship sailed on to the Friendly Isles, and on the 19th anchored off Tongatabu: Sacred Tonga, whose ponderous old King ruled, in kindly manner, an archipelago of about a hundred and fifty lesser islands. The romantic charm of South Sea atolls – the compulsive appeal, from a distance, of some brightly beached, palm-bannered, sea-girt paradise – have often been blunted and derided by closer acquaintance with the reality of a hot and shabby, comfortless little port; but Tonga, by all accounts, has never disappointed its visitors, and there were those aboard *Challenger* – even among the scientists – who found in the laughing, friendly Tongans an attraction that blurred, for a little while, their deeper regard for calcareous algae, echinoderms, *Peripatus*, and land planarian worms. Moseley, that admirable man who wished he had seen less of Sydney's hospitable white colonists and more of Australia's gifted Aborigines, primly observed that Tongan girls were 'most accomplished coquettes'; and Sub-Lieutenant Lord George Campbell – who wore a monocle that

Queen Charlotte   *King George*

King George Tupou and his consort.

fascinated the islanders – loudly proclaimed his affection for a five-year-old child who, while he left her for a few minutes, tried to enhance her beauty by scrawling some bright blue lines across her face. Tonga, on the evidence of the *Challenger*'s people, does indeed appear to give substance to the romantic or sentimental belief that somewhere in the Southern Pacific there still existed – a hundred years ago – an earthly paradise only slightly dimmed by the Wesleyan missionaries who were busily improving it.

The Tongans were tall, powerfully built, muscular and merry, and many of the older ones had grown immensely fat. Their land was rich and fertile, there was no great need to work laboriously to make a living, but a sort of ingrained, communal sense of responsibility ensured that what had to be done was done punctually. Earlier in the century the islands had been distracted by war – for some years relapsed into anarchy – but by 1850 or thereabouts George Tupou was their master and he, baptized in a Wesleyan font, made Tonga a Christian kingdom. The missionaries introduced some tiresome, petty legislation – they disliked the appearance of bare-breasted girls and the agitation of native dancing – but the stabilizing influence of their teaching was of lasting benefit. The King, their most distinguished convert, lived until 1893, when he was succeeded by his great-grandson George Tupou II whose daughter was Queen Salote.

Flat and green, palm-tufted, Tongatabu lies low upon the sea, and in 1874 the small town of Nuku'alofa was dominated in a very modest way by a small white church, the bungalow which was the King's house, and an administrative building distinguished by a wooden tower. Reed mats made walls for the native houses, which were simply furnished with a kava bowl, more mats, and wooden pillows; but nature had added the decoration of coco-palms, oleanders and scarlet hibiscus, and immediate hospitality offered the kava-bowl full of a liquid less intoxicating than some had hoped. In the old-fashioned way of preparation the root of *Macropiper methysticum* had been chewed by young girls or boys, and water or coconut milk added to the pulp; but the missionaries had prohibited chewing, substituted grating or grinding, and an essential ingredient may have been lost.

Moseley, who had read Darwin's work *On the Expressions of the Emotions*, was immediately struck 'by the unusually marked development of facial expression. The muscles of the forehead during animated conversation are contracted and relaxed incessantly, and in a most varied manner. . . . In affirmation the head is jerked slightly upwards, the eyebrows being raised at the same time. I asked one of the missionaries who visited the ship about this matter, and to test it he pronounced the word for yes, and involuntarily threw up his head. The gestures accompanying the language are necessary to its perfect use.'

The men wore their hair in a 'sort of mop sticking straight up from the head', parti-coloured by the application of coral lime so as to variegate a natural black with locks of rusty red. Young Campbell identified the hue as reddish yellow or light yellow – he was looking at girls rather than men – and wrote enthusiastically: 'Picture to yourself dark brown almond-shaped eyes, dark eyebrows, a flat South Sea Island nose ('tis like no other), large but well-formed lips, the ready laugh displaying rows of perfect teeth, a halo of curly yellow hair, all set on a graceful, straight, lithe figure, draped in a costume which shows it off to perfection.' The costume was a kilt of tapa-cloth made from the bark of the paper mulberry – soaked and hammered till it was light and thin – and not all the girls wore the upper garment prescribed by the missionaries. Campbell's enthusiasm was renewed by the alacrity with which they accepted his cigars – incessantly they laughed and called for 'schmoke' – but his appreciation of the 'real sonsie lassies' by whom he was surrounded did not prevent him from learning something about them which, at that time, seems to have escaped Moseley and his questing mind: the coral lime with which they coloured their hair was effective also in repelling vermin.

There were horses and cattle on Tonga, sheep on the tall, neighbouring island of Eua, but no indigenous mammals except bats: a big Fruit-bat came out in large numbers as evening darkened. On coral reefs small heron waded, kingfishers and swifts were common, there was a small bright green Fruit Pigeon, a Great Fruit Pigeon with a harsh, drawling voice. There were two sorts of parrot, both scarce, and lizards were abundant. It is clear, however, that on Tonga no lesser form of life rivalled humanity in interest, and one reads, with respect for an extreme sort of conservation, that 'to protect the morals of the natives, seamen were fined if they remained on shore after 9 p.m.'.

'*The girls here were spreading great pieces of Tapa in the sun to dry, and only one or two were in legal costume*'. *Lord George Campbell was fascinated, and casts his shadow as he photographs them.*

Then *Challenger* sailed to the west, or west-by-north, and a passage of barely forty-eight hours, that included a pause for dredging in shallow water, another at greater depth, took her from a Polynesian people to a predominantly dark, Melanesian stock, from a low flat island to an ancient high-pitched crater surrounded by a barrier reef. Though there had been a close historical connection between them, the people of Fiji were almost as different as their scenery from the Tongans, and on Matuku Island – *Challenger*'s first Fijian landfall – the natives seemed much less attractive than old King George's cheerful subjects. Their houses were dirty, built on filthy dark flats by the sea-shore, and Moseley saw nothing to praise except the agility of a boy who crossed a mangrove swamp, from top to top of the sprawling mangroves, without falling into the mud from which they grew.

But the view from the top of the old volcano, 1,200 feet high, was magnificent: white surf on the encircling reef, a vertical precipice falling into the crater, light green grass contrasting with dark woodlands, and the scarlet blossom of the Araba (*Erythrina indica*) that comes into full blossom in August, when yams must be planted, and so starts the Fijian calendar. On the honey of the Araba flowers the little parrot called a Lory – jet-black and red and green – was feeding, and with it were small Honey-birds. Swallows flew about the denuded rim of the volcano, and hopping across the mud of the mangroves far below was a small, clownish, jumping fish called *Periophthalmus*. It had upward-staring, bulbous eyes, strong pectoral fins that gave it strength to leap across the surface of mud or water, as much as a foot at a time, and it preferred jumping to swimming.

At some distance from Matuku, moreover, the dredge brought up a great prize from a coral bottom 320 fathoms deep. Shells of the Pearly Nautilus are common

LEFT: *The island of Matuku, Fiji, from the entrance through the Barrier Reef.*

RIGHT: *Lt Swire drew – not very accurately – the Nautilus with its siphon, described by Campbell, and tells with glee how it squirted water all over Wild, who was engaged in a more serious drawing.*

enough, and most people have seen and admired their spiral symmetry and gleaming pallor; but the living animal is very rarely caught, and the *Challenger*'s specimen excited great interest. It swam round and round in a shallow tub, moving backwards – with its bright shell foremost – and propelling itself in small jerks in a manner that posed a serious problem for young Campbell. He was writing home again, and he told his parents that it appeared to move by filling itself with water, and then ejecting it from its. . . . He pauses, and presently continues: 'I have just enquired as to what I ought to say, and am told that the water by a tube goes into the "mantle", and from there is ejected by the "siphon", so there!'

The ship lay off Matuku for only a few hours, and went on to Kandavu, southernmost of the Fijian group, where a very good harbour had lately been adopted as a port of call by mail steamers running between San Francisco and Sydney; and for their greater safety it was expedient to survey it. The islands of Fiji, first sighted by Tasman, were more closely discovered in 1789 by Captain Bligh of the *Bounty*, whose sailors had mutinied not far from Tonga and set him and his eighteen loyalists adrift in an open boat. Bligh, without arms, could not exploit his discovery, and sandalwood traders in the early 1800's were the first Europeans to establish a foothold there. The islands are scattered over a vast area – 40,000 square miles says Moseley – and number about 240, of which by far the largest are Viti Levu in the west and Vanua Levu in the north; between them is the small island of Ovalau, and

Periophthalmus kolreuteri

Goro Goro Ovalau, Fiji. A nineteenth century lithograph.

thither went *Challenger* before returning to Kandavu to complete its survey. But Moseley and others, both naturalists and officers, remained at Ovalau where the ship's barge was left to give them passage to some lesser islets, and thence back to Kandavu.

Moseley, indefatigable, explored coral reefs, and with Lieutenant Suckling, RN, a Fijian corporal and two native prisoners to help him, climbed a steep mountainside at Ovalau, and breathless with wonder and exertion found himself and his emotions trapped, as it were, in a cage of local scenery; a rocky mountain stream, cascades tumbling into black basins, ferns and mosses, plantains and scarlet hibiscus growing among the rocks, orchids hanging from the trees, little parrots flying above them: all the beauty of a South Sea island was concentrated about him, and having crossed to the other side of the hill he heard that in a village not far away there was preparation for a dance, so off he went to enjoy that too.

On their way to the village he and Suckling met many natives 'dressed in their best, with bright new girdles of yellow and scarlet dyed Pandanus leaves, bodies and hair freshly oiled, ornaments displayed, and faces painted black or red or a mixture of both'; and a young Mbau chief 'besides having his hair whitened, his face was blackened for the *meke*' – the dance, that is – 'and the contrast between black and white was most effective'. In the village chief's house there was kava to drink, and because Fiji was less inhibited than Tonga the root of *Piper methysticum* was chewed, not grated. Only 'young men with good teeth were chosen to do the chewing', and they paid great attention to cleanliness; but in spite of that Moseley disliked the kava, which reminded him of a popular medicine called Gregory's

Fijian cannibal

Mixture. Nor was the dance a success, for the girls they expected failed to appear, and he and Suckling hired a canoe to take them to Levuka where Suckling's schooner lay. A few hours later Moseley and his *Challenger* shipmates, who were waiting for him, set off in their barge for the minute island of Mbau under the east shore of Viti Levu. Formerly a native fortress of great strength, and notorious for the cannibalism practised there, Mbau in 1874 was the residence of King Thackombau.

The King, says Moseley, 'was visited in the morning by two of our people who took him by surprise. He was found lying on his stomach, reading his Bible.' In his younger days Thackombau had been a great warrior, and so addicted to cannibalism that he enjoyed the reputation of having 'partaken of 2,000 human bodies'. He was known, declares Moseley, 'to have cut out, cooked and eaten a man's tongue, in the man's presence, as a preparation to putting the rest of him in the oven, and that merely to spite the man because he begged hard not to be tortured, but to be clubbed at once'. Some twenty years before, when Thackombau was threatened by serious rebellion, King George of Tonga had come to his assistance and helped him to defeat his enemies. They had both become Christians, with the help of Wesleyan missionaries, but conversion appeared to have affected them in curiously different ways. Thackombau – again lying on his stomach, with his Bible on the mat beside him – questioned his visitors in the liveliest fashion. He wanted to know what sort of animals lived in the deeps of the sea; the naval strength of Britain, Germany, France and other powers; he was interested in everything. The benign King George of Tonga, on the other hand, had 'said nothing at all during our interview', and it had been impossible to interest him in anything.

The redoubtable King Thackombau was not photographed by Challenger's *people, but his son-in-law Timothy was. 'Timothy weighs 22 stones' is the note under the picture* LEFT *in Moseley's album. Lydia, King Thackombau's wife* RIGHT, *cannot have weighed much less.*

At the corner of an ancient, ruined temple on Mbau there was an upright stone against which 'the heads of the human victims destined for the oven were dashed. In front of it, in old times, bodies have been heaped up till they formed a pile ten feet high.' Another stone, used for the same purpose, was surrounded by slabs of coral perforated by boring molluscs, and against that second stone so many heads had been hammered and broken that nearly all the holes in the coral held human teeth: 'The slabs were quite full of them'.

There have been many attempts to explain or excuse the practice of cannibalism. Revenge may have been one reason for it, protein deficiency another. Belief in a magical inheritance of the victim's bravery and skill at arms filled many cooking pots, and as many others may have been boiled to give the victors a well-filled assurance of victory. In Fiji, however, the practice was so rife that mere gluttony is commonly thought to have inspired it: a dead human being was called a 'long pig' and eaten for enjoyment. That, however, may be too simple an explanation, for on Mbau – according to Moseley – victims were presented 'to the god Denge'; and there is the curious fact that a chief of Namosi in Fiji used always to eat human flesh after having had his hair cut.

Moseley was much interested in the subject, and learnt that in older times a chief had been expected to give distinguished visitors a cannibal's meal, and that young women were supposed to be the best eating. Europeans were not much liked, because their diet was too rich; baking, in an earth oven, was the Fijian way of cooking, and

'Murderers (Viti levu), Fiji. They were caught dragging the naked body of the missionary's wife by the hair through the jungle in order to eat it. I saw them in penal servitude at Ovalau Island', writes Moseley.

there was a certain vegetable, perhaps a sweet potato, that was considered the proper accompaniment to long pig. Baked meat was eaten cold as well as hot – a dish of cold cooked flesh was often sent as a present – and it was properly eaten with a four-pronged wooden fork.

The King found them a pilot, to take the barge up the broad Rewa river in Viti Levu, and they rowed between tall trees festooned with creepers till at dusk the big Fruit-bats flew out, coots and water-rails grew noisy in the reed-beds, and a German sugar-planter gave them hospitality. They went down-stream again, bought clubs and spears and kava bowls, and found their way to a village called Nakello where a great dance was to take place. They called on the chief and watched his small son being dressed and decorated for the occasion. The chief himself shaved the boy's head, all except 'a vertical ridge, which was left intact at the back, and looked some-what like the crest of a Greek helmet'; and smeared the shaven parts with a thick coating of vermilion paste. The guests were given kava and very nasty 'puddings', and the chief showed them two war-clubs which had killed a large number of illustrious enemies, and were kept carefully oiled 'just as we oil our cricket bats'.

The purpose of the dance – an annual affair – was to collect tribute, not for the chief, as it had been in the past, but for the local branch of the Wesleyan Missionary Society; and a great crowd of people assembled. 'The girls were most of them without covering to their breasts, but the upper parts of their bodies were literally running with coconut oil, and glistened in the sun. The men and boys were painted in all imaginable ways, with three colours, red, black, and blue. There were Wesleyans with face and body all red, some with them all black, others with one half of the face red, the other black. . . . Some of the men had remarkable head-dresses. One of them, for instance, had sticking out from the front of his head, and secured in his hair, a pair of light thin twigs of wood which were a yard in length. They were slightly bent over in front of his face, and at their extremities were fastened plumes of red feathers. . . . The most interesting dances were a club dance and a fan dance, in each of which a large body of full-grown fighting men, some of them with grey beards, performed'; but the extraordinary feature of the whole performance 'was the extreme order and decorum of this concourse of three or four thousand people. The representative of the power which has tamed these savages was a little missionary, with battered white tall hat and coat out at elbows, who stood beside us and took no prominent part in the ceremonies, but yet had full sway over the whole, no dance having been prepared without his previous sanction.'

The Wesleyans had conquered the Cannibals.

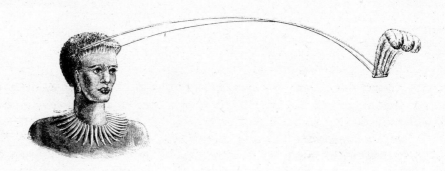

12 The people of Cape York

So far it has been fairly easy to follow the course of *Challenger* from the Antarctic ice to Australia, from New Zealand northwards to Tonga, thence west (perhaps a little north of west) to Fiji; but difficulties will increase because the Pacific is a vast ocean – over 9,000 miles from Bering Strait to the Antarctic Circle, 10,000 miles across its Equatorial waistline – islands cluster in it more thickly than raisins in a dozen Christmas puddings, and the *Challenger*'s course took her from one archipelago pudding to another. From Fiji she sailed west to the New Hebrides, west again to Cape York – at the tip of the long, hot peninsula that thrusts northwards out of Australia towards New Guinea – and then through the Torres Straits to the geographical confusion of the Banda Sea between Arnhem Land, western New Guinea, and Celebes. It is there that the armchair navigator may begin to find the voyage hard to follow.

The ship left Fiji on August 11th, and busily returned to her old routine of trawling and sounding. In 1,350 fathoms, however, the trawl was caught on the bottom, the weather was wet and changeable, and in a sudden fierce rain-squall on the 13th the fore-topgallant mast and flying jib-boom were carried away before sail could be shortened. But trawling was soon resumed, and the Report shows that after diversion ashore the main purpose of the voyage was again being energetically pursued: 'There were many very productive hauls with the surface nets between the Fiji Islands and the New Hebrides, pteropods, heteropods, and pelagic foraminifera being specially abundant. With the exception of a very large cylindrical species of

117

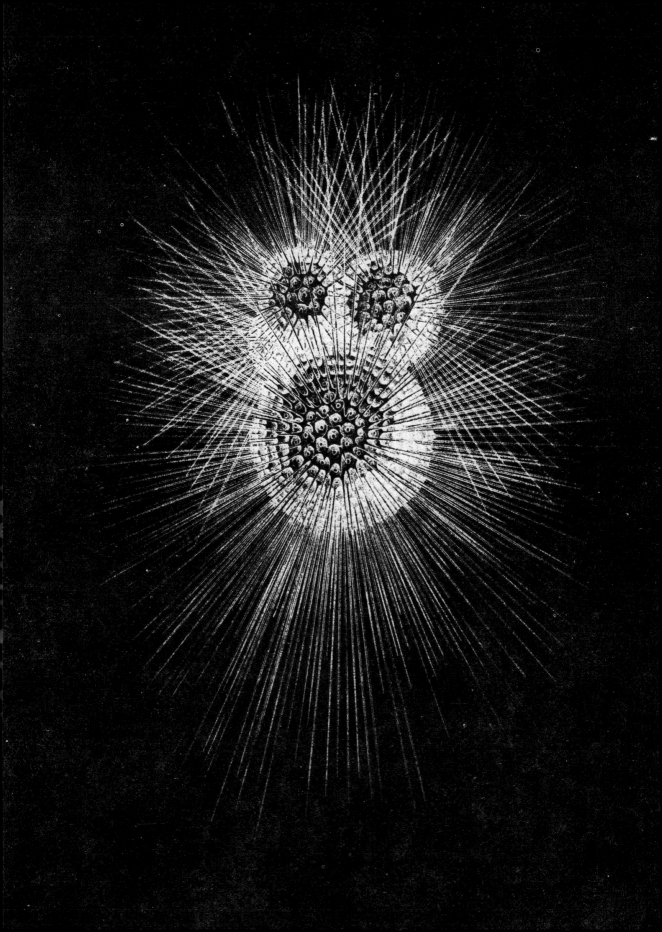

ABOVE: *the flying fish* Exocetus.

LEFT: Globigerina, *one of the foraminifera, drawn by Mr Wild.*

Etmodiscus, diatoms were very rare both on the surface and at the bottom. It was observed that the large foraminifera, such as *Sphaeroidina dehiscens*, *Pulvinulina menardii*, and thick-shelled *Orbulinae* were procured in greatest abundance when the tow-net was dragged at a depth of 80 or 100 fathoms. . . . Flying Fish (*Exocetus*) were especially abundant during this trip, and at night frequently dashed aboard ship near the exposed lights.'

With a fresh breeze blowing and rain darkening the sky, three islands of the New Hebrides were sighted soon after noon on the 17th: Tongariki, Makura, and Three Hills. It was Captain Cook who gave the archipelago its accepted name, but it had also acquired a name or reputation of another sort. The Melanesian natives were said to be dangerous and treacherous, perhaps by reason of innately distempered minds, but possibly because their relations with Europeans or Americans had been so unhappy as to convince them that all strangers were enemies. There are about thirty islands in the group – as well as islets and isolated rocks – and all are mountainous, some volcanic, and in their hot and humid climate densely forested. The explorers would, indeed, see little more of them than their forests and high-reaching hills, for the Hebrideans' evil reputation persuaded Captain Nares that it would be unwise to let his scientists go ashore except on one island to which they had a sort of introduction; and even there they were not allowed to move off the beach.

Before leaving Fiji they had taken aboard some Hebridean labourers who had been employed there, and wanted to go home. Their native island was Api, twenty miles long, rising steeply from the sea, and except for a very few, small, cultivated patches, covered with almost impenetrable forest. The ship steamed close in to the shore, where a coral beach lay in front of a valley invisible under its trees, and a few islanders appeared, some of them waving green branches which may have signalled

119

The Report's *illustration of the landing of natives at Api.*

friendly intention. They were all armed, however – their numbers increased – and the Captain, going ashore in the first boat, unostentatiously wore a revolver. The returning labourers quickly found acquaintances or relations, and there was no overt hostility.

The New Hebrideans were not prepossessing. A small people, seldom above five feet in height, they were darker than the Fijians, poorly shaped, and clad only in a wrap-around of some dingy fabric. They were not, however, entirely unsophisticated, for among them were some who, like the *Challenger*'s passengers, had worked in Fiji or Queensland. Most of the men wore, hung from the neck, small triangular ornaments cut from the shell of the Pearly Nautilus, and broad, flat, tortoise-shell bracelets; they wanted knives, pipes and tobacco, but were not eager to trade, and would not part with their bracelets at any price, nor with their featherless, bone-tipped arrows which, when poisoned, they carried wrapped in a plantain leaf.

It was a visit from which neither side got much profit – the naturalists, confined to the beach, felt frustrated, the Hebrideans may have wondered why the foreigners wanted to collect shells and spiders – and after only two hours on a totally unknown island the boats returned to the *Challenger* and sail was made for the west. The next port of call, Raine Island on Australia's Great Barrier Reef, was twelve days distant, and sounding for temperature resulted in a curious discovery. On August 19th, in 2,650 fathoms, the bottom temperature was the same as that at 1,300 fathoms: 35.8°F. From Api to the Barrier Reef, indeed, the bottom temperature was constant at about 36°F, and that temperature was also found, throughout the passage, at 1,300 fathoms. The inference, according to the Report, is that 'the uniform temperature of the water from the depth of 1,300 fathoms to the bottom is caused by the

120

Lt Channer's caricature of the same occasion. The friendly native LEFT *is menaced first by Pelham Aldrich, then by Wyville Thomson; Channer himself comes next, followed by two seamen.*

Coral Sea being cut off from colder water by an elevated ridge on the floor of the ocean over which the greatest depth of water cannot exceed 1,300 fathoms'.

Raine Island, no more than three-quarters of a mile in length and not far from Cape York, lies at the entrance to the passage commonly taken through the Barrier Reef, and was marked by an abandoned beacon-tower, substantially built, and sixty feet high. The island was inhabited only by birds, but they existed in such numbers that their flight cast a shadow on the land, and the mingling of their voices made a deafening noise. There were flocks of Turnstones on the shore, but they and a heron and a small gull appeared to be casual visitors. The residents were Landrails so tame they could be caught by the hand, whose full-fledged young were already running; 'Wideawake' terns, their young also fledged; Noddies, like those seen on St Paul's Rocks, still sitting on their eggs; two species of gannet nesting on bare

The natives of Api, photographed on board before they disembarked.

The Frigate bird Tachypetes aquila.

ground – the Booby of St Paul's Rocks and a bird, almost white, with a naked blue head and a ferocious eye with a bright yellow iris – and a third, smaller species, with red feet, nesting in low bushes; and Frigate Birds whose nests were platforms of twigs and grass matted by dung, and whose young were covered with 'frills of a rusty coloured down'. On the last few days of her passage from the New Hebrides the ship had been attended by birds, more numerously than ever before – long-tailed Tropic Birds, flocks of diving terns, Boobies perching on the yards, sometimes a Frigate Bird – but the multitude on Raine Island, and the din they made, were a marvel surpassing beyond accountancy all previous experience.

When the shore-party had had their fill of bird-watching, the ship sailed again, but in that reef-strewn coral sea had to anchor at night. Coral reefs may show as patches of sand above the sea, more dangerously as shadows beneath its surface, or a thin white line of breakers; and on the following day, as she continued her passage to Cape York, Captain Nares himself went up to the fore-top to order her course. He knew the coast well – he had served before on the Australian station – but to those seeing it for the first time it was a view not only desolate but curiously mena-cing. Low hills were visible, thickly wooded, and glaring sand in a shimmer of heat. Off the little ghost-town of Somerset, which was their destination near the very tip of the peninsula, lay a small island bare of vegetation – as was the Cape – except for

'Twelve feet in height, red pinnacles looking like the chimneys of pottery kilns.' Termite nests, Cape York.

Screw-pines or *Pandanus*, but ludicrously decorated with enormous termite-hills. Brick-red towers, as much as ten feet high, the termite nests stood as thickly as kiln chimneys in the Potteries, thought Moseley.

At one time the Queensland Government had attempted to plant a colony and establish a sea-port at Cape York. A detachment of Marines was sent there, and two bold men drove up a herd of cattle over a thousand inhospitable miles. But everything went wrong: the Cape was appallingly hot, no settlers were attracted, and according to report the neighbouring Aborigines were very hostile and speared a Marine whenever they got the chance. In 1874 the intended colony consisted of a few half-ruined houses, a grog-shop, a police barracks that housed a dozen native constables, a postmaster who was also superintendent of the police, a couple of subordinate police officers, a missionary who had a steam pinnace lately presented to him by the London Missionary Society, and some white loafers who lived in tents or shanties near the beach. A few hundred yards away were the poor remnants of three aboriginal tribes, and others, more truculent, lived farther inland, whose occasional bickering – or so it was said – was quelled with great zest by the native constables.

Moseley, though previously inclined to think well of Aborigines, could find nothing to say in praise of those who lived near Somerset. Their camp was an oval space, hidden by bushes, at the centre of which were some heaps of smouldering wood ash; round them was a shallow depression, caused partly by use – that was where the 'Blacks' sat or lay – and partly by the accumulation of ashes at the centre and a periphery of ashes and other refuse that had been thrown out. The dormitory, that is, lay between an open fire-place and a kitchen midden, and was sheltered by the large leaves of a fan palm that had been stuck into the soil. When Moseley first went there – early one morning, to look for a guide – there were twenty-one people in camp: six adult males, four boys between ten and fourteen years old, two old women, two of middle age, and the rest were girls or young women.

During the day the younger men and women went out to look for food, but the two old women – almost as thin as skeletons but with swollen bellies – sat miserably inactive, sometimes scratching themselves with a pointed stick, or vacantly looking at a visitor in the hope of his having brought tobacco or some biscuits. These poor Blacks appeared to have no property except a few baskets of plaited grass, for the collection of food; a large number of gin bottles to store water; and several bamboo tobacco pipes obtained by barter from the Murray Islanders who occasionally called at Cape York. With little else to do, the Blacks had devised a curiously elaborate manner of smoking, which Moseley describes in detail:

'The tobacco-pipe is a large joint of bamboo, as much as two feet in length and three inches in diameter. There is a small round hole on the side at one end and a larger hole in the extremity of the other end. A small cone of green leaf is inserted into the smaller round hole and filled with tobacco, which is lighted at the top as usual. A man, or oftener a woman, opening her mouth wide, covers the cone and lighted tobacco with it and applied her lips to the bamboo all round it, thus having the leaf cone and burning tobacco entirely within her mouth. She then blows and forces the smoke into the cavity of the bamboo, keeping her hand over the hole at the other end, and closing the aperture as soon as the bamboo is full.

'The leaf cone is then withdrawn and the pipe handed to the smoker, who, putting his hand over the bottom hole to keep in the smoke, sucks at the hole in which the leaf was inserted, and uses his hand as a valve meanwhile to allow the

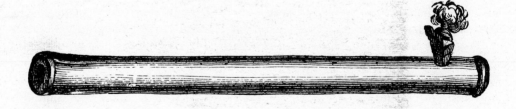

ABOVE: *bamboo tobacco pipe.*

RIGHT, ABOVE: *the village of Ngaloa, Kandavu, Fiji, painted by Mr Wild.* BELOW: *foraminifera in elevation and section. The average foraminifera measures well under one millimetre in diameter.*

requisite air to enter at the other end. The pipe being empty the leaf is replaced and the process repeated. The smoke is thus inhaled quite cold. The pipes are orna-mented by the Blacks with rude drawings.'

Baskets of plaited grass, discarded bottles, and some bamboo pipes: that was all the visible property of the camp, but hidden in nearby bushes – concealed from sudden attack – were several small spears and a throwing-stick. No knives, no other weapons or any tools except pointed sticks, hardened in the fire, that were used to dig up the roots of wild yams, and stones, one round and flat, the other long and conical – stones that had been found, not shaped – with which they pounded and crushed the large seeds of a climbing bean. They ate also shell-fish and snails, snakes and grubs, and some were seen breaking up drift-wood to find Teredo worms. Unlike the Aborigines in the south they had not learnt to climb trees in pur-suit of opossums, nor did they hunt the wallaby. They lived on creeping things and roots, and fish that they caught with four-pronged spears.

The younger women wore a tattered wrap-around, some of the men had old shirts, but Moseley's guide – a man called Longway – went stark naked, as did his son, a boy of about ten. One day when they were with him, Longway begged him to shoot some parakeets; which, to his regret, Moseley did. He killed a little, close-flying flock of half a dozen with a single shot, and Longway refused to go farther until he had eaten them. He and the boy lighted a fire of grass and sticks, pulled some feathers from the birds, and threw them into the fire to singe what remained. Then, before they had even been thoroughly warmed, the birds were pulled out, and Longway and his son ate the bleeding carcasses and most of the guts.

Neither they nor others in the camp could learn to count above three: 'Piama, labaima, damma' – so far they were confident and exact, but all higher numbers were lumped together as 'nurra'. Sometimes Moseley would put down five or six objects, and ask them to count. They would arrange the objects in pairs, or pairs and a singleton, and say 'Labaima, labaima, piama'. Even a man who had often worked for white people had never acquired any knowledge of numbers: Moseley shot two dozen birds of one sort or another – perhaps more parakeets – and asked how many there were in the bag. 'Six', answered Longway. Nor, as it seemed, had they any faculty of memory, for once when Longway was elated by the promise of two shillings, if he could find a Rifle-bird for Moseley to shoot – and had been constantly repeating to himself, 'Two shillings!' – he grew tired before the day was over, went back to camp to smoke his bamboo pipe, and when Moseley followed, to pay him, he was quite astonished and had evidently forgotten all about his promised reward. What money they earned they spent on biscuit: they knew they could get more biscuits for a florin than for a shilling, but that was the extent of their know-ledge.

Moseley was able to correct a much mistaken contemporary belief about the

The Rifle-bird of Paradise Ptilorhis alberti

LEFT: *Mr Longway, drawn by Swire.*
RIGHT: *Mr Wild's drawing of the Aborigine camp near Somerset. He was struck by their condition, 'occupying the lowest step on the ladder of civilization . . . a palm leaf their only dwelling.'*

skills and implements native to Cape York. All sorts of savage weapons could be found in anthropological collections in England – all labelled 'Cape York' – though the plain and visible fact was that the local Aborigines had no wealth of equipment, no discernible talents. The mistake had arisen because Cape York was 'a sort of emporium for savage weapons and ornaments'. The pearl-shellers, who fished for *Trochus* shells from Thursday Island, trafficked with many islands between Cape York and New Guinea. Murray Islanders brought bows and arrows and drums for barter. The harbour police in Somerset dealt in such curios, buying them to sell again to passengers in passing steamers, and the Aborigines of Northern Australia had consequently been given credit for skills they did not possess. No Australian native, thought Moseley, used bow and arrow; javelins labelled 'Cape York' had come from the Admiralty Islands; and Moseley himself had acquired a large drum that otherwise might have gone to some provincial museum as an example of culture on the Gulf of Carpentaria, though its origin in fact was New Guinea.

On the long peninsula that lay like a bake-house wall beside the great stewing-pot of the Gulf, birds and butterflies gave most pleasure, both to naturalists and others in the ship's company, for bird-life was brilliantly abundant, and there were enormous, slow-moving butterflies. There were little warblers that fed among the blood-red flowers of the Coral-tree; parakeets that flew about in small screaming flocks and filled themselves to the beak with honey; and true Honey-birds. The White-crested Cockatoo was wary, difficult to approach, and the Great Black Cockatoo even more difficult. The most sought-after was the Rifle-bird (*Ptilorhis alberti*), one of the Birds of Paradise: about twice the size of a Starling, velvety black with iridescent green breast and crown – more iridescence in the tail – it was a shy bird but could be lured by imitating its call because its jealous nature resented intrusion on its territory. After great exertion Moseley had managed to shoot one.

128

In the heyday of Queen Victoria naturalists had few inhibitions, and his comment after the event records only a virtuous satisfaction: 'The male in full plumage is indeed a splendid object', he says.

Mound-birds, that bury their eggs and run off like barnyard fowls, were easily shot, as were Bush turkeys, that build huge mounds, and Swallow-shrikes. More unexpected is young Campbell's admission that they also shot butterflies. They were very large – either sky-blue or yellow, green, and black – and they defied the net. Many were blown to pieces by impatient guns, but Campbell, loaded with Number 12 shot, sensibly waited till one of the yellow and green sort was reasonably far away, and 'down it came, a glorious fellow, and not the least injured'.

They spent a week in the intense heat of Cape York – 'You drip, drip', says Campbell, 'and wonder what chance you have of reaching home in a solid state' – and putting to sea again, landed briefly on a couple of small islands in the Torres Straits to be rewarded with some exceptionally large oysters; more birds of brilliant plumage, among them a Painted Quail and a fruit pigeon gorgeously dressed in purple, green, and scarlet; and the curious spectacle of native graves ornamented with bones of the Dugong or sea-cow: a ponderous animal that suckles its young – cleverly using flippers to hold the infant to its breast – and at one time thought to be evidence for the existence of mermaids.

The Straits were named after the Admiral of a small fleet sent out by Philip III of Spain to search for a southern continent. De Torres left Callao in December, 1605, and the following year found the New Hebrides where he encountered misfortune: there was mutiny in his fleet and, abandoned by his consorts, he sought a way to the Philippines to refit, discovering the straits to which eventually his name was given. In the same year a little Dutch ship, the *Dove*, put out from Bantam in Java and presently entered the Gulf of Carpentaria. For the next fifty years or more

Dutch navigators explored and roughly charted much of Australia's east coast – of which they formed no high opinion – and in 1642 Abel Tasman, sailing from Batavia, discovered the large island that he called Van Diemen's Land, but which now preserves his name. Not until 1688 did an Englishman go so far, and he, the first of his nation to see Australia, was William Dampier, supercargo in the *Cygnet*, whose crew had become buccaneers. But Dampier, despite the bad company he kept, was literate, wrote about what he had seen, and went back to see more. Then in 1770 that superlative seaman Captain Cook – in the topmost class with Magellan and Drake – was sent out in HMS *Endeavour*, formerly a collier, to observe the transit of Venus. That he did in Tahiti, and went on to discover New Zealand and, by accident, the Great Barrier Reef, where he nearly lost his ship. Continuing his voyage to the north, he named and doubled Cape York, and turned eastwards through the Torres Straits a hundred and four years before the *Challenger*'s arrival.

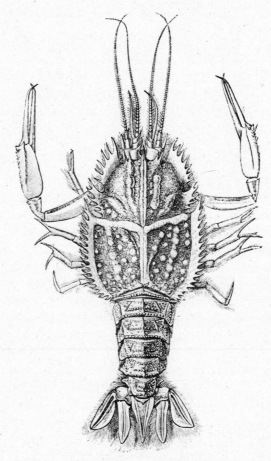

Polycheles crucifera

13 For sale: Birds of Paradise

'On our way to the Aru Islands we crossed the Arafura Sea, which lies to the west of New Guinea.' So says Moseley, with less than his usual accuracy. The Arafura Sea lies south of the long, westward-tapering tail of New Guinea, between it and Arnhem Land, and east of the island of Timor. The Aru Islands number about eighty and the one that lies nearest to New Guinea is separated from its large neighbour by about seventy miles of shallow sea. Some of the islands are isolated only by narrow creeks, rather like rivers, and formerly they may have been continuous with New Guinea, of which, in a zoological sense, they are still a part. They are low-lying, their eastern coast is defended by coral reefs, and much of their surface is covered with a virgin forest of screw-pines, palm trees, tree ferns, and a sort of gum. Their inhabitants were Papuan, or partly Papuan, in origin, and it was formerly rumoured, and perhaps believed, that somewhere in the interior there lived a tribe of people called Korongoeis, whose skins were white, and whose hair was fair; but to the *Challenger*'s naturalists the islands' appeal depended on the fact that in their forests there flew Birds of Paradise, whose breeding, for a long time, had been as obscure and mysterious as that of the Korongoeis.

For its first knowledge of the existence of the most beautiful of all birds, Western Europe was primarily indebted to Magellan, whose circumnavigation of the world began, at the mouth of the Guadalquivir, in September, 1519. He and his fleet of five ships passed through the Straits which bear his name, and entered the Pacific where he was so fortunate as to find good weather. He reached the Moluccas – the

The King-bird of Paradise or Ribbontail. Paradisea regia. *It is coloured red, chestnut, orange, carmine, purple and golden green.*

islands between Celebes and New Guinea, between the Philippines and Timor, which later became part of the Dutch East Indies – and there a local ruler, known as the King of Bachian, gave him, as a present for the King of Spain, two dead birds, about the size of thrushes, which had small heads, long beaks, slender legs, but apparently no wings. Instead of wings they had long, plume-like feathers of various colours, and they were said never to fly except when the wind blew. Magellan did not live to convey this curious present to the King of Spain – he was killed in the Philippines – but one ship of his fleet completed the voyage, aboard which was an Italian adventurer, Antonio Pigafetti, who wrote an account of that momentous adventure in which he recorded that in the Moluccas the birds were called '*bolon dinata*', or divine birds, and it was believed that their home was 'a terrestrial Paradise'.

In subsequent years many brightly plumaged skins were brought to Europe, from which the feet had been cut off, and a romantic belief was propagated that the birds made no contact with the earth; and the Great Bird of Paradise of the Aru Islands was given the splendid but misleading name of *Paradisea apoda*, or Footless Paradisian.

Comparatively little was known about the family until a few years before the *Challenger* crossed the Arafura Sea; but in 1869 Alfred Russel Wallace, an uncommonly daring ornithologist – for New Guinea was full of perils and murderous people – published an account of his exploration of some parts of that vast island, and described the extraordinary pleasure with which the male Bird of Paradise – there are more than forty species – recognized his beauty and displayed it for the admiration of his duller-suited harem. Even in captivity they retain their innocent self-absorption and perform their elaborate dances without inhibition; but vanity and their beauty led to their slaughter in increasing numbers, for though their environment gave them some protection, they needed much more.

Some sorts, such as the Twelve-wired Bird of Paradise, lived in swampy coastal districts, where approach was not easy, but many others – the great majority, indeed – preferred the thickly forested highlands; there are Sickle-bills that breed at heights of between 6,000 and 9,000 feet, and MacGregor's Bird *(Macgregoria pulchra)* – called after the very able and energetic Lieutenant-Governor of Papua when Papua became a Crown Colony – has an even higher habitat between 11,000 and 12,000 feet. But harsh terrain and tropical foliage were not enough to deter their hunters when fashion-mongers and fine ladies were eager to buy dead birds at rewarding prices.

From early times, indeed, the plumes of a Bird of Paradise have been coveted, and men, not women, were the first to adorn themselves with the splendours of a King-bird or Ribbon-tail. Before military dress became clay-coloured or drab green, warriors of all races advertised the perils of their profession by decorating their persons, and about the middle of the sixteenth century a traveller reported that in Constantinople the Janissaries of the Sultan of Turkey's bodyguard wore plumes which they obtained from the Arabs, and which may have been taken – in what was beginning to be a world-wide trade – from *Paradisea apoda*. It was in the later years of the nineteenth century, however, that the trade was so grossly expanded as to menace the existence of Birds of Paradise. In 1884 Germany annexed northern New Guinea and the large Bismarck Archipelago, and commercial development, which began immediately, included the systematic killing and selling of Birds of Paradise. Nor was Britain less blameworthy, for in 1895 a single London warehouse sold 750,000 plumes, mainly of Egrets and Birds of Paradise'. In 1913, Congress in the United States prohibited their import, and Canada, Holland, and a few other countries followed that benign example; but it was not until 1921 that the British House of Commons felt itself capable of defying feminine interest and the millinery trade, and passed the Plumage Act which belatedly followed American legislation. It must not be expected, then, that the *Challenger*'s naturalists, in pursuit not of profit but of information, would refrain from killing the exquisite creatures that they

OVERLEAF: *The voyage of the* Challenger *1872–76. 1 Portsmouth. 2 Lisbon. 3 Gibraltar. 4 Madeira. 5 Tenerife. 6 St Thomas. 7 Bermuda. 8 Halifax. 9 Fayal. 10 San Miguel. 11 St Vincent. 12 St Iago. 13 St Paul's Rocks. 14 Fernando Noronha. 15 Bahia. 16 Tristan da Cunha. 17 Simon's Bay. 18 Cape Town. 19 Pr. Edward's Is. 20 Crozet Is. 21 Kerguelen. 22 Heard Is. 23 Melbourne. 24 Sydney. 25 Wellington. 26 Kermadec Is. 27 Tonga. 28 Fiji Is. 29 New Hebrides. 30 Cape York. 31 Aru Is. 32 Ki Is. 33 Banda Is. 34 Amboina. 35 Ternate. 36 Zamboanga. 37 Ilo-Ilo. 38 Manila. 39 Hong Kong. 40 Zebu. 41 Camiguin Is. 42 Basilan. 43 Humboldt Bay. 44 Admiralty Is. 45 Yokohama. 46 Kobe. 47 Miwara. 48 Honolulu. 49 Hilo. 50 Tahiti. 51 Juan Fernandez. 52 Valparaiso. 53 Messier Channel. 54 Port Churruca. 55 Punta Arenas. 56 Elizabeth I. 57 Falkland Is. 58 Monte Video. 59 Ascension. 60 Vigo.*

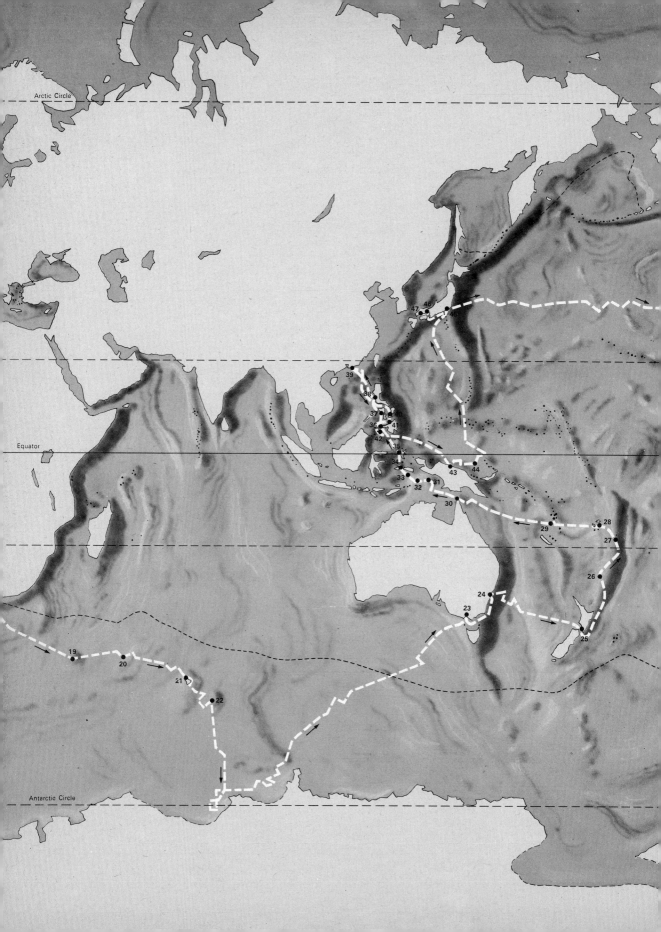

Equator

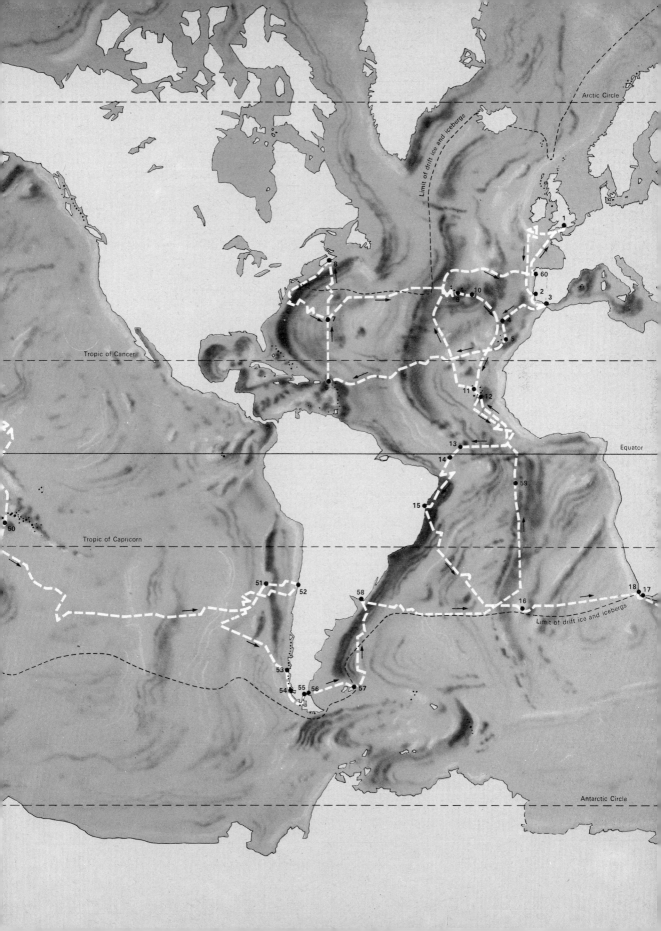

heard and saw among the feathery tops of tall trees on the Aru Islands. They shot as many as they could, for even scientists still lived in a state of relative innocence: they all knew of the relationship between man and his environment, but not yet were they fully aware of man's increasing power to destroy his environment and endanger himself.

The Aru Islands were sighted on September 14th, six days after leaving Cape York: the short voyage had been lengthened by dredging, and sounding had shown that the Arafura Sea, shallow all the way, was seldom deeper than 40 fathoms. Anchoring off Dobbo, the capital, on the 15th, the ship was promptly visited by the chief traders of the islands, and Dutch half-caste missionaries. The traders were Malays from Macassar, and they came in state. Their boats flew the Dutch flag; the traders, between a double row of paddlers, wore gold-embroidered coats and white trousers; the missionaries, in ancient, tall top-hats and black tail-coats, sometimes conspicuously ill-fitting, carried silver-headed sticks. They all looked hot and uncomfortable, and soon changed into a simpler native costume, for each had had the forethought to bring sarong and baju with him.

Dobbo, on the small island of Wamma, was only a village consisting of three rows of houses, divided by two narrow streets. Built on heavy piles and thatch-roofed, the houses stood on a strip of sand that reflected a glaring heat, and on a nearby beach were Macassar trading ships. Most of the Dobbo fleet had gone off to Singapore at the end of the south-east monsoon, and only about three hundred people remained in the village: twenty Chinese, ten mop-headed islanders, and the rest Malays who were about to start fishing again for trepang (or *bêche-de-mer*), pearl-shells, and tortoise shell. The price of tortoise shell was fifteen shillings a pound, pearl-shells two shillings a pound, and the skin of a Great Bird of Paradise cost ten shillings. Tizard, the Navigating Officer, knew the China Seas and the coast of Borneo, and had learnt Malay; with his help Moseley and the others engaged guides who led them on their excursions ashore. When it came on to rain, the guides, showing commendable common-sense, took off their scanty clothes, wrapped them in a pandanus leaf, and walked naked till the rain had stopped; and Moseley himself was capable of a timely ingenuity. He had a very active guide who, in the airless heat of a dense forest, walked too quickly for his comfort; so bending to examine a large stone he pretended to find it interesting, and told his guide to pick it up and carry it. Thus burdened – with a heavy stone and Moseley's vasculum – the man's pace was suitably reduced, and when he returned to the ship Moseley dropped the stone overboard. It was an expedient, he says, which had served him well on other occasions, and 'can be recommended to naturalists'.

In spite of its diminished population the village was a lively place, giving shelter not only to human beings, but also to a tame cassowary, yellow-crested cockatoos, red and green parrots, a wallaby, ducks and fighting-cocks. Young Campbell disliked the Malays' 'hideous habit of chewing betel-nut making their mouths, in many cases, really sickening to look at. It dyes the gums and lips a brick red, and

Mop-headed islanders from Aru.

Vivid pictures of Dobbo, chief port of the Aru Islands, are painted in the journals of the Challenger's voyage. Spry was impressed by the neatness of the village – shown ABOVE *from the landing stage – and one rather wonders why. On the left is a native chief with his son; on the right a Malay merchant with his daughters. Wild was very taken with the native chief's intelligence, and pronounced him 'one of those men who in any clime are sure to rise above the general level.' But Lord George Campbell was very scathing about the Malay merchants who, wearing 'white trousers and on their close cropped heads the absurd little Malay caps . . . appeared very much thunderstruck and stupid.'*

The chief merchant's son being rowed out to Challenger, *as drawn by Pelham Aldrich.*

blackens the teeth, besides eating them away, till eventually nothing but black stumps are left.' In fairness, however, he adds that betel-nut chewers do not suffer from toothache, and generously describes how, when the chief merchant's son 'came off to the ship one day, an umbrella held over him, and paddled by his Papuan slaves, attired in a most gorgeous yellow garment, his long black hair hanging down to below the shoulders, oiled, curled, and wavy, he really looked extremely handsome.'

In one of the houses he sees Chinese sprawling on their beds and smoking opium, and on a mat at another door the skins of some Great Birds of Paradise drying in the sun, 'and very beautiful they looked, their long silky golden plumes, bright chocolate-coloured wings and bodies, and emerald throats'. Though the heat was too great 'for anything but a salamander' he revelled in the lush scenery of Wokan, a neighbouring island, where he and the others went shooting: 'Both in the deep shadow of the woods, and in the sunshine on the shore, butterflies, the most gorgeous and varied, and of all sizes – from a huge bird-winged sort to tiny blue and yellow gems – fly rapidly in the air, or flicker hurriedly through the lower foliage; scarlet dragonflies come staring motionless at you, then with one jerk, go yards away; dull-coloured little lizards glide rustling across the path; snowy cockatoos scream harshly, and some have shockingly dirtied their plumage; and listen! *Wauk, wauk*, that's the "great" bird of Paradise; *whree*, that's the little "king" bird; there booms low the note of a pigeon; there chatter a flock of lorriquets; and on the dark coral shores blue kingfishers and lonely grey herons are on the lookout for fish.'

He shoots a few of the little King-birds: 'Their colouring is exquisite; snow-white breast, green band around the throat, and crimson-velvet plumage, while from the tail two stiff, bare shafts fall down, ending in flat spirals, coloured metallic green,

RIGHT: Challenger's *course from Cape York to Japan, as illustrated in the* Report. *Her passage through the Philippines is hard to follow but essentially she undertook the same route twice, on her way to and from Hong Kong.*

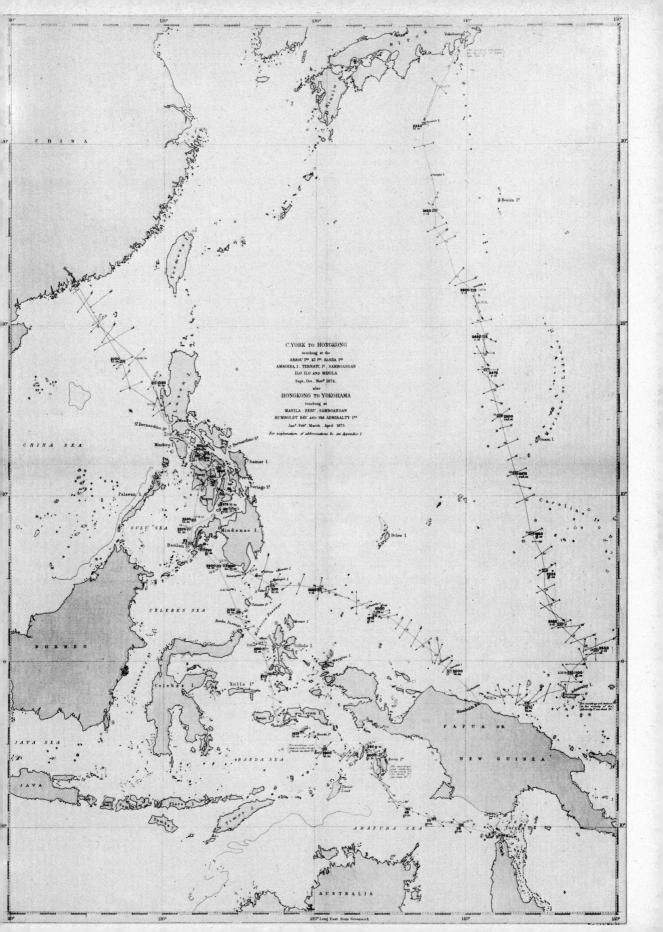

C. YORK TO HONGKONG
touching at the
ARROU Iˢ, KI Iˢ, BANDA Iˢ
AMBOINA, I, TERNATE Iˢ, SAMBOANGAN
ILO ILO AND MANILA
Sept., Oct., Novʳ 1874.
also
HONGKONG TO YOKOHAMA
touching at
MANILA, ZEBU, SAMBOANGAN
HUMBOLDT BAY AND THE ADMIRALTY Iˢ
Janʸ, Febʸ, March, April 1875.
For explanation of abbreviations &c see Appendix I.

and under the wings are two emerald tufts of feathers, visible when the wings are outstretched.' A few Great Birds were killed, but none in full dress, and it may have been too early in the year for courtship and its plumage; only the little King-bird wore his best. Once, high up in a tree, Campbell saw 'the leaf-roof beneath which the natives hide while watching for the arrival of the paradise-birds, shooting them one by one with a silent, blunt-headed arrow'. It was a curious arrow, with a blunt knob instead of a point, and at short range could stun a bird without spoiling its plumage; but except at short range it was inaccurate.

The islands and their waterways were fairly thickly populated – friendly people in their long huts in the woods; canoes, large or small, constantly coming or going – and 'I must not forget to tell you,' writes Campbell, 'that one young lady whom we met in the woods was principally dressed in beads, pretty loops about her throat and ears and over her hair; armlets, anklets, and bracelets also of beads'. By the Malays such primitive charm was less appreciated: they called the natives 'pigs', and a native chief a 'pig-Rajah'. In comparison with the Papuan people the Malays, of course, were sophisticated, but Campbell, and others of his sort, preferred the Papuans. To them the ship was a great attraction, and one day a big canoe, full of men, came alongside and 'took possession. . . . They were very excited and interested in everything they saw, and with a stick measured the whole length of the upper deck from taffrail to bowsprit; others watched the carpenters repairing a boat, and begged for an awl; the young fellows climbed actively up the rigging and stood triumphantly on the royal yard, shouting, gesticulating, and laughing with delight. . . . What stories they will tell of the "great canoe" when they get back to their homes!'

Despite enervating heat the *Challenger*'s people appear to have spent a happy week among the Aru Islands, and though the naturalists deplored their failure to find *Paradisea apoda* in full plumage, Moseley, a minute or two before he heard its cry – '*wauk, wauk*' – had the uncommon experience of shooting a large Fruit-bat 'with a young one hanging at its breast'. It was on September 23rd that they left the little archipelago and headed for the Ki Islands, a hundred and fifty miles to the west, where a fleet of boats came out to meet them. Shaped like whale-boats, they were built without iron nails, their strakes being fastened with rattan and bamboo dowels, and stiffened by inner beams; their crews used paddles with long pointed blades, and chanted at their work with a drum for accompaniment. The effect of that stylish approach was spoiled, however, when the crew-members of one boat came aboard, all of whom 'were in the most horrible state of skin disease, their skins being in a rough scurfy condition in many cases all over the body. I have not seen elsewhere such bad cases of vegetable itch. . . . The men kept constantly scratching themselves violently, and life can be hardly worth living in Great Ki Island. Yet the disease is easily cured.' So says Moseley, and curiously adds – but he was an Oxford man – 'After all, the natives are no worse off than were Cambridge under-

RIGHT: Paradisea apoda, *the Great Bird of Paradise*

their fight right up in front—and making what we took for signs of attack with their missile weapons on each other—at a sound like "wush"! sharply made—they simultaneously changed feet, and retired from one another—at the next "wush"! they again advanced—After repeating this 6 or 7 times the dance concluded—Like all the Natives we have seen, they are excellent "timists" if there is such a word—

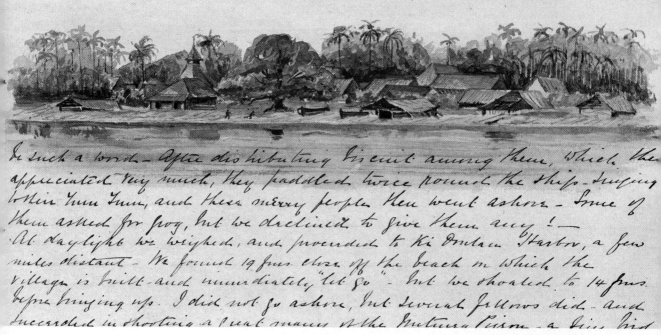

After distributing biscuit among them, which they appreciated very much, they paddled twice round the ship—singing to their Tum Tum, and these merry people then went ashore—Some of them asked for grog, but we declined to give them any!—
At daylight we weighed, and proceeded to Ki Doulan Harbor, a few miles distant—We found 19 fms close off the beach on which the village is built—and immediately "let go"—but we shoaled to 14 fms before bringing up. I did not go ashore, but several fellows did—and succeeded in shooting a great many of the Nutmeg Pigeon—a fine bird

AMBOINE.   Pl. 156.

Bassar ou Marché au quartier Malais

graduates in the middle of the seventeenth century, and they used to be nearly physicked to death into the bargain.'

Despite their constant itching, the Ki islanders, who had a reputation for their skill in boat-building, took great pleasure in examining the ship, 'ran all over it and climbed into the rigging', and performed a dance on the quarter-deck. In pursuit of game they used a very ingenious, light and slender arrow, cut from a species of Canna: 'The strips are so cut that the stiff midrib of the leaf forms the shaft of the arrow, and portions of the wings of the leaf are left on at the base of the arrow to act as feathers. The point is simply sharpened with a knife.' They were so small and light, says Moseley, that they made very little show in flight, and no noise; and among the birds they would kill were large, heavy nutmeg pigeons weighing as much as two pounds. The Ki Islands were as handsomely decorated as the Arus, with birds and brilliant butterflies and little green lizards with bright blue tails; but after a day or two *Challenger* moved on to the more important Banda Islands, famous for their cultivation of nutmegs and burdened with a history that exposes colonialism in its most unpleasant aspect.

There are twelve islands, charmingly named: Great Banda, Neira, Goonong Api, Kraka, Pisang, Kapal, Waii, Rhun, Naailaka, Swangi, Rozengain, and Poeloe – of which Goonong Api, or 'Fire-mountain', was an active volcano. Malays and Javanese had visited them before the arrival of Europeans, and in 1512, when the Portuguese came, the natives lived in a loosely governed Mahomedan republic. The Portuguese established a factory to trade in spices, and dominated the islands for nearly a century. Then came the Dutch with three ships and 700 soldiers and ousted the Portuguese, but were opposed by the natives who succeeded in ambushing and killing a Dutch Admiral and forty-five soldiers or sailors. The Dutch determined on a war of extermination which, with varying success, lasted from 1609 till 1627, when on Great Banda a last remnant of eight hundred, who had resisted till then, surrendered and were deported to Batavia. The Dutch secured a monopoly of the nutmeg trade, and imported slaves to do the work.

In later and gentler times labour was imported from Java, but according to the Report it was 'difficult to induce the better class of men to emigrate', and not easy to maintain discipline over those who did. 'Here, as elsewhere, the native does not appreciate hard labour'; nor, as it seems, did the European overseers who sat on their verandahs 'smoking, with plenty of cooling drinks at hand'. Tropical abundance, one infers, was what really maintained the island's economy, and nutmegs were a source of pleasure as well as of wealth. 'The nutmeg is the kernel of a fruit very like a peach in appearance, which makes an excellent sweetmeat when preserved in sugar.' The owner of a plantation, a very wealthy Malay native of Banda,

LEFT, ABOVE: *the village of Ke Dulan, Little Ki Island.* Challenger *anchored nearby, and 'we had a grand dance on the upper deck, a number of tum tums being brought up from the canoes'.* BELOW: *the covered market at Amboina, 'full of fish, fruit and vegetables, and the Malay smells paramount everywhere'.*

145

said that about one male tree to every fifty females was planted on the estate; he had a superstition that if a nutmeg seed were planted with its flatter side uppermost, it would be more likely to produce a male seedling. Formerly, before the Dutch Government renounced its monopoly of the growth of nutmegs in the Moluccas, the trees were strictly and most jealously confined to the island of Great Banda. The utmost care was taken that no seeds fit for germination should be carried away from the island, for fear of rival plantations being formed elsewhere; seeds were, of course, often smuggled out. The Government destroyed the nutmeg trees on all the other islands of the group. It was, however, found necessary to send a commission every year to uproot the young nutmeg trees sown on these islands by the fruit pigeons *(Carpophaga concinna)*. As agents for the dissemination of plants and trees, fruit pigeons were of prime importance.

The *Challenger*'s people were received by the Dutch Resident at Banda, and other Europeans, in the kindliest fashion and entertained in different places by a Malay band, Javanese musicians, and dancers wearing parti-coloured garments and silver filigree helmets decorated with Bird of Paradise plumes. On an expedition to a nutmeg plantation the party set off in the steam pinnace accompanied by the Resident's large and ornately decorated canoe: bow and stern rose to high, carved pinnacles, large banners flew, and a Malayan crew of eighteen raised their paddles vertically between each stroke, with drums and gongs to keep the time. On the weather side of Great Banda there was an awkward sea, but native labourers on the plantation came down to carry their visitors ashore in arm-chairs, and waiting for them were a dozen musicians and a couple of dancing girls. Their music sounded

The resident's canoe, Banda

Mohamedan mosque in the square at Ke Dulan – see Pelham Aldrich's watercolour on page 144. Moseley was interested in its curious architecture, but Lord George Campbell more interested in the Mohamedans. 'They were very particular as to our not going in, and ostentatiously obstructed the doorway.'

like that of a string band, but was produced by a dozen bell-shaped gongs and what might be called musical glasses were it not for the fact that they were made of bamboo. On the hill-tops where the nutmegs grew the undergrowth had been cleared, the gardened jungle looked rather like a park, and orchids grew on tall Canary trees. Returning to the shore, the visitors were entertained by the dancers in red and yellow garments and silver helmets, who performed a war-dance to the accompaniment of gun-fire. Later, on the island of Neira, they were taken to a club house, an important feature in all the Dutch settlements in the Far East; and there learnt that the common custom was to rise at daybreak, take a light breakfast of fruit and coffee, and attend at one's office till 11 a.m., by when the day's work was virtually over. Aboard *Challenger* there was more activity, and the purpose of the expedition was not forgotten: dredging in fairly shallow water, the pinnace brought up, among other specimens, numerous Monaxonid sponges, to one of which – a new species – was given the name *Amphilectus challengeri*, and a scientific description of entertaining density: its striking external habit is characterized, we are told, 'by a smooth acuate skeleton and an equianchorate parenchyma spicule', as its picture may demonstrate.

The next port-of-call was Amboina, chief port of the Moluccas, and still in the Banda Sea but a little closer to China. West and north-west of Amboina is the large island of Celebes, separated from Borneo by the Macassar Strait; and to the north – but with a host of islands between – are the Philippines, and north again, Formosa. Amboina had a history at least as violent as that of its neighbours, and of larger distinction. It was, of course, initiated by the Portuguese who, with the marvellous and imaginative energy that characterized them in the sixteenth century, mobilized and despatched, in 1521, a fleet of nine ships whose commander built a fort and began what proved to be a long and difficult process of pacification. Not until 1580 were the Portuguese firmly established, and by then they were extremely unpopular. So unpopular, indeed, that in 1609 there arrived, by native invitation, a Dutch fleet under Admiral van der Hagen, who opened fire and called on the Portuguese Governor to surrender. The Governor was apparently a man of pacific habit, and the Portuguese capitulated without fighting. The Governor died, however, as his wife, who was sensitive about honour, decided that the honourable thing was to poison him.

The Dutchmen's easy success did not lead to peaceful occupation, for the natives were soon as eager to be rid of them as previously they had been to expel the Portuguese; and the situation was complicated by the appearance of some Englishmen who established a small settlement in 1615. The Dutch were resourceful and ruthless; in the Far East they pursued an imperialist policy with an efficiency that assured success, and they bitterly resented competition; the English factory survived only until 1623, when the Dutch destroyed it, and tortured and killed the English merchants. Cromwell compelled the United Provinces to pay their widows and offspring £300,000 in compensation, and, more memorably, the poet Dryden

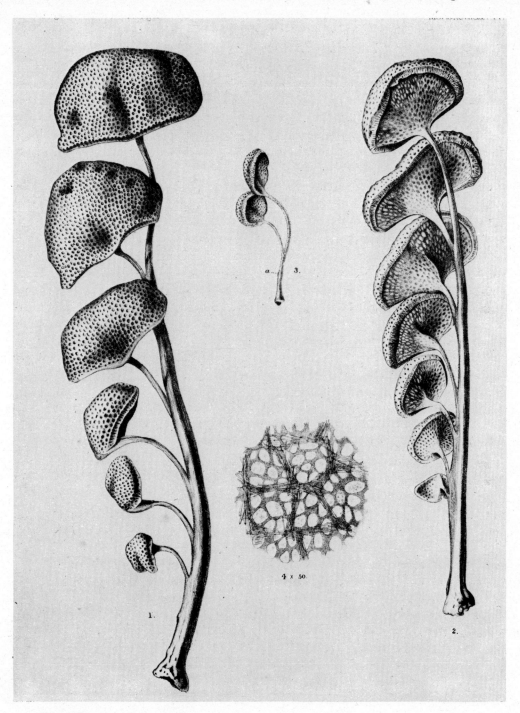

Monaxonid sponge, Amphilectus challengeri. *The enlargement shows the spicules.*

found in the massacre inspiration and material for his tragedy, *Amboyna*. Then, between 1796 and 1814, the island was twice taken by the British, and twice returned to the Dutch; who finally lost possession of it and all their East Indies when they were re-styled Indonesia and proclaimed their independence.

In 1874 the Governor had jurisdiction over all the neighbouring islands, of which the largest was Ceram; and the particular importance of Amboina lay – or lately had lain – in its monopoly of clove cultivation. What the nutmeg was to Banda, the clove was to Amboina, and though the tree grows naturally throughout the Moluccas, the Dutch ensured their monopoly by destroying it in all places other than the favoured island. It is a mountainous island, rising to some 4,000 feet, and more than twenty miles long. Its little town was tidily planned, with two long streets facing the sea, the better houses guarded by fine Croton hedges, and the naturalists were much impressed by the scrupulous care with which the old fort was maintained: all within was perfectly ordered and spotlessly clean, though one of its guns – when, punctiliously, salutes were exchanged – fell off the parapet into the ditch.

Campbell, as usual, saw and appreciated all that was picturesque: 'The canoes are a great sight: both here and at our first anchorage they came alongside full of fruit and eggs, and literally crowded with lories and cockatoos; while occasionally a cassowary, with legs tied, lies prostrate at the bottom of the canoe. These cockatoos are not the Australian yellow-crested species, but those gentlemanly-looking old fellows whose white feathers curl like moustaches over their beaks, and their erected crests show pink underneath. They sit solemnly along the sides of the canoes, while the lories are tied by their legs to bamboo perches, and are always moving and bobbing about, never at rest. They are quite lovely, one kind coloured crimson, and another green, blue, and purple.

'The Malay fisherman fish by torch-light, with spears and nets, and it is a pretty sight at night to see hundreds of canoes, each with two or three torches, putting out from the huts and villages along the bay, looking, when they get all together, like some large town in the distance. Then in the early morning they all come paddling back – whole fleets of them – keeping close together, abreast in a row; and as they pass the ship, by way of a little show-off, they strike up in chorus a boatman's song, keeping time to the double knock of their paddles against the sides of the canoes.'

And Moseley – also as usual – discovered yet another of nature's oddities and eccentricities: 'Some of the smaller trees growing on these ridges are covered with the curious epiphytes, *Myrmecodia armata* and *Hydnophytum formicaum;* these are plants belonging to the natural order *Cinchonaceae*. Both plants are associated in their growth with certain species of ants; as soon as the young plants develop a stem, the ants gnaw at its base, and this activity causes the stem to swell; the ants continuing to irritate and excavate the swelling, it assumes a globular form, and may become larger than a man's head.

'The globular mass contains within a labyrinth of chambers and passages, which are occupied by the ants as their nest. The walls of these chambers, and the whole mass of the inflated stem, retain their vitality and thrive, continuing to increase in size with growth. From the surface of the rounded mass are given off small twigs, bearing the leaves and flowers.

'It appears that this curious gall-like tumour on the stem has become a normal condition of the plants, which cannot thrive without the ants.'

Butterflies, sea-shells, and deer were other attractions on Amboina; but the deer, though numerous, seem to have been able to look after themselves, and the shells, for which the island was famous, were so dear that no one bought them. Of the butterflies – some of them large and brilliant – six new species were captured, and from the shallows of the sea several new species of brachyurous crabs. Then the ship put to sea again, heading north towards the Molucca Passage. She had lain for nearly a week at Amboina, and her new destination was the island of Ternate, an active volcanic cone rising from the sea to a height of over 5,000 feet. Immediately to the east of it lies the very much larger island of Gillolo which in 1874 was said to be almost unknown, and since Indonesian independence may – from a European point of view – have become even more remote. *Challenger* had a calm and easy passage through mild seas decorated with islands of differing size and shape: past Obi, past Batchian, past the old volcano of Makian, split in two by eruption in the mid seventeenth century, which, erupting again in 1862, is said to have killed some 6,000 people. Dredging and sounding prolonged the voyage, but at daylight on October 14th the ship's company were rewarded by the sight of ten volcanic cones, several in eruption; then, under steam, the ship entered the channel between

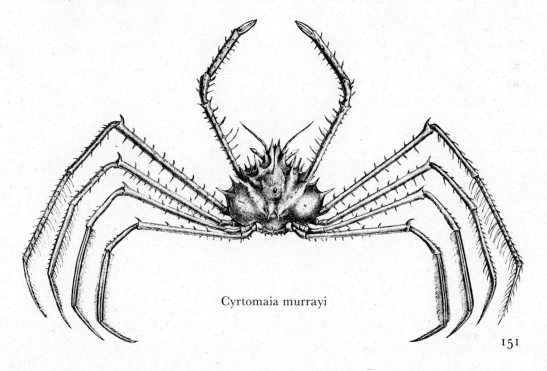

Cyrtomaia murrayi

Ternate and its neighbouring volcano on the island of Tidore, and anchoring off the coaling pier on Ternate saluted the Dutch Resident with thirteen guns.

The Resident, van Musschenbroek, was himself a naturalist and received his visitors in the most agreeable fashion, presenting them with a good collection of snakes and corals – as well as much information – and arranging a ball in their honour at which the musicians, who were Malays, played indefatigably though they knew only one tune. In the natural scene, however, there was no lack of variety. The tall, twin volcanic islands were green to the top, and beneath their wooded slopes were plantations where, in marvellous profusion, grew cloves and cinnamon, nutmegs and peppers, pineapples, durians, oranges and limes, bananas and bread-fruit; and to animate the vegetable picture flocks of green and crimson lories flew among the trees with a rushing sound. In the little town were the usual Dutch, Chinese, and Malay quarters – square, whitewashed houses with verandahs, bamboo huts – fishermen carrying a catch almost as brightly hued as birds, Chinese children chattering home from school, wild men from Gillolo, Malays in gay calico, and white residents sedately strolling. Westwards from the Aru Islands the voyage had offered a succession of entrancing views, and Ternate, almost on the Equator, seemed to concentrate and show under its steep side all the riches of tropic islands.

Papilio alcidinus, *a butterfly which for its own protection mimics in colour and shape an unappetizing day-flying moth.*

Native boats off Tidore, with its volcanic cone in the centre.

Campbell evolved an engaging theory that among parrots of a certain sort the red ones were female, the green ones male; and as if to demonstrate the superiority of scientific practice Wyville Thomson bought the birds he had been admiring – 'All the parrots and lories at one fell swoop,' says Campbell, 'and with a yet feller swoop poisoned and skinned them all on board.' On Ternate lived a Mr Brown who dealt in Birds of Paradise, sending Malay sailing boats or 'proas' to New Guinea to collect them; it was a dangerous trade, for sometimes his agents were killed, and occasionally a proa did not return. According to Campbell, Brown had specimens of sixteen different species – of which Wyville Thomson bought many – as well as three living birds, one of them a Great Bird of Paradise in full plumage. There were also Mahomedan dealers, and the price of a skin varied from eight to fourteen shillings. Some of the Malay collectors were expert in preparing and preserving bird-skins, which they mounted on a small stick, embedded in tow stuffing and protruding from the tail, so allowing the bird to be handled without touching the feathers.

Moseley was determined to climb the Peak of Ternate, the Resident gave him four Malayan guides, and Lieutenant Balfour agreed to go with him. They spent a night in the house of a Dutch official, at a height of about a thousand feet, and set off before daybreak. The path was steep, the ground slippery after a heavy shower, but when daylight came they were above the last of the cultivated land and on the verge of a forest that clothed the mountainside from 2,000 to 4,000 feet. Higher than that was a dense growth of tall reeds, and at 4,800 feet they found an ancient, outer crater, covered with bushes and tree-ferns and inhabited by deer and wild pig. Above that was recently ejected lava. The terminal cone

153

showed no vegetation, rose on a slope of 30 degrees, and was about 350 feet high. As Moseley and Balfour began to climb the Malayan guides turned tail and ran, for they believed that immediate eruption would be the consequence; and Moseley admitted that there was some risk in the ascent. The cone consisted of masses of basaltic lava, varying in size, and from the interior of the crater rose thick smoke. They tried to climb down, but twenty yards was as far as they could go without danger of suffocation; and then, returning to the rim of the crater, they were rewarded with a superb view of Gillolo, Tidore, and many distant islands. They had been climbing for five hours.

The volcano of Ternate

14 *Mindanao and Zamboanga*

From the Moluccas to the Philippines, to Hong Kong, and the Philippines again: the names, at least, are becoming more familiar, but it is doubtful if, in Europe, Luzon and Cebu and Mindanao are much better known than Amboina and Great Banda. In the United States it is different: people there have had much occasion to examine the geography, politics, and ethnic confusion of an archipelago, daunting in its size, that has nurtured life – animal and vegetable – in astonishing profusion, but appears never to have given human beings a truly peaceful and settled habitation. Of the average person in Western Europe it may not be untrue to say that he knows the Philippines were discovered by Magellan, but took little interest in them until, in December 1941, the Japanese attacked Pearl Harbor, landed on Luzon, and General Douglas MacArthur withdrew into prepared positions on the Bataan peninsula that almost encloses Manila bay, where he settled down to endure a five months' siege. This is no place for an assessment of MacArthur's soldierly genius, but it would be ungracious to omit a reference to the man who first compelled the world at large to pay attention to an immense assembly of islands – there are said to be 7,000, though only a dozen or so are large – whose early history is obscure and their later centuries dark with dispute. In 1874 they were still a Spanish possession, but Spanish rule had long lost its early vigour, and the friars of a once able and heroic church had become rich, corporate landowners. Discontent was growing fast.

On their way to the Philippines – trawling deeply in the Celebes Sea – the naturalists added to their already huge collection of marine 'animals' some more specimens

Pile dwellings of Lutaos, a village of Moros on the island of Basilan.

of the long thin fish called *Ipnops murrayi*, first captured near Tristan da Cunha, and a number of new Asteroids or starfish. Asteroids of one sort or another are found in all the oceans, and *Challenger*'s contribution to knowledge of the group, both from a geographical and a zoological point of view, was the most important ever made: she brought home 150 forms new to science, and twenty-eight new genera were established. Almost as remarkable as that, however, is the catholicity of interest shown by the seafaring 'philosophers', and as soon as he goes ashore Moseley's attention is diverted from starfish to the curious pile-dwellings of the Filipinos.

On October 24th the ship arrived at the small town of Zamboanga, at the tip of the long peninsula that dangles from the western extremity of the large, southerly island of Mindanao. Behind the town were paddy fields, bright green and swampy, where wisps of snipe flew wildly and domestic buffaloes wallowed; along the beach was a row of houses that appeared to be moving into the sea on stilts. All the native buildings were pile-dwellings, or modifications of them, but some had taken to the sea more completely than others.

Opposite Zamboanga, across a narrow strait, was the island of Basilan, and there a community of Moros had built houses that stood, quite isolated from the shore, on piles projecting from a shallow bay. They had been built close together, and many

Dwelling house at Zamboanga, connected to the shore by a gangplank.

were connected by broad, ricketty gangways. The main house – or main part of a house – usually stood on three rows of piles, and out-buildings were supported by others where needed. There was always a platform in front of the entrance to the house, and behind it might be another shelf to carry a canoe. At Zamboanga, where also there were Moros, there was the same sort of construction, but the houses stood closer to the beach; at low tide they were not entirely surrounded by water, and their inhabitants could walk ashore on a plank. These Moros – so Moseley suggests – had been partially tamed by the Spaniards, and had acquired enough confidence to live almost on land.

Other races, such as the Bisayans – who were Malays – lived inland but built their houses in the same way. Their architecture retained the ancestral pattern devised, for protection, by remote forebears; and though the style, when first taken ashore, kept in some measure its original sanitary advantage, that was lost when it was discovered that more rooms could be added by closing the spaces between the piles. A fence of palm leaves made a pig-shed, walls of matting improved it, and when planks were nailed across there was a proper room. The next step might be the substitution of stone pillars for wooden piles, and walls of masonry could then take the place of planks. In a house thus improved the ground-floor would be an addition to the first storey, which had indeed come first. Moseley watched a new house being built, and the old sequence was maintained. 'The roof and first storey were built first, complete upon the piles, and the lower structure added afterwards.'

Ingeniously he suggests that a verandah, if there was one, represented 'the platform originally intended for the inhabitants to land on from canoes'; and after noting the wide geographical distribution of pile-dwellings – from Switzerland to the Gulf of Maracaibo, from New Guinea to Central Africa – confesses that he has been surprised 'by the remarkable resemblance of many of these Malay houses to Swiss chalets. In the chalet the basement enclosed with stone walls is usually only a cattle-stall, the first storey is the dwelling-house, and, as in the Malay building, is constructed of wood. It seems possible that the chalet is the ancient lake-dwelling gone on shore.' And if the chalet has a balcony, that, of course, is the verandah which was initially the platform on to which you stepped from your canoe.

He returns to his immediate environment to speak of the Moros, who were also called 'Lutaos'. They were Mahomedans who kept themselves apart from other races, and were thought, says Moseley, to have settled in Mindanao in the seventeenth century. It may be, however, that they arrived much earlier. In the twelfth and thirteenth centuries there were Arabs in Ceylon, in such numbers as to control its trade, and in the stories of *The Thousand and One Nights* – there is great variation in their dating – the tales of Sindbad the Sailor are evidence, in a popular way, of adventurous seafaring. By the Portuguese the Arabs were called Moors, and Ibn Batuta, the greatest of Moorish travellers and a native of Tangier, was in China about the middle of the fourteenth century; when the original Moros of Mindanao were, perhaps, already in residence. In Campbell's opinion they were 'fine wild fellows', and in Moseley's sober judgement 'a fierce and warlike race, pirates by profession at all events not long ago at Basilan and Mindanao, and still so at the Sulu Islands. . . . The men are short and broad-shouldered, with powerful chests and

158

thickset bodies, and extremely active. Their features are of the Malay type, but peculiar. Their eyes are remarkably bright. Their colour is light yellowish brown. They have often a slight beard and moustache. They wear bright-coloured shirts and rather tight-fitting trousers, buttoned close round the leg at the ankle. The Moro women are short and small, and delicate-limbed, most of them very handsome when young; many of them are very light-coloured in complexion; their eyes, like the men's, being extremely bright. They are fond of bright yellows and reds in their dress, and are very fully clad. The men are armed with circular shields and spears, and formerly at least they used suits of armour made of plates of buffalo horn linked together with wire.'

Campbell, in his customary way, records the picturesque, and describes a pretty little street-scene in Zamboanga: 'Along the centre runs a sluggish stream, the banks planted with trees, and steps leading down to the water. The houses on both sides were occupied by Chinamen's shops, whose owners were sitting at their doors placidly smoking. In this stream, along the whole length of the street, were women and girls, half-immersed, washing their clothes and themselves. Women plump, pretty, and graceful; women the reverse; women with their hair down – a thick, black, wavy mane – and women with it up, some pounding away at linen, some washing their hair, and some skylarking – inflating their garments with air, throwing themselves on the top of the water, bobbing and floating about on this impromptu air cushion, till the air escaping again reduced the drapery of these damsels to their original wet and clinging condition. It was a busy, pretty scene, and absorbed our attention a good deal.'

The Chinese excite an equal admiration. They occupy, he says, 'nearly the whole of two streets, have excellent shops, large and well fitted up, where everything can be got and of the best quality, from portmanteaus to pâté de foie gras, from bewitching velvet – silver, gold, and silk embroidered – slippers to Bass's bottled pale ale, from Chintzes of gorgeous pattern to Messrs Blackwell's jams and pickles, from cotton-stuffs of all colours and qualities to delicately woven *pina* or silken-stuffs.' Pina was a fabric, something like muslin, woven from the fibre of pineapple leaves on primitive hand-looms: it was work for women, and at its finest the stuff was marvellously light and transparent. Young men of fashion wore embroidered pina shirts, which were expensive.

Campbell had never seen rice growing before, and the vivid green of the well-watered paddy fields pleased him immensely, as did the variety of fruit trees that grew about the native villages. There were mangos, oranges, durians, pomelo or pompelmoose, guavas, bananas and breadfruit, coco and areca palms, and one regrets that he had not the hardihood to sample a durian. That legendary fruit, which grows to the size of a large melon, is said to have the most exquisite flavour of anything emerging from soil or tree, but a smell so horrible – putrid and vile – that few can defy it to give their palate pleasure. Campbell smelt an opened durian, and fled.

He must have had an easy, engaging manner, for he seems to have been received with instant friendliness wherever he went. He and a companion, having hired ponies, rode off for the day and lost their luncheon-bag crossing a river deeper than they thought. It did not spoil their enjoyment. They were puzzled by water-buffaloes that, in the heat of the day, stood so deep in deep pools that only their horns, ears, noses and eyes were visible. They rode through a smiling landscape, with paddy fields brilliant beside darker palm groves, a brown river rippled and frothy, and in the distance the Basilian mountains intensely blue under a blazing sun. But they were hungry, and they had lost their lunch. Then they met a cheerfully grinning native carrying a large sugar-cane which he both chewed and used as a walking-stick, to whom they said hopefully, 'Banana? Banana!' '*Si, si*', he answered, and they followed him to a hut beside the river, and there, in the shade of pomelo and durian trees, they were given bunches of bananas newly plucked, tumblers of coconut milk freshly tapped, and soft-boiled eggs. There were girls who fried bananas for them – ran up and down ladders, pretending to be busy – and when, having paid their host, they told him they would soon be back, he appeared to be delighted.

The officers of some small Spanish gunboats entertained the *Challenger*'s officers and naturalists with a display of native dancing – girls in solitary undulation, a spirited and convincing war-dance by grimacing Moros – and to add a little realism the headman of the Moros showed his *kris* – a long dagger undulant as the girls – with which he was said to have killed his two dozen enemies. They were 'a capital lot of fellows', the Spanish officers, and a champagne supper concluded the evening's entertainment. Then the voyage was resumed, to Ilo-Ilo on the island of Panay, a well-to-do but dirty town in a populous island, and from there to Manila in its almost

'The body sways gently to and fro, but the feet, excepting a slight shuffling movement, contribute nothing to the display.' The boys danced too, but all Challenger *eyes were on the girls.*

land-locked bay. The capital city had come down in the world since the beginning of the seventeenth century, when it was the commercial metropolis of the Far East: Dutch competition, Malay pirates, hostile Chinese, and its own incompetence had hampered administration and progressively weakened the rule of Spain, and in 1874 the population of Manila was not much more than 90,000, and it offered little in the way of entertainment except the tobacco factories. They employed thousands of women who sat on the floor beside low tables on which, with small wooden mallets, they beat the tobacco leaves before rolling them into cigars. The noise was deafening, the heat uncomfortable, and Campbell was reminded of penguin rookeries on Inaccessible Island. He admits, however, that the women, most of them young, were scrupulously clean, 'and it was vastly nicer to be stared at and grinned at by these girls than to be screeched at and have holes dug in one's leg by penguins.'

From Manila to Hong Kong in rough, monsoon weather; and Campbell, in a lordly way, declares that he sees no need to describe a place so well known. It is

161

The journal of Pelham Aldrich LEFT *ends at Hong Kong, for he left the ship to return to England with Captain Nares.*

worth mentioning, however, that in the thirty-odd years since the island was ceded to Britain in 1841, a city of handsome buildings had been well designed and raised in solid dignity to stand complacently against their background of romantic beauty; and to the great relief of Parliament the colony had for some years been self-support-ing.

The ship remained there from November 17th until January 6th, 1875, but little was added to the history of the cruise except an event that all on board deeply re-gretted. Captain Nares was appointed to command the ships *Alert* and *Discovery* on an arctic expedition which, it was hoped, might reach the North Pole, and he sailed to England accompanied by his First Lieutenant, Pelham Aldrich. To succeed them came Captain Frank Turle Thomson, of HMS *Modeste*, and Lieutenant Carpenter, of HMS *Iron Duke*, both ships being on the China Station, who joined *Challenger* on January 2nd. She was by then lighter of a considerable burden, for all the zoological and other specimens acquired since leaving Sydney had been landed at Kowloon and packed in 129 cases and several casks for transmission to England; a procedure which was followed in other ports.

British residents in Hong Kong, and naval and military officers stationed there, made members of the expedition warmly welcome, and hospitality awaited them also in Canton. The hosts may sometimes have been surprised by unusual topics of conversation, and on one occasion, at least, Moseley must have created conster-nation. He was invited by a Hong Kong merchant to a Chinese dinner and, for a

To succeed a man both distinguished and popular as captain of the Challenger *was a daunting task. Frank Turle Thomson* RIGHT *looks apprehensive, but he soon made his own contribution to the voyage.*

start, spoke admiringly of the flowers that decorated the room in which the party assembled. But a little while later he was less tactful.

'The dining-table', he writes, 'was closely packed with dishes of most varied kinds, tastefully ornamented and arranged. There were absolutely no bare spaces, a display of profusion being evidently intended. I was astonished to find as a condiment in the sauce of some stewed pigeons, specimens of the well-known but curious *Cordyceps sinensis*. This is a fungus which attacks and kills the caterpillars of certain moths; the fungus penetrates the tissues of the living larva, and after the latter has buried itself in the ground in order to assume the pupa state, the fungus throws out above ground a long stem from the dead body of the larva.

'The dried dead caterpillar, with the fungus outgrowth attached, is one of the many Chinese delicacies which, while they seem so strange to us, are generally prized because, in addition to their gastronomic qualities, they are credited with exercising certain invigorating medicinal effects. The caterpillars are sold tied up in small bundles, and the article is called "the summer grass of the winter worm".'

It is a pity that there is no record of his host's behaviour when, with sudden recognition, Moseley exclaimed, '*Cordyceps sinensis*! A fungus which attacks and kills caterpillars. It penetrates the tissues. . . .' Sub-Lieutenant Campbell cannot have been present, or we should know more about that interesting occasion.

Challenger put to sea again on January 6th, leaving a crowded harbour to the accompaniment of much music. As well as the hundreds of junks and sampans that

163

were its usual traffic, there were foreign ships – French, Russian, Austrian and German – and British men-of-war whose bands, one after another, saluted her as she steamed through the Lyemun Pass and steered for Lema Island, where sail was made and the fires put out. She was in Manila again on the 11th, and Moseley had time to comment, with some asperity, on native dress, appetite, pastimes, and religion. Such people as Bisayans and Tagalogs and half-castes never tucked their shirts in, but worely them loosely flapping: a ludicrous habit, he thought, which reminded him of the Australian Aborigine's description of an Anglican clergyman as 'white fellow belong Sunday, wear shirt over trousers'. He was revolted by an extraordinary luxury, generally enjoyed, which consisted 'of ducks' eggs which are brooded until the young are just beginning to be fledged, and are then boiled. It is a sickening sight to see these embryo ducklings swallowed at the roadside stalls, which are common at every street corner, piled high with half-hatched eggs.' He disapproved, with good reason, of the large, razor-sharp blades with which fighting-cocks were spurred; and acidly he observes that 'Papal indulgences for sins, and even for crimes, are still sold in the Philippines, by the Government, at its offices all over the country, at the same counters with tobacco, brandy, lottery tickets, and other articles of which the Government retains the monopoly'.

Cebu was next on the programme, where Magellan had foolishly intervened in some trifling war between the Rajah of Cebu and a neighbouring ruler, and was tragically killed on a small, offshore island. The Rajah had let him build a chapel and celebrate mass; he had accepted baptism, and most of his subjects followed his example; but their habits suffered no change, and still they spent five or six hours a day eating half-cooked meat and drinking heavily. Their domestic animals were dogs, cats, pigs, goats and poultry, all of which were eaten. Cebu was a pretty place, but the heat was excessive and mosquitoes were troublesome. Tobacco was cheap and plentiful – even small children smoked cigars – and much Manila hemp was exported. There were curlews and white egrets on the shore, very handsome orioles, and fine reddish-brown hawks. But for the naturalists Cebu's chief attraction was the siliceous sponge commonly called Venus' Flower Basket *(Euplectella aspergillum)*, which was found in abundance at 100 fathoms in the channel between Cebu and Bohol. The natives used a simple but ingenious dredge to fish for them: a bamboo triangle, armed with thirty-six hooks and weighted with stones, that swept a path fourteen feet wide.

About eighty miles eastward of Cebu was Camiguin where in 1871 a volcano erupted from low ground, in two months threw up a hill two-thirds of a mile long, destroying all vegetation for many miles, and by 1875 had grown to a height of almost 2,000 feet and was still vigorous. Most of a population of 11,000 had fled, and the cone was too hot to climb. There appeared to be no crater, but from cracks in the red dome-shaped mass small fires glowed at night, and by day there came a column of smoke. Small hot streams ran downhill, in which green algae grew. 'At the source of one of these streams,' says Moseley, 'as it issued from beneath the volcano, the

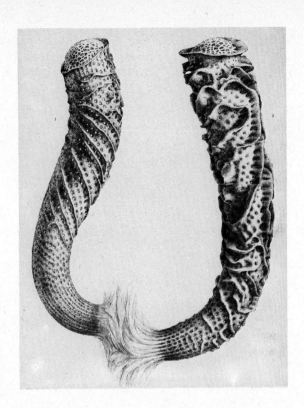

Euplectella aspergillum,
Venus' Flower Basket

water had a temperature of 145.2°F, and was thus too hot to be borne by the hand. Here there were no algae at all growing in the water. There were, however, small green patches on stones projecting out of the bed of the stream into the air, and also along the margins of the stream where they were not bathed by the hot water itself, but only soaked up the moisture and received the spray occasionally.' The fact is interesting, he concludes, 'as showing that green algae of some considerable complexity may have commenced life on the earth in its early history, before the water on its surface had anywhere cooled down to a temperature sufficient to be borne by the human hand, and which may have been strongly impregnated with various volcanic gases and salts.'

The ship returned to Zamboanga, where the scene had changed. The rice had been harvested, the paddy-fields showed a yellow stubble, in the dry season many streams were low but roads deep in dust. Bunkers had to be replenished – there would be no further opportunity for coaling till they reached Japan – and the Spaniards were both helpful and generous. They themselves were short of coal – their stock was down to 200 tons – but they let *Challenger* take half of what they had, and supplied convicts to help with the loading.

A few miles inland, where a stream ran down a highland glen, a party of seven – four officers and three men – enjoyed, under canvas, a few days' shore leave before setting off into the immensities of the Pacific. They shot between thirty and forty birds, of about eighteen different species, and what Campbell calls a flying lemur and Moseley, more accurately and at greater length, describes as 'the well-known aberrant flying insectivorous mammal *Galeopithecus philippensis*'. It is like a flying squirrel, he adds, and has 'membranes of skin stretched between its legs and out on to its tail; so that, supported on this as by a parachute, it skims through the air in its leaps from tree to tree with a partial flight'. The Philippines are extraordinarily rich in bird-life, but apparently the *Challenger*'s people found no opportunity for purposive search and study; there is no record of rare and unexpected ornithological capture, and Campbell's final comment on the islands strikes a sombre note.

The cemetery at Zamboanga was a long, high wall in which, in five rows, were openings – 'like ovens', was Moseley's suggestion – in which the bodies of the dead were closed with a dressing of quick-lime; and after three years the bones were removed to a common charnel-house.

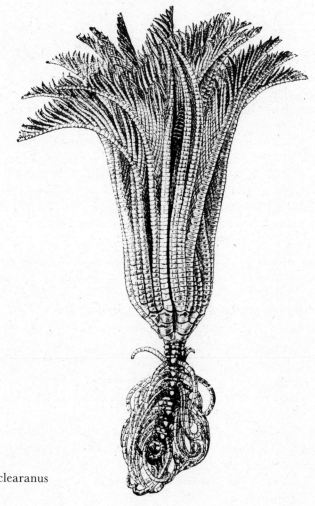

Pentacrinus maclearanus

15 New Guinea and the wood-carvers

Challenger's zig-zag cruising in the Atlantic, at the start of her slow and stately circumnavigation, must have seemed in retrospect little more than a homely exercise in comparison with her voyaging in the Pacific. The Pacific dwarfs all other oceans. The Atlantic is less than half its size, and of the total surface of our Earth the Pacific is almost a moiety. It is a vast, gibbous basin rimmed on the one side by the whole coastline of the American continent from the Gulf of Alaska to the friendless islands off Tierra del Fuego; on the other by the ragged northern edges of eastern Asia, by Japan and the Philippines and the Great Barrier Reef; and *Challenger*'s course would take her from Zamboanga to the north coast of New Guinea, not far below the Equator; from there to Japan, where Moseley, in happy contrast to New Guinea, would be delighted to find 'nearly a mile of continuous bookshops'; thence to the Sandwich Islands, now called Hawaii; south from there to Tahiti in the thick confusion of the Society Islands; over to Robinson Crusoe's island of Juan Fernandez off the Chilean coast; and so down to the difficult entrance, the treacherous passage of the Straits of Magellan, and the returning gateway to the Atlantic. For those who did not enjoy long voyages – perhaps a majority of those on board – it was a formidable prospect.

New Guinea was only a secondary objective – no more than a flying visit was anticipated – and the real purpose of sailing eastwards was to go far enough to make a fair wind of the north-east trade to Japan, and thereby save coal for sounding and dredging. Dampier, in the year 1700, had gone round the north-west end of New

Guinea, and sailing along the Equator reached the meridian of 150°E in twenty-one days: since his time, apparently, no one had set and followed that course, but it was hoped that what Dampier did, the *Challenger* could do. That hope was disappointed, however, and *Challenger*, even though occasionally steam was used, took twenty-six days to reach the Admiralty Islands and the meridian of 147°E.

In the matter of dredging, however, the voyage was quickly and richly rewarded, for off a group of small islands not far from the southernmost tip of Mindanao two hauls were extraordinarily productive, and brought up, from a deposit of blue mud, twenty-two specimens of teleostean fishes – fishes whose skeletons were completely ossified – and over 150 specimens of invertebrates, most of which belonged to new genera or species of deep-sea animals. Many were crinoids – echinoderms with a calyx-like body – and 'the philosophers' found academic entertainment in giving them such names as *Metacrinus moseleyi, Metacrinus murrayi,* or *Myzostoma wyville-thomsoni* and *Promachocrinus naresi* in gratitude to Captain Nares.

As the ship approached the coast of New Guinea she passed through long lines of driftwood, twigs and branches and uprooted trees, stems of cane and tattered palm-leaves – evidence of the torrential force of some fairly large river – and all that debris was alive with minute inhabitants, while under it swam great shoals of little fishes, and dashing through it went troops of dolphins and squadrons of small sharks. More surprising was a large flock of phalaropes that accompanied it, for in Britain the phalarope *(Phalaropus hyperboreus)* is a visitor from the far north, and to see it roosting on driftwood from a New Guinea river was unexpected proof of its versatility.

There was no difficulty in distinguishing the land. The intention was to anchor in Humboldt Bay, which lay just on the westward side of the meridian that was Dutch New Guinea's eastern frontier. The high, solitary peak of Mount Bougainville rose on the east side of the Bay, and the Cyclops Mountains were clearly visible; as, perhaps, is the significance of their names. Louis Antoine de Bougainville was a French soldier, mathematician, and navigator who sailed round the world in the 1760s: he was one of the very few people to whom, in 1875, the world owed a morsel of information about an island more than 1,500 miles long, and in its broadest part almost 500 miles across. As for the Cyclops Mountains, the significance of their name lay in the fact that behind them lived a people almost as mysterious, and perhaps as dangerous, as that pastoral community of which Homer tells, whose chief, Polyphemus, had made a meal of some of Odysseus's unhappy companions.

The Dutch, those busy exploiters of the Far East, laid early claim to western New Guinea, and their suzerainty as far as the meridian of 141°E was recognized in 1828;

RIGHT: *some of the exotic forms of radiolaria collected by* Challenger.
OVERLEAF: *Mr Wild's portrait gallery of Humboldt Bay 'savages'. 'The head of one was encircled by a crown of bright scarlet [hibiscus] flowers while the head of the others was stuck all over with large white feathers', he writes. Lord George Campbell says, 'their faces, ugly enough as nature fashioned them, they make still more hideous by artificial means.'*

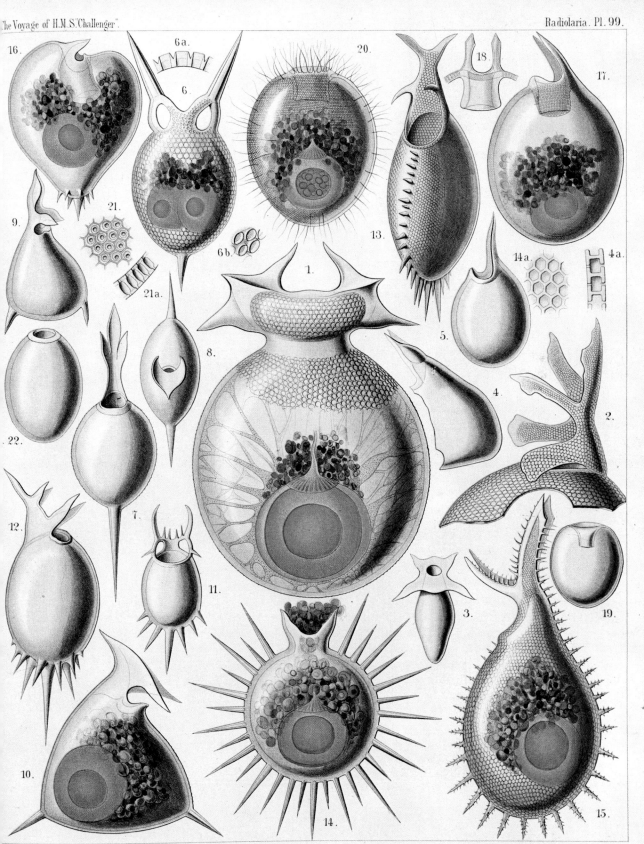

F.Haeckel and A.Giltsch.Del.

E.Giltsch Jena, Lithogr.

1–15. CHALLENGERIA. 16–18. PHARYNGELLA. 19,20. ENTOCANNULA.
'21.22. LITHOGROMIA.'

but the Dutch had done almost nothing to explore that large dominion, and apart from coastal survey there had been, before 1870, only tentative and minimal investigation of the eastern, Papuan half of the island. For all one knew, in 1875, Polyphemus or his like might still have been a local potentate. Thirty years after that, indeed, there is ample evidence of a pastoral people disastrously separated by mutual fear and suspicion that bred a murderous inclination towards all strangers. In 1883 Australia had begun to realize the strategic importance of New Guinea, and a year later Britain proclaimed a protectorate over the south coast, and its hinterland, of the eastward half of the island; a proclamation that was quickly followed by German annexation of the north coast and its neighbouring islands. The first Administrator, and later Lieutenant-Governor of Papua, was Sir William MacGregor, an heroically energetic explorer; and in the course of time he was followed – at first as Chief Justice, later as Lieutenant-Governor – by Sir Hubert Murray, a man of outstanding ability and deep sympathy with the Stone Age natives for whose care he became responsible. Murray travelled far, saw much, interpreted liberally, and wrote objectively about his Papuans. One of his stories – to which must be given a date in the early years of the present century – was about his cook, a man called Oala, who told him that the people of his district had lately found an unknown old man asleep on a hill, and promptly killed him. Murray, horrified by the tale, had denounced the murder, and at that Oala became indignant. 'Do you think', he asked, 'if I found an old man or a baby asleep, do you think that I wouldn't kill him? My word, I would kill him all right'.

Returning to his house, Murray related that curious conversation to his wife and some friends who were present. Among them was a young man who was both shocked and incredulous. He was friendly with Lohia, a native of his own age who appeared to be quite devoted to him; and to test the truth of Murray's story he went out to look for Lohia, and said to him, 'If all the white men went away and left me behind, and you found me asleep under a bush, what would you do?'

Lohia thought for a little while, and then replied, 'Well, if I were sure that you were asleep, I would kill you myself; but if I thought you might wake up, I would get my brother to help me'.[1]

Cannibalism was a widespread habit, and though it might be excused by a general protein deficiency in a monotonous diet of sago and yams, it had also acquired a ritual value. It was a natural pleasure, and spiritually fortifying too. In fairness to the Papuans, however, it must be noted that Murray – by no means blind to their common faults and their defects in character and behaviour – was convinced of their singular aptitude for improvement. They were easy to reform and willing to be reformed, he said; and he, who had travelled widely in their country, knew that their

LEFT: *four examples of the smaller objects from the sea's bottom.* ABOVE LEFT: *off the Cape of Good Hope, magnified 35 times, 150 fathoms.* ABOVE RIGHT: *off Australia, magnified 35 times, 410 fathoms.* BELOW LEFT: *from Torres Strait, magnified 35 times, 155 fathoms,* BELOW RIGHT: *foraminifera from the South Pacific, magnified 25 times, 1,450 fathoms.*

[1] Lewis Lett; *Sir Hubert Murray of Papua.*

Canoes of Humboldt Bay natives seeking gifts come to surround Challenger *from the village of Ungrau.*

tendency to homicide was largely a product of the fear that their own environment had created. Not all of it was mountainous, but much was savage, inhospitable country where fertile areas had to be jealously guarded; many people lived in tiny communities, cultivating their food-gardens under high ridges difficult of access, where any intrusion was a threat to survival. All strangers were enemies; and as such, to their great astonishment, were *Challenger*'s naturalists feared.

As the ship entered the bay, after sundown, lights glimmered or flashed from the shore, and were answered from the south side of the bay. The signal-fires multiplied, and across the water there came hoarse and angry shouting. At Ungrau and Tobaddi were villages built on piles, and the alarm they gave was answered by the people of Wawah. Against the light of torches could be seen the darkness of bodies quickly passing, and as the anchor was let go, a light appeared close to the ship. A canoe had come out to reconnoitre, but was wary of too near an approach. The light vanished, then reappeared a little closer, and in the canoe a man stood up and made a loud, incomprehensible speech. Aboard *Challenger* responsive lights were waved in token of friendship, but there was no friendly reply. The first canoe had been joined by others, and they remained at a safe distance, shouting again, but the only word that could be distinguished sounded like 'Sigor! sigor!' In some of the canoes were two boys who, at either end, carried paddles, and between them, on a small platform, a full-grown savage whose tall turban of hair was decorated with scarlet hibiscus flowers and cassowary feathers. In the nearest boat the man in the middle – an exhibi-

174

The village of Tobaddi. 'The houses rest on piles', writes Moseley, 'the roof rises as high as 40 ft.'

tionist, perhaps – blew his smouldering torch to a blaze, and in its light his wild features and halo of flowers and feathers made a striking picture.

It was thought, mistakenly, that the cries of 'Sigor' were demands for tobacco, and cigars on a string were let down over the side (there was an abundance of cheap cigars on board, bought in Manila). They were greedily accepted, and these natives of coastal villages were sophisticated enough to simplify and increase donation: they tied empty coconut shells to the string, and let them be hauled up to show that more than one at a time could be given. A coloured handerkerchief or two were thrown down, and lured by them and more cigars the fleet of canoes drew alongside, but none of their occupants could be persuaded to come aboard, nor even to approach near enough to take a gift from hand to hand. Some held up four-pronged fish-spears, and precariously – the ship was rolling, the spears were sharp – cigars were transferred on them. Biscuits were not welcomed, for no one knew what to do with them. They did, apparently, know something about guns, for one of the natives, by expressive pantomime and shouting 'Boom!', demanded one. He was disappointed, and presently the fleet returned to shore.

In the morning the canoes came out again, with five or six men in some of them, and surrounded the ship with a din of deafening demand. The anchorage was uncomfortable, for a big swell was running into the bay, and at 7 a.m. *Challenger* weighed anchor and stood in towards a small cove under Point Caillié. There was a moment of perturbation and panic – perturbation aboard ship, panic in the canoes – when the screw began to turn, for the natives drew their bows, and on the deck above them there were, perhaps, those who sought shelter from the anticipated flight of arrows. But then it was seen that the natives were aiming their bows at the turbulence created by the propeller, which apparently – but only for a little while – they thought to be some unknown submarine monster. Their fear subsided, however, and they followed the ship as she steered towards the cove. Sixty-seven canoes were counted, with an average of three men in each, who from time to time shouted in the sort of encouraging way that accompanies an American football game: '*Wah, wah*', they shouted, and '*Oh, oh, oh!*' Some had large perforated shells which they blew to make a great booming sound; and the observant naturalists were able to identify their trumpet-shells as a *Triton* perforated on the side of one of its upper whorls, and a *Strombus* perforated at the apex of the spire.

Ahead of the ship the Cyclops Mountains rose to heights of about 6,000 feet, and a sheltered cove was visible, with one or two islets in it. The rising sun lighted the fleet of canoes and the savages who manned them: naked but decorated body, blackened face, a nose with the septum pierced for the sinister addition of a boar's tusk – if the points were turned up, they meant war, but peace if they slanted down – and above all a frizzy, feathered, bulbous head of hair. The water grew deeper as the ship approached the shore, and the anchor was dropped in 36 fathoms. There *Challenger* lay sheltered from the swell, and many of the natives, making signs of drinking, pointed to a part of the bay where a stream ran down. Their motive was obscure, but they knew enough about ships to realize that fresh water was a recurrent need; and their steadfast refusal to come aboard probably showed that, in the past, they had been badly treated by some unknown visitor. They were eager to barter, however, and as soon as the ship anchored again the canoes surrounded her, and on their four-pronged spears the natives offered weapons and ornaments in exchange for hoop-iron and small hatchets. 'Sigor' did not mean cigars, but iron; and hoop-iron, in lengths of six or eight inches was accepted as currency, though the small hatchets, of poor quality and manufactured only for trade, were much preferred: they would not last long, but they were better than stone axes. Nothing would induce the natives to barter their trumpet-shells, but a hatchet would buy an elaborate breastplate confected of beads and the tusks of wild boars, and in exchange for hoop-iron, necklaces, armlets, and tortoise-shell earrings were offered, with bows and arrows and daggers made of the long bones of a cassowary. A hunger for iron was undoubtedly more persistent than an appetite for human flesh.

There was an embarrassing situation when Moseley and others attempted to go ashore. It still seemed possible that the bay could be surveyed and the fringes of the land explored, and a boat that took some officers to a small uninhabited island was unopposed. But Moseley's boat met trouble. When it was near the shore a native, standing on the platform of a small canoe between the boys who paddled it, offered a yam for sale. It was refused, and he showed an arrow instead. He put the point to his neck, pretended to push it in, and mimed the agonies of death. Then he offered the yam again. Again it was refused, and he repeated his performance with the arrow. Those in the ship's boat ignored him, and moved slowly towards the shore. Hurrying to the nearer end of his canoe, the yam-seller fitted an arrow to the string of his bow, and pointing the arrow at Moseley, contorted his face 'into the most hideous expression of rage, with his teeth clenched and exposed, and eyes starting'. Calmly, as befitted a naturalist, Moseley explains that 'this expression was evidently assumed to terrify us as an habitual part of the fight, and not because the man was really in a rage'. But as he shifted his aim to Moseley's companions – now to Buchanan, now to von Willemoes Suhm – 'we were in a dilemma'.

The Humboldt Bay arrows were five feet long, flat at the inner end – there was no notch to hold the rattan string – and unfeathered. More like small spears than arrows, they were much too long for the bows; but the bows, cut from solid palm-wood, were very powerful and for ten or a dozen yards the arrows, before losing direction, flew with immense force. The boat's crew was fully armed, and the naturalists had loaded shot-guns, but apparently the menacing native and his friends knew nothing about firearms, and while he still postured the boys with him were exuberantly delighted by his warlike display. 'We, of course, would not shoot the man in cold blood,' says Moseley, but 'if we had fired over his head he would certainly have let fly one arrow at least, and he was within six yards of the boat'. It was indeed a dilemma.

A stroke or two with the paddles brought the canoe up to the stern of the boat, the warrior caught hold of the gunwale, and to share the spoils another canoe also closed in. On a seat lay a large tin vasculum; the two warriors began struggling between themselves for possession of it, and while they were engaged with each other the boat was turned, and discreetly the sailors rowed back to the ship. In the vasculum were some trade knives and three bottles of soda-water, and Moseley consoled himself for his loss by speculating on the consternation that would ensue when, in the innocence of a pile-dwelling, the bottles were opened.

It was difficult to account for the truculent native's apparent ignorance of firearms, for the Dutch had often been to Humboldt Bay, and in one of the canoes that first approached the ship there had been the man who, by mime and babble, had asked for a gun. But there is evidence elsewhere – notably in Sir Hubert Murray's reminiscences – of a curious irrationality in the natives of New Guinea; a forgetfulness of purpose; an errant mind; and the yam-seller's indifference to Moseley's shot-gun may have been characteristic of a racial capacity to elude reason or reality.

Before the boats were hoisted in, the pinnace put out for the shore, carrying Captain Thomson, Wyville Thomson, Murray, and the artist Wild, who wanted to make a sketch of the village. The houses of the village stood on a platform built on piles, and as the pinnace approached a few natives came out, carrying bows and arrows. One of them drew his bow, pointed an arrow at the pinnace, then changed his mind and offered to sell bow and arrow for 'sigor'. There was noisy protest when a sailor jumped

OVERLEAF: *Humboldt Bay warrior, nose tusks turned upwards, on the platform of his canoe.*

on to the platform, but presently a native agreed to take Murray ashore in his canoe, and another took the two Thomsons. They shot a few birds, and the natives, now friendly, showed a lively interest in their sport and were unimpressed by the noise of a gun going off. Their houses were prettily designed and neatly built, their construction being strangely at variance with primitive arrows, clumsy stone-bladed axes, and ineffectual stone-headed hammers.

The visit to Humboldt Bay was sadly disappointing, but the Report could not have been more judicious in its comment: 'Unwillingness on the part of the natives to allow the parties to land and explore the country rendered it necessary either to pay respect to their wishes, or to proceed in the investigations at the risk of an embroil- ment with them. Much as it was wished to explore a part of the world so little known as is the district of New Guinea around Humboldt Bay, it was considered unjustifiable to use force for the purpose, or even to land any explorers where a momentary im- pulse on the part of a savage might possibly lead to the sacrifice of many lives.' The situation was accepted, and the ship left New Guinea on a course, a little north of east, for the Admiralty Islands. There a reception awaited her that was as amiable as Humboldt Bay had been unpleasant, and a remarkable discovery was made: the islands – small and virtually unknown – were the home of craftsmen whose work was as delectable as it was unexpected.

For a day or two the weather was fine, with a light westerly wind, but the wind was variable, it headed them, then fell away altogether, and the passage was tedious. It took a week to cover 300 miles, and thick cloud obscured the view, rain fell heavily, as they approached the islands. They had to lie-to until the sky cleared, and then Captain Thomson steamed along the edge of the D'Entrecasteaux Reef that lies north of the main island, rounded its eastern point at dusk, and anchored the ship safely in 18 fathoms. A stiff breeze was blowing, but as *Challenger* came in several canoes put out, under sail, from islets that rose above the reef – as if growing from it – and natives in a state of great excitement, waving paddles in friendly gesture, wanted to start bartering at once. '*Laban, laban!,* was their cry, and in the Admiralty Islands *laban* meant what *sigor* meant in Humboldt Bay. It was thought prudent, however, to defer trade till the following morning, and obediently the canoes went home again. It was March 3rd, and for seven days *Challenger* lay in what was called Nares Har- bour. Rain continued for most of the time.

Le Maire and Schouten, Dutch navigators, sighted an archipelago which they called Twenty-four Islands in 1616. They thought the main island was Ceram in the Moluccas, but the group may have been the Admiralty Islands. Perhaps, however, their true discoverer was that admirable seaman and navigator, Captain Philip Carteret, who in HMS *Swallow* saw and named them in 1767. He was attacked by a dozen canoes, from which spears were thrown, and repelled them with musket-fire. One of the canoes, which was captured, was fifty feet long, made from a single tree and furnished with an outrigger; its contents were six fine fish, a turtle, some yams,

RIGHT ABOVE *hand carved food bowls and* BELOW *gourds and a turtle skull from the Admiralty Islands.*

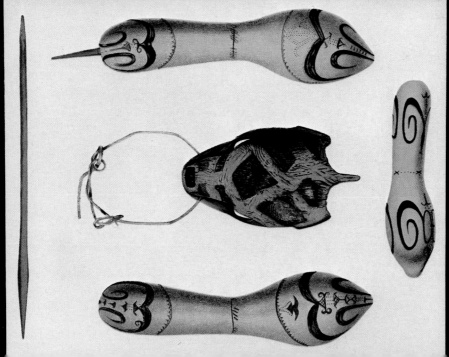

PTILOPUS JOHANNIS ♂ et ♀.

and a coconut. Bougainville spoke of the islands a year later, and La Pérouse may have seen them before losing his ship and his life near the New Hebrides in 1788. It was while looking for La Pérouse – at the instigation of the Parisian Society of Natural History – that Bruny D'Entrecasteaux made, in 1792, the first running survey of the group; but the earliest landing on the islands, by anyone other than natives of the Pacific, was made by the master of the American clipper *Margaret Oakly*. An occasional whaling ship may have visited them, and a year before *Challenger*'s arrival Lieutenant-Commander Saunders in HM Schooner *Alacrity* had seen enough – however brief his visit – to report that the natives were 'friendly and well-disposed'. Nothing more was known of the islands and the islanders: for rather more than a hundred years their existence had been recognized, but the inhabitants appeared to have lived uncommonly secluded lives.

Admiralty Island – the main island, that is – rises from low-lying coastal land to nearly 3,000 feet in gentle undulation from deep bays, some fringed with mangroves and others within a natural breakwater of coral reefs. It was only the north-west corner of the island, and islets in the vicinity of Nares Harbour, that *Challenger*'s people explored, but within that area friendly or, at least, commercial relations with the natives were established at daylight on the 4th, when canoes came crowding round the ship, and hoop-iron was again broken up for currency. 'Trade-gear' was manufactured in Sydney for the single purpose of Polynesian commerce, and 'the philosophers' – in innocent acceptance of an iniquitous practise – had spent about £300 on the purchases of almost worthless axes with soft iron blades, butcher's knives of no better quality, red and blue cotton cloth, beads and pipes and tobacco. It is pleasant to record that the natives, as innocent as the naturalists, hurriedly prepared for barter shell-hatchets and models of canoes which were at least as badly made as the stuff from Sydney. They combined a lively knowledge of barter – which argued some experience of commerce – with such extreme ignorance that many accepted old newspapers in the belief that they were a fine, delicate cloth; happily the rain set in again, and dissolved both paper and credulity.

They had, too, a sense of humour that set them apart from the natives of New Guinea. They offered for sale pieces of tortoise-shell, and to prove its fine, stiff quality pretended, with expressive grimaces, to be unable to bend it; and then, when the sailors played the same trick with thin pieces of hoop-iron, they saw the joke and enjoyed it. They were lighter in colour than the natives of Humboldt Bay, they dressed their hair in a different style, and more than one member of the expedition noted that many had curiously Hebraic features. As conspicuous as their noses, moreover, was the fact that their canoes were better built than any seen alongside *Challenger* except those of the Fiji and the Friendly Isles. On the evening of the 3rd, when a strong breeze was blowing, they had come boldly out under sail, and it seemed likely that they were accustomed to voyaging as far to the east as New Britain, and perhaps

LEFT: Ptilopis johannis (*named after John Murray*), *Fruit Pigeons from the Admiralty Islands*

'For ethnological reasons we measured them in every way, and got a good photograph of one,' Lord George Campbell.

farther; they made signs, indeed, to show that the manganese ore, with which they often blackened their bodies, came from somewhere in the east.

Sub-Lieutenant Swire made a fine, detailed drawing, and wrote a full description of an Admiralty Islands canoe which deserves attention because he was busily employed during the ship's stay in Nares Harbour, but still found time to examine with scrupulous care the local boats. He and others, under Tizard, made a tolerably complete survey of the coastline of the harbour and of its waters, and he says: 'I didn't enjoy myself at all. It was wet, hot, and uncomfortable, and I got all the skin burnt off my arms, so that, on the whole, I vote Nares Harbour an infernal hole.' He was, however, fascinated by the local canoes and their construction.

They were much larger than those seen at Humboldt Bay, and of superior construction. They varied in length from thirty to fifty feet, and basically consisted of a single tree hollowed-out by fire and adze. Its sides were heightened by a single strake, and topped by a gunwale. One side was cut flat, the other rounded, and from the latter projected the outrigger: when sailing the outrigger was always to windward, so the flat side was the lee side. About midships was a raised platform, high in the middle, attached by a strong stitching of bamboo fibres. Both ends of the canoe had a raised 'duck back' to shed water when going to windward, and were decorated with

184

The Admiralty Islands canoe. The outrigger platform, loaded with stakes, is the place of honour, the seat of the head man or chief.

cowrie shells and designs in red and white. The outrigger beam – also flat on the lee side – was attached by four poles and complicated lashings. The mast was stepped on the lee gunwale, and a smaller spar on the raised platform: that secondary spar had a forked upper end, into which the mast was fitted and 'boused down taut by a shroud led from the top of the mast to the platform'. The square sail, of matting, was spread by a gaff at the top, a boom at the bottom, and hoisted with one corner uppermost, the opposite corner made fast to the foot of the mast, so that 'it looked like the ace of diamonds'. The crew might number ten or more, and they used sharply pointed paddles.

The islanders' technical skills lacked balance, however. They could build a sea-worthy boat, but they had no bows, slings, or throwing sticks: their only weapons were light, flexible lances with heads of obsidian or volcanic glass, of which they possessed a vast number. There were great flocks of pigeons in the woods, but no better means had been found of trapping or killing them than the laborious exercise of climbing a tree to surprise a roosting bird. Costume was minimal: women wore two bunches of grass, one in front and one behind, and men a belt of white bark – or a rough cloth made from bark – and a white cowrie shell perched jauntily, like a very small bowler hat, on the glans penis. Against a skin blackened by manganese ore the

Food bowls

white shell and the white belt were obviously decorative, and of the islanders' artistic sense there was the truly remarkable evidence of the wooden bowls that were the principal items of cottage furniture.

It is difficult to write soberly of these bowls, for their beauty and the craftsmanship that made them would demand high praise wherever they had been found; and the marvel of their beauty is much enhanced by the remoteness of the islands whose naked people had discovered, for domestic use, an ideal of symmetry and a formal decoration appropriate to it. Their only tools were big sea-shells with sharpened edges, and to measure the truth of a circle or the slope of a cavity they had no instrument other than eyes and fingers of extraordinary precision.

The islands were heavily forested. There was an abundance of wood on their rolling hills, no lack of shells on their beaches. But less obvious was the provenance of a craftsmanship of fastidious exactitude, and speculation is bankrupt when one asks why people, who had never thought it necessary to give themselves clothes, should discover the propriety of making works of art to hold a meal of sago and roast pork.

The bowls, which were fairly shallow, stood on four short, sturdy feet, and some were very large: according to Campbell, as much as three feet in diameter. Two of the handles, rising above the level of the brim, were usually cut in delicate spirals and ornamented with perforating carving. Occasionally the handles represented the head and tail of a duck or a crocodile, or perhaps a couple of human figures. Some of the bowls were blackened, others a bright reddish-brown. Except for them there was little furniture to be found in a house, which typically looked like an elongated haycock – though styles varied from island to island – and had a heavily thatched roof supported on two stout posts. Wide shelves, one above another, ran from post to post and carried spears, food, and food-bowls; and there might be a bed-place of rough boards against a wall. Everything was rough; there was neither neatness nor anything for comfort as, for example, there had been in Fijian houses. The Admiralty

186

Islanders had not yet begun to think of comfort; they were satisfied with few luxuries.

A sense of design more expert and elaborate than that demonstrated in the food-bowls was shown in the ornaments that men sometimes wore on forehead or breast. A round white plate ground down from the shell of a Giant Clam had a hole in the centre for suspension, and in front of it was fastened a thin circle of fretted tortoise-shell that showed, through the apertures, the white background. 'The patterns are of endless variety,' says Moseley, 'no two being alike, and show all kinds of combinations of circles, triangles, toothing, and radiate patterns. Symmetry is evidently striven after, but with the appliances available the execution falls short here and there of the design. Nevertheless these ornaments are very beautiful.' Both food-bowls and the fretted ornaments had their counterparts in the Solomon Islands, and the ornaments resembled also those worn in the Marquesas: the Marquesas are so far away that traffic with them can never have been possible, but the Solomons, where craftsmanship was highly developed, lie within a thousand miles or so, and with them – though it seems improbable – there may have been communication of some sort.

In the comfortless houses of the islands there were decorated gourds, occasionally a decorated human skull – perhaps with eyes of pearl-shell set in black clay – and in the club houses hung decorated turtle skulls. The obsidian-headed spears and obsidian knives – sharp enough to be razors – bore also elaborate ornament. But each object, or class of object, had its own specified style of ornamentation: curved patterns were never used on spears, but only on gourds; diagonal lines, red or black,

Admiralty Island spears. The central one BELOW *has its tip, made of hardwood, painted to look like the obsidian heads to left and right.*

187

were the proper decoration for spears and bracelets. Even fish-hooks had their beauty, for they were cut, without a barb, from trochus shell and made lures that needed no bait. Add music to the visual arts, but music of less distinction; for according to Moseley the natives had no idea of tune. As musical instruments, however, they had perforated conch shells, a simple Jew's harp made of bamboo, Pan pipes, and drums made of hollowed cylinders of wood. Women danced, quick-stepping in a ring, but men apparently did not, or at least were not seen dancing. Ornaments, however – bracelets and fretted breast-plates, nose-rings and ear-rings – were worn by men, and men only; women went unadorned except by a sparse, indigo-blue tattooing.

Botany and native habits occupied Moseley during the week that *Challenger* lay in Nares Harbour. The botany of the islands was quite unknown, and often he waded up to his middle to collect orchids and ferns that hung, a couple of feet above the water, from the immense horizontal branches of trees that grew, wave-washed, at the very edge of the sea. An orchid and one of the tree-ferns he found were both new to science; as also were fifty-five words of the local language that he had had some difficulty in acquiring. The natives were willing enough to tell him the names of the birds he shot, but turned sullen and suspicious when asked the word for a nose or an arm, which everybody ought to know. He also discovered the very odd fact that 'in the process of learning the art of counting, a term for the numeral ten had been reached by the natives before eight and nine had been named'; so eight and nine were expressed as ten minus two and ten minus one. 'Up to ten counting is done on the fingers, and after that eleven, twelve, etc., are reckoned on the toes.' The advantage of going bare-foot was obvious.

Lord George Campbell – observant in his own way – sought entertainment rather than knowledge, but his eyes were keen, his intelligence lively, and his letters are full of interest. When Captain Thomson first went ashore – on the nearest of the islets that rose from the long reef, where a village could be seen under coco-palms and breadfruit trees – Campbell saw how the natives waved the boat away from a bad landing-place, and pointed to a better; and when the Captain went ashore they seemed to understand firearms but were still a little frightened when their visitors shot a few nutmeg-pigeons and other birds. They also showed – on that first morning – signs of jealousy when women approached: the women were promptly ordered back into their huts. To a tall man, who appeared to have some authority, the Captain gave an old white hat, which he accepted with pleasure. Later in the day the white-hatted man, who was christened Otto, guided them to a small island about which nutmeg-pigeons flew in clouds. Otto and his men filled a large canoe, the pinnace took it in tow, and the natives were delighted to move at such speed across the sea. The pigeons provided fresh meat, but no sport; to shoot them was too easy, and Campbell soon grew tired of killing. More catholic in their appetite than others they had met, the Admiralty Islanders gladly accepted ship's biscuits in fair exchange for their help.

On the following day Campbell discovered the impenetrability of the island forests: a few large Casuarina trees, others hidden and swamped by a creeper like convolvulus; tall Pandanus palms with aerial roots falling from a great height; a sago-palm swamp, heavier woods beyond it, and birds twittering or crying in a dense foliage that hid them from sight. On another island Captain Thomson was patiently making friends with natives who grew angry as presents were distributed: angry because they did not get enough, or others got more than they deserved, and angry especially when anything was offered to their women, who had no entitlement to favour.

On March 6th the weather was squally, the pinnace was sounding outside the reef, and Campbell in the whaler was waiting inside. 'The surf on the reef was glorious, mountainous lines, now black, now white, subsiding with a thundering crash.' During a great gust of wind and darkening rain a large turtle went drifting past, but no one had a rifle ready for it. Then out came two canoes, whose occupants boarded the whaler, and one of them was delighted with Campbell's soft white hands, 'with my boots, my coat, and everything about me, over which he purred and cooed as if I were a baby'. The pinnace came in, they all landed, and a congregation of natives received them joyfully. There was a tall stockade among the trees, apparently intended for defence, though obviously permeable, and when the tourists divided, and went their chosen ways, Campbell and two natives, inside the stockade, met three women who accompanied him to help, as stalkers or gillies, with his shooting. 'Two of them were oldish and ugly, the third was a sonsie young lassie. They were much excited, pointing out the birds, cowering away as I aimed and fired, but delighted as the birds fell. This nice girl was with me all the time, on which account she came to be known as "Campbell's girl". My girl, I must tell you, was slightly tattooed about her face, blue dotted lines around her eyes and cheeks, and also she, like most of them, would perhaps not have suffered by a slight scrubbing. One of us made signs to her that if she would come to the boat, we would beautify her with beads, and you should have seen the angry look of the men! Crossly they told her to be off, and then, as angrily, an older woman snarled at them, stamped her feet, pointed a finger of scorn, pshahed and hissed like a veritable snake. Though apparently the property of the male sex, I fancy the inferior sex have much their own way here as elsewhere.'

On the outer side of that island were two villages, one numbering about thirty huts, the other smaller. To Moseley the houses had seemed rough and comfortless, but Campbell thought them 'excessively clean and neat, each surrounded with a fence, over which one gets by stepping-stones. The ground is floored with coral sand; cocos, sago-palms, and tidy wee gardens of the yam plant grow in and around them.' On the island where Moseley complained about having to wade waist-high to gather orchids and tree-ferns, Campbell thought that 'a prettier beach than on this island there could not be: large trees, covered with blossom, at close intervals, with great boughs growing quite low down and stretching far over the water. Walking in the shade along the strip of coral sand, covered with rare shells and corals, one had constantly to climb over these boughs or wait for a retreating wave, then run round before the next came swashing in beneath them right up to the huge trunks.' He adds, regrettably, 'the only bird we got here was a fine eagle', and continues: 'These woods are lovely as only tropical woods can be, but they are woods, not forest. Trees there are of enormous girth here and there, but the majority of them are more remarkable for great height than thickness. The foliage above is extremely dense, and the under-growth a tangled greenery of rare, unknown, and beautiful ferns. . . . Enormous ferns, whose every leaf is only to be measured by the fathom, grow between the forks of branches, and every tree is more or less entwined with a creeper of some kind or another: one very beautiful kind, which, wreathing round some straight and branch-less stem, encloses it within a cylinder of great jutting-out green leaves. The butter-flies are hardly worthy of the woods they live in, being all very dark-coloured.'

From ferns to sociology again: 'In the afternoon the Captain went to Island C with the idea of giving some presents of beads to the women, for they as yet appear not to have profited at all by our visit, which of course our chivalry can't brook. As usual when this policy of gratuitous presents is carried on, the men crowded round, and there was no chance for the women. So they threw strings of beads among them over the heads of the men, which made them very excited and cross – so much so that Otto and one or two others were extremely anxious that the Captain should go away at once. . . . This savageness on the part of the mob is pure selfishness, not jealousy in the sense of their not wishing us to have anything to say to their women; that feeling was totally absent after the first day.' Poor women! Denied the right to decorate themselves, except by sparse tattooing, they were also refused permission to accept presents. And the men who were so selfish were gifted craftsmen, natural artists.

Sexual jealousy being no bar, Campbell and others went where they wished, in-quisitively looking into private houses and the public buildings designed for worship, utility, or social purpose. They were shown 'how to make fire by rubbing two sticks, a small pointed piece rubbed hard in the groove of another. Everybody, men, women, and children, were quite at their ease and most amiable.' And then: 'Waiting by myself on the shore for the others to come down, I was minutely examined by some women, in which I lent them my very best aid. They stooped and felt my boots, so I put my foot up on a canoe. From the boots they turned their attention to my socks, which they pulled down, and were much puzzled and delighted with my white skin. I firmly believe they thought our hands and faces painted; my arms too they thought much too nice. In short they admired me immensely, and I felt much flattered.' But then again presents were given, and more trouble broke out: 'This is always the way: give them nothing and they could not be more civil and pleasant; open a bag of trade-gear and the demon of jealousy makes them savages at once'.

At Zamboanga goats and pigs had been bought, with the intention of stocking some uninhabited island; and when it became impracticable to go there, the goats were offered to the Admiralty Islanders, who indignantly refused them. They ap-peared to be frightened of goats, and did not know that female goats yielded milk. They were skilful fishermen in waters where waves broke high and savagely on coral

Wild drew the carved figures in front of the temple ABOVE *in detail for the* Report, *but painted an expurgated version for his own book* At Anchor.

reefs, but they lived in fear of crocodiles. Campbell and his friends discovered, one day, a river forty yards across and bridged at its entrance by a shallow bar on which small breakers crashed in foam. They were about to cross when they saw that their native attendants were horrified. On the sand a large crocodile had left the signature of its great body, and the river – as gesticulation made clear – was so full of the brutes that it was judged dangerous even to wade in the shallows. The river appeared to have its source somewhere below the tallest land visible from the anchorage: a long, forested ridge with three volcanic nipples at its highest part. It was there, perhaps, that the islanders found obsidian for their spears and knives, but *Challenger*'s people had no time for deeper exploration.

Campbell describes a hut that he calls a temple because, as well as being larger than domestic dwellings, its doorway was guarded by 'two rudely and obscenely carved figures of a man and woman painted black, red, and white'. They were, perhaps, rain gods; and as the interior of the temple was decorated with the skulls of human beings, turtles, pigs, and the marsupial Cuscus – they hung from a thick, central pillar, painted red and white – it would seem that funerary rites were of some importance in the islands' way of life. The dead, however, inspired little reverence and the natives were always ready to exchange a skull for a trade hatchet; and how they disposed of their dead remained obscure. Moseley says flatly that they were buried, but offers no evidence for sepulture; and Campbell cannot rid himself of a dark, improbable suspicion that the dead were eaten. The morbid interest that both men and women showed in the whiteness of his skin may have prompted that unpleasant thought.

He and most of his shipmates, says Campbell, were glad to leave the islands; and offers, for a sufficient reason, the fact that they had been so closely confined. Rough weather, a reef-ringed sea, and as soon as they went ashore an almost impenetrable forest opposed them. They were as narrowly circumscribed as, in many parts of the world, primitive peoples had always been, isolated by impassable desert, the menace of mountains or jungle, and fear of the unknown. They had tasted, for a little while, one of the distinguishing flavours of primitive life, but though they did not like it – or did not like it enough to plead for another week of it – they had obviously found it of absorbing interest; and to those who read of their experiences it may seem that their anxious view of Humboldt Bay and its denizens, and their seven days in Nares Harbour, were in a humane or anthropological assessment the most rewarding episode of the whole voyage. Humboldt Bay gave them a glimpse of the unknown perils of the vast, fear-ridden island of New Guinea, notorious for the splendour of its Birds of Paradise and the menace of its mountains and hungry mountaineers: they saw no Birds of Paradise but they had been threatened by the seaside neighbours of the mountaineers. Then, in the virtually unknown Admiralty archipelago, they had met people of a wildly unbalanced culture: the islanders were seafarers who built fine boats, craftsmen who carved works of art with sharpened clam-shells, but had found no means of killing for their food the multitude of birds that flew above them, and seen no need to clothe themselves or allow their women the communicable pleasure of adornment and dressing-up. The islanders who carved with unerring skill their beautiful, great wooden food-bowls were, at the same time, so limited and so ingenious as to know that eight equalled ten minus two but could not be more simply expressed; and, less practical than the savage people of Humboldt Bay, had not discovered the relatively simple art of shooting, with a bow, arrows that could far out-distance their small spears. In a human context the Admiralty Islanders were comparable with the most fascinating discoveries that dredge or trawl had brought up from the hitherto unknown depths of the ocean.

Less than seventy years after the *Challenger*'s visit, the main island of the Admiralty group was re-named Manus, and heavily fortified by the Americans in their Pacific war against Japan. After the defeat of Japan the fortifications of Manus were, with great effort, dismantled, and a few years later it was rumoured that they must be restored. It is improbable that anything now remains of the culture that Campbell, Swire, and 'the philosophers' investigated and enjoyed.

16 *The pleasures of Japan*

At the very beginning of the long passage to Japan there was a moment of alarm when the ship, steaming out of Nares Harbour, came suddenly into shoal water and, before the engines could be stopped, passed over a coral patch in less than 4 fathoms. Outside the harbour the sea deepened to the safety of 150 fathoms, and the familiar routine of dredging, and sounding for temperature or depth, was resumed. Throughout the passage the wind was light and variable, averaging force two or force three, never exceeding force six, and often falling to a flat calm.

On March 23rd – thirteen days after leaving Nares Harbour – a sounding of 4,475 fathoms, or rather more than five miles, was recorded in latitude 11° 24′ north, longitude 143° 16′ east, between the Caroline Islands and the Marianas. That was the greatest depth observed, and as it had not been anticipated the sinkers, weighted only by three cwt., went down slowly and the first sounding was thought to be inaccurate. The line was hove in, and four cwt. attached. Even so, the sinkers needed thirty-six seconds to drop 25 fathoms from 4,400 to 4,425; thirty-eight seconds from 4,425 to 4,450; thirty-seven seconds from 4,450 to 4,475; fifty-two seconds from 4,475 to 4,500, and it was concluded that the weights struck the bottom between 4,475 and 4,500 fathoms. The two thermometers sent down were both broken by pressure, and mixed with the mud brought up in the sounding tube was some mercury which, falling faster than the sinkers, reached the bottom first, and the tube fell precisely where the mercury had fallen.

The tube had sunk about three or four inches into the bottom-ooze, and the layer

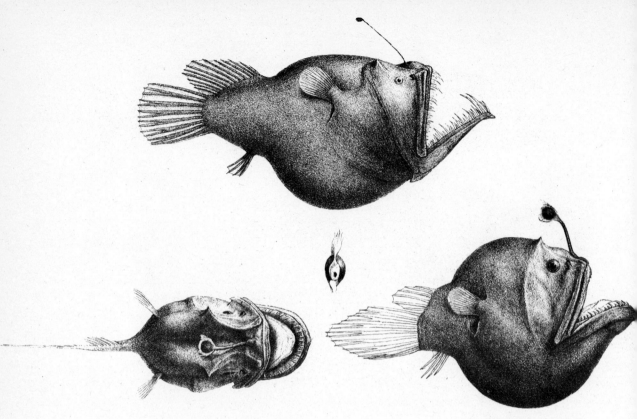

Deep sea fish. TOP: Melanocetus murrayi, *2,450 faths.* LOWER: Ceratius bispinosus, *360 faths.*

that formed the upper surface of the ocean's pavement was a reddish or chocolate colour, more than half of it a 'radiolarian ooze' consisting of siliceous shells and skeletons. The deeper layers were a pale straw colour, and looked like the diatom ooze found in the Antarctic; also in the clay-like deposit in the tube were pellets of manganese peroxide and fragments of pumice. Pumice and radiolarian ooze were brought up throughout the passage from a floor that was fairly level – apart from the great chasm in latitude 11° north – at about 2,450 fathoms; and surface flora and fauna were richly varied and everywhere abundant.

'In the region of the Counter Equatorial Current, between the Equator and the Caroline Islands, pelagic foraminifera and mollusca were caught in great numbers in the surface nets, surpassing in this respect anything previously observed' – but no profusion of molluscs, no abundance of rhizopods, could dispel the evergrowing boredom that pervaded the ship as day broke calm and windless, or almost windless, and there was nothing to be seen but the vacant expanse of a vast, featureless ocean. Somewhere below the horizon there were islands – scores of islands – but in a passage that lasted more than thirty days not one of them was sighted. Even birds were rarely seen. When *Challenger* had left the Tropics behind her the Northern Albatross appeared – she acquired a constant escort of those large, unhurried birds – but except

Lophius naresii, *from the Admiralty Islands*

for them she was visited only by a single red-tailed Bos'un Bird, a Noddy, five exhausted swallows that settled on the rigging, a few finches, and a bird that looked like a thrush. The sails hung flat, Japan was still far away, and though the ship was officially described as a steam corvette, her engines remained silent. Coal was conserved for occasional dredging and the final task of pushing against unknown currents, in inshore waters, to anchorage or harbour at Yokohama.

'A most tedious voyage,' says Moseley. 'The vastness of the expanse of water in the Pacific Ocean, in proportion to the area of the dry land, was pressed most strongly upon our attention.... A fact often brought home to me before, during the *Challenger*'s cruise, was forced on our notice on this voyage to Japan, namely, that the inmates of a sailing ship, on a long voyage, suffer far more from too little than from too much wind. We were constantly becalmed.'

Campbell does not condescend to mention those thirty-two vacant days – they were not worth remembrance – but Swire took note of the fact that since leaving the Philippines the sailors had been living on salt meat from the harness cask, officers on 'preserved meat' – which cannot have been improved by tropical heat – and that towards the end of the passage the issue of water was restricted. He records, too, a visible and audible improvement of temper when, ten days out from Nares Harbour,

195

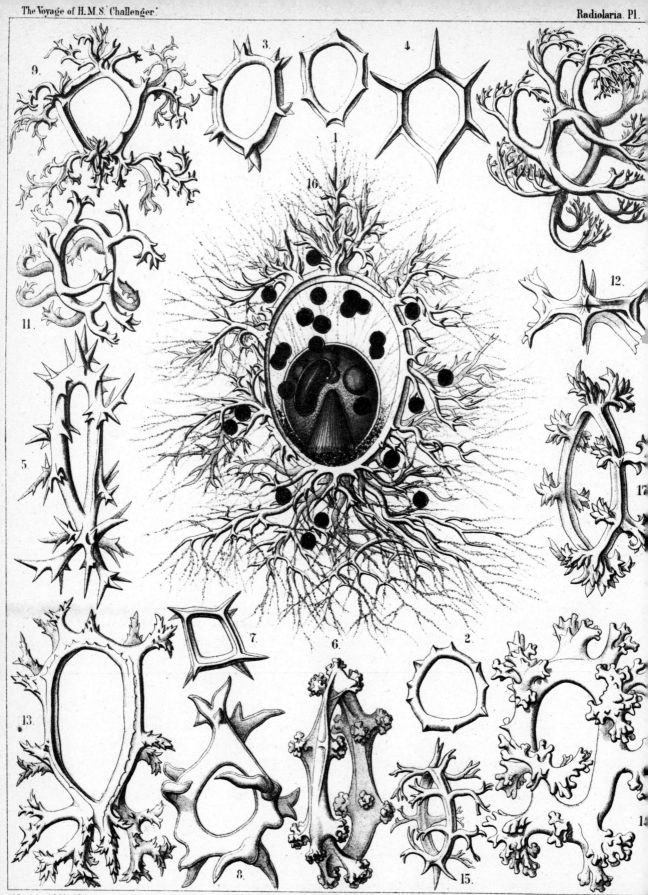

E.Haeckel and A.Giltsch.Del.

E.Giltsch, Jena, Lith

1 - 8 LITHOCIRCUS, 9 - 17 DENDROCIRCUS.

a good fresh wind began to blow, and for a day or two the ship made five or six knots: 'The change among us all when this wind set in was marvellous. Away went cloudy faces and surly manners, and all was once more as pleasant as ordinary sea life can be.' But the good wind failed them, and not until the coastline of Japan is sighted, on April 10th or 11th, is Swire again in an exhuberant mood. Then he watches sharks, porpoises, and dolphins coming out to meet them – dolphins 'rushing through the water like an azure flash of light' – and 'a spanking breeze drove us foaming up the Gulf of Yedo'. Over a mass of clouds Fujiyama showed the noble symmetry of his white head; in Yokohama letters from England were distributed; 'and every soul in the ship felt more amiable than he had done for the last three months'.

To Swire, after a month at sea, Japanese women seemed 'the neatest little ladies I have ever seen'; and he is much taken by their liberal and ingenuous use of cosmetics, a practice not yet common in England. 'They powder their necks and foreheads and rouge their lips,' he writes. 'There is not the slightest deception about it, and powder and rouge are as much part of a Japanese *musume*'s dress as are gloves of that of an English lady.' In Japan, in 1875, there was indeed more than powder and rouge to attract the interest of European visitors, for unlike Hong Kong – which Campbell had dismissed as 'too well known to need description from me' – it was still a country of which the rest of the world knew very little.

In the sixteenth century, and the earlier years of the seventeenth, the Japanese had become warily acquainted with Portuguese and Spaniards – with their seamen, merchants, and missionaries – but after some experience of western foreigners and their ways, they retreated into a wilful seclusion. Great feudal lords were the rulers of Japan, who, knowing that the invention of firearms had eventually proved disastrous to feudal practice and pretensions in Europe, may have prudently decided that they, on their large estates, could live more happily if their neighbours were prevented from buying guns. By 1640 Japan had deliberately cut herself off from the outside world, and as late as 1825 the ruling Shogun had declared that any foreign ship, trying to enter harbour, would be repelled by force.

Shrewdly, however, an interdict on western learning had been relaxed, foreign books were greedily imported, and gradually distrust abated and a rising mercantile class – that distrusted the nobility more than any foreigners – demanded the opportunities of foreign trade. In 1854 Commodore Perry obtained a commercial treaty for the United States, and during the next ten or twenty years there were far-reaching political and social changes. For seven centuries the titular Sovereign supreme in theory, had in fact been subject to a military dictatorship – often challenged by dissent, sometimes broken by anarchy – embodied in the Shogun, the dominating feudal potentate of his generation; and in 1867 the last Shogun was persuaded to resign – persuasion was accompanied by a minimum of bloodshed – and the young Emperor Mutsuhito, under the title of Meiji, was restored to the

LEFT: *radiolaria. Numbers 1–8:* Lithocircus; *9–17:* Dendrocircus. *In the centre: the living form.*

power of which one of his predecessors had been stripped in the latter years of the twelfth century. His task was heavy, but he had able advisers, and Japan was ready for a benign and profitable revolution. The long established feudal regime was methodically converted into a national government, and the foundations of an industrial state were soundly laid. Young Samurai – heirs of the military caste – were largely responsible for the transformation of their country, and though traditionally they were both hot-headed and hot-blooded, the only extravagance of which Japan was now in immediate danger was a somewhat indiscriminating fervour for western ideas.

Europeans were not given open freedom to move and live where they pleased – rights of residence and trade were strictly limited to the treaty ports – but liberty to travel could be obtained without much difficulty, and the whole temper of the country, in 1875, was such as to ensure, for *Challenger*'s scientists and officers, the kindliest of welcomes. After thirty-two days at sea Moseley, the devoted naturalist, quickly rediscovered the pleasure of a crowded street, a busy town, and with an enthusiasm hardly inferior to that of young Swire, responded to the charm and friendliness of the ordinary Japanese whom he met, and to the splendid physical power of Japanese coolies. He soon made friends with a Mr Dickins, a barrister practising in Yokohama who was not only 'an accomplished Japanese scholar', but 'deeply versed and interested in all branches of science'. Dickins, otherwise unknown or uncelebrated, may either have been a pioneer with a nose for profit in far places, or an eccentric seduced by the exotic appeal of Nō plays, the colour prints of Utamaro, and the tea ceremony. He was obviously a useful and entertaining guide, and after travelling with him from Kobe and Kyoto to Yokohama, Moseley wrote: 'I have never met with any persons, whether naval officers or members of other professions, or ordinary travellers who have been to Japan, who did not wish to go there again, so charming are the people, and so full of interest to everyone is the country and its belongings'.

'No traveller,' he continues, 'can fail to be impressed by the great powers of endurance shown by the Japanese coolies. Two coolies will drag a man in a jinriksha a distance of thirty miles in six hours, along a road anything but good. The same two men dragged me at a fair pace thirty miles on each of two successive days. When great speed is required, three coolies are taken, and as they run they encourage one another all the way, and when several jinrikshas are travelling together the shouting reminds one of a pack of hounds in cry.' Moseley the tourist is quite as admirable as Moseley the scientist, for as well as a constant interest in all he sees, he has a remarkable capacity for enjoyment. One is thankful that no one told him how short was the life of a rickshaw coolie, for that would have saddened him.

At Kobe he was delighted to see a 'Sacred White Horse' in a temple stall, and having bought a measure of boiled maize for it, clapped his hands together, in the attitude of prayer, 'in memory of ancient reverence for the white horse in my own

RIGHT: *Japanese in ceremonial dress.* FAR RIGHT: *a Japanese girl in walking costume. Painted on silk.*

country'. He discovered with some surprise the popularity of pilgrimage, and recalled the curious sight of 'a string of blind pilgrims on the road, travelling on foot,
holding on one behind the other, and led by the one man who could see'. It was in
Osaka that he found 'nearly a mile of continuous bookshops', and wisely bought a
large collection of illustrated books. On the high road to Kyoto – it strode along a
great embankment above a broad river – he observed the intensive cultivation of
wheat and rice and rape, and noted with approval that scarecrows wore rice-straw
raincoats and the large mushroom-like hats of Japanese peasants. In a hotel at Kyoto
he had his first experience of sleeping in a room whose walls were made of paper; and
looking down on Kyoto, the Holy City of Japan, from one of the hills that rise above
it, he thought it the most beautiful city he had ever seen: 'Everywhere are groves of
Cryptomerias surrounding the holy places and monasteries, and above the groves
in all directions rise the high temple roofs and porches'.

The road to Yokohama was not much used by Europeans – there was an easier and
cheaper route by sea – and Moseley was pleased to observe that he and Dickens were
of as much interest to the Japanese as the Japanese to them. 'I was especially worth
seeing,' he says complacently – with a rather strange complacency – 'since I had a
reddish beard of some length. The Japanese consider beards and moustaches excessively ugly, and they even used to put false beards and moustaches, often red in
colour, on the face-pieces of their suits of armour, in order to assist the warriors in
terrifying their enemies.

'It was amusing to watch the faces of the people in some of the towns as they glared
at us. I saw one woman look as if suddenly taken ill, on meeting me unexpectedly at a
corner. Others burst out into fits of laughter. Everywhere the idea uppermost in the
minds of parents was that we were a sight which the children should on no account
be allowed to miss. Mothers darted into the back premises and rushed back with
their children, and often when we were halting came and planted them in front of us,
and pointed out to the children, with their outstretched hands, the various points of
interest in the Tojins.

'I was', as Mr Dickins pointed out, 'a first-rate Tojin'; and he explains that 'Tojin',
originally meaning a Chinaman, the only sort of foreigner that the Japanese used to
see, had come to mean a foreigner of any kind, and was also a term of reproach. He
discusses the difference in colour between Europeans and Japanese: in comparison
with the uniformity of black hair and yellow-tinted skin the diversity of European
colouring must seem astonishing. He proceeds to a description of the *maquillage* that
women favoured in 1875, and goes far beyond Swire's superficial examination: 'An
even layer of white is put on over the whole face and neck, with the exception of two
or three angular patches of natural brown skin, which are left bare at the back of the
neck, as a contrast. After the face is whitened, a dab of red is rubbed in on the cheeks
below each eye. The lips are then coloured pink with magenta, and this colour is put

LEFT: *Osaka, 'Venice of Japan', 'an ever-moving mass of white sails of junks and boats'.*

on so thickly that it ceases to appear red, but takes on the iridescent metallic green tint of the crystallized aniline colour.' It is difficult to visualize the appearance of a woman so heavily lacquered, and as if to excuse a lack of clarity he adds, 'I suppose the idea is that such thick application of paint shows a meritorious disregard of expense'.

He then makes the uncomplimentary suggestion that 'this form of painting the face seems to be exactly of the same nature as savage painting, and possibly is a direct continuation of it'. In China, he says, when a man of distinction was buried, servants used to be buried with him. Now, in lieu of servants, figures made of pasteboard and paper are burnt, and the pasteboard heads 'are painted with streaks, some of which are put on in almost exactly the same style at the angles of the eyes as those of modern Japanese actors. It seems a fair conjecture that the streaks on those heads are a direct survival of an actual former savage form of painting, which was once in vogue in China, probably used to make fighting-men hideous.' Two illustrations are offered to reinforce his theory: of a Japanese actor's painted face, copied from a theatrical picture-book; and of the head of a figure sold for burning at a Chinese funeral. The resemblance between them may substantiate his conjecture that theatrical convention was derived from a practice once common in China, but to pretend that a woman's use of cosmetics had the same savage ancestry implies the belief that women paint their faces, not to attract a man's attention, but to frighten-off her competitive female friends: a caustic opinion for so genial a man.

Of tattooing he says that 'the art has reached far greater perfection in Japan than anywhere else. Formerly all the coolies were tattooed, often all over the body, but now the practice is forbidden by the Japanese Government as barbarous.' It seems, however, that the art survived proscription, for he goes on to say: 'So rapidly is the work done that an elaborately finished design of a dragon or Japanese girl covering all the front of the forearm will be completed in a couple of hours. Very little pain is caused by the process, and not any or only a little scarcely perceptible bleeding. The area tattooed is slightly inflamed subsequently, but not so much as to cause inconvenience of any kind, and it becomes quite healed in eight or ten days.

'The results produced are astonishing in their softness, their correctness and delicacy of outline and minuteness of detail. In a representation of a fish or dragon every scale is separately shaded, often with two strengths of shading, and in birds every feather is separately finished. In some cases large figures on the backs and shoulders of coolies are made to stand out in relief by means of an even dark shading, extending over the whole background', and he adds the puzzling statement – only, perhaps, to be resolved by admission to the royal archives – that 'the artists recommend themselves to Europeans by each asserting that he is the man who tattooed the Duke of Edinburgh'.

Moseley has little to say about the theatre – his notes are quite perfunctory – and,

Tattooing in pink and blue covers the entire bodies of the coolies RIGHT.

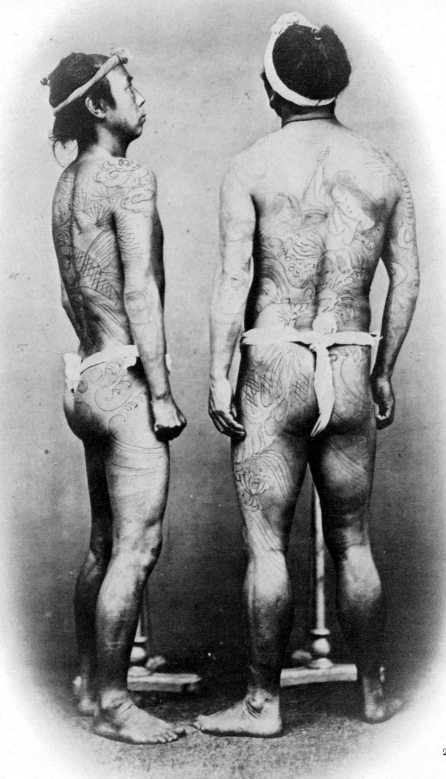

203

like many others, he may have found a Nō play boring. He has, however, a charming reference to the Hairy Ainus, the aborigines of Japan, who had the reputation of being not only dirty and drunken, but hospitable and polite. In one of the books that he bought in Osaka there was a picture of Ainus hunting seals or sea-otters. They were in canoes, some armed with bows and arrows, others holding rod and line and trolling, as a lure, a fox's brush. They made the lure dance about on the surface of the water, and the seals (or sea-otters) followed in a shoal.

Swire and Murray were both inquisitive about the manner of judicial execution, and at Kobe Swire went to look at the place of execution. It was a square clearing in a grove of small fir trees, at a corner of which was a shed where the victim was taken to drink as much saké as he wanted. Then, reconciled to death or possibly anaesthetized, he was led to a hole surrounded by a wooden fence. He knelt, and his hands were tied behind his back. The executioner, armed with a sword, cut off his head with a single blow, and the head fell neatly into the hole. Swire, however, is merely repeating what someone told him. Murray was more conscientious, and at Osaka watched an execution. According to him the condemned man was accompanied by a 'confessor' – so Murray calls him – with whom he spoke for a long time before he knelt and announced his readiness to die by shouting to the executioner '*Uroshi!*' – which is said to mean 'Come on!' Both accounts appear to bear out Swire's belief that 'a politer and more even-tempered people does not exist than the Japanese'.

'A charming country and charming people' was Campbell's opinion. He and some friends went by train from Yokohama to Yedo – now called Tokyo – and spent a night at an Engineering College, one of three colleges staffed by Englishmen. In the morning they took passage in rickshaws of the Government's postal service, and Campbell discovered that of the thousands of coolies who made an arduous living between the shafts, many were disbanded soldiers, formerly in the private armies of

Bearded like Moseley himself, the Ainu photographed LEFT *with his spouse has dignity quite unlike that of the other Japanese.*

The rickshaw man poses for Moseley's camera on the road near Kobe.

the great feudal lords who, when the Emperor resumed authority, had surrendered most of their privilege. Campbell writes of their journey at considerable length, and with a sustained enthusiasm for all he saw, did, or heard in Japan: or almost all, for Japanese food – those shreds of seaweed and bamboo, unknown vegetables and scraps of anonymous fish in little pots and platters – were not to his liking, and in comparison with Japanese guitars and flutes he thought the music of the bagpipe – even the tuning of a bagpipe – like the music of the spheres.

Their destination was Nikko, about ninety miles north of Tokyo: a mountainous place of temples, shrines, and monuments, now a National Park. They started on a fine May morning, they admired the carefully cultivated fields, orchards heavy with bloom, cranes stepping daintily in the muddy paddy-fields, and far ahead of them, violet-tinted and capped with snow, the mountains about Nikko. They spent a night in a tea-house, waited on by pretty girls kneeling politely before them, they slept between paper walls, and bathed in a huge, communal wooden tub. There is laughter and kow-towing as they take their leave, they meet a wedding party and a painted, doll-like bride, they cross a river in a big, flat-bottomed boat, and the country grows more picturesque as they approach the hills. They stop in a provincial town and order an elaborate Japanese dinner: Campbell dislikes it all except the courtesy of a kneeling girl who, with much laughter, takes his chop-sticks – those futile instruments – and obligingly feeds him. Then they call for singing girls and dancing girls, and Campbell is careful to make it clear that geishas are models of propriety.

On the following day their coolies pulled them uphill along a great avenue of Cryptomerias broken by villages, variegated by groves of young bamboo, ornamented by road-side shrines and gentle Buddhas. They meet a great lord or *daimio*,

205

'Almost an unbroken line of splendid Cryptomerias', said Campbell of the road to Nikko. 'This splendid avenue . . . I believe unrivalled in the world.'

travelling 'in a box slung on a pole' and accompanied by a dozen retainers; two-sworded travellers, aloof and incurious; shaven-headed priests; messengers, almost naked, running with letters in a split bamboo; heavy-laden pack-horses and, as they approach the mountains, more and more pilgrims. Nikko is a single long street, a rushing stream, a river crossed by two bridges, one plain and serviceable, the other 'gorgeous in vermilion paint, supported on either bank by huge granite columns looking as old as the river itself'. That was the sacred bridge over which the Shogun was carried in state, twice a year, to visit the temples that lay hidden beyond dark fir-woods. To the fame of Nikko nothing contributed more than the sepulchres and sanctuaries of Iyeyasu and Iyemitsu, the first and third Shoguns of the great Tokugawa dynasty. The former was buried with stupendous pomp in 1617; the latter, his grand-son, was assassinated in 1650 while visiting the tomb. And now, on Campbell's enthusiastic pages, comes a record of almost orgiastic sight-seeing, and one can hardly blame him, for the splendours of Nikko were fabulous, and the nearby country was fantastically beautiful.

The tomb of Iyeyasu was simple: under tall Cryptomerias on the slope of a hill was a light-coloured bronze urn on a circular base of three steps, and in front of it was a stone table on which were a censer, a lotus-cluster, and a stork with a candle-stick in its mouth. Lower down the hill, to ward off evil influence, was a cylindrical copper column, forty feet high, topped by lotus flowers from whose petals hung little bells; a pagoda of the seventeenth century, five storeys and a hundred feet high, had

206

The outer court of a temple at Nikko. The golden gate, ornately decorated and roofed in the centre of the picture, is a focus of the shrine at the head of the steps.

the signs of the zodiac carved round its base; the Gate of The Kings was decorated with the figures of unicorns, lions, tigers, elephants, mythical animals, and tree-peonies. There was a sumptuous stable for the sacred horses, a granite cistern for holy water. There was a quadrangle of gilt trellis-work, cloisters covered with carving of the most intricate and elaborate sort, black and scarlet lacquer, ribbons of mosaic, birds, flowers, and trees frozen for eternity and brilliantly coloured. There were temples full of priests in flowing robes of scarlet, yellow, and violet. . . . That, and a great deal more, was Nikko.

They left on a route different from that by which they had arrived, their luggage on a pack-horse. There was heavy rain, then brilliant light again. 'Beautiful, beautiful!' exclaims young Campbell with Celtic exuberance, and catalogues the shape and colour of highland glens blessed with the music of clear, running streams and luxuriant with the bright growth of laurel and tawny maple, feathery bamboo and copses splashed with the pink of cherry blossom. They are walking now, and go through country where silk-spinning and weaving is a cottage industry. 'It is the prettiest work imaginable. The cocoons, each the size of a bantam's egg, are placed in boiling water, kept so by charcoal fires underneath. A girl sits in front with a piece of wood in her hand with which she keeps all the cocoons in a corner of the pan, then with one hand catches the threads of a dozen or more cocoons, which, manipulated in a puzzling way, all unite into one between her rapidly moving fingers, and then is wound on to a small reel which she turns with her other hand. The cocoons go bob, bobbing, and turning round and round until all the silk is off. . . .' And again: 'In another street we found a busy scene. Down each side ran a rapid burn turning five hundred little water-wheels which were connected with the machines in the houses lining the road. From these, as we pass, come out crowds of women and girls. My ideas of silk will always in future be associated with this street, its five hundred wheels flashing in the sunlight, and its hedge of girls, all looking so clean and fat and happy.'

Is it possible that Japan, before the reformation of 1868, was a tolerant and relatively contented country despite the rule of shoguns, the great lords called daimios, and the menacing presence of two-sworded samurai? If the evidence of Campbell, Swire, and Moseley can be accepted – if the majority of people were as well-mannered and happy as they declare – the shoguns and daimios and samurai cannot have been very oppressive; for it is impossible to suppose that a general habit of civility, a national tendency to laugh and be gay, were the product of a few short years of reformation. The symbol or cynosure of reform was the Emperor himself, and in his presence no gaiety was permitted, as Campbell, again in Tokyo, presently discovered. He was the junior member of a party granted an audience.

'I must tell you,' he writes, 'how a deputation of us was presented to the Mikado. We went in three carriages, and in full dress, the Ambassador's English escort riding ahead and in rear. Arrived at the palace, we were received by the household officials, dressed in uniforms of European fashion. In the room where we wait, which has the usual painted paper walls, is a table and handsome gold-lacquered chairs. We sit down and smoke. Sir H. Parkes goes in first, and delivers an autograph letter from the Queen, just received, after which we all troop in Indian file. We walk through several rooms until we arrive in that where the Mikado is standing by the side of a chair. We bow as we enter, range ourselves in line, bow again and advance diagonally (this formation consequent, I imagine, on the shyness of those on the left of the line), the Minister on the right front-extreme, I almost on the left rear-extreme. Three steps and bow; three more steps forward and again bow! three more, and again bow!! and yet three more, and again bow!!! By this time we have arrived close to the Son of Heaven, who stands quite motionless. The Minister has the honour to present us one by one; we bow low as our names are recited. The Mikado does not speak, I think, but one of the attendant officials says that the Mikado is very glad to see us. He does not look like it, neither bowing, smiling, nor speaking. We retire as we entered, only backwards this time, and it is all over. The Mikado's uniform is rather good, well cut, gold-striped white trousers, and a swallow-tailed coat laden with gold embroidery.'

He comments, indeed, with an asperity rare in him, on some of the less publicized effects of reformation. Buddhism, he says, means beautiful carving, painting, and colouring, but Shintoism – the Mikado's religion and now the orthodox faith – means utter simplicity and bare wood. For centuries, however, the two religions have co-existed, tolerated each other, and each has accepted something of the other's ritual. So the reforming government has proceeded to purify the accepted faith and its manifestations; and, in consequence, 'magnificent buildings ornamented with *chefs*

The Mikado   *Emperor Mutsuhito*

d'oeuvre of carvings and paintings, with columns lavishly lacquered with gold, and the floors with vermilion and black; with ceilings and friezes of exquisite pattern and colouring, are ruthlessly pulled down and scattered to the winds, while their army of priests is dismissed and told to get a living elsewhere'.

From Yokohama *Challenger* sailed to Kobe in the Inland Sea, and from Kobe a railway took some of her people to Osaka, which Campbell calls the 'Venice of Japan, the pearl among her cities'. But Campbell, in love with all Japan, except its music and its food, cannot be expected to remain faithful even to an oriental Venice. He goes to Kyoto, riding in a rickshaw. He is filled with admiration of the running

men between its shafts, and shows more understanding of them than Moseley displayed. Each rickshaw was pulled by two men, 'strapping, fine young fellows, graceful and strong. They ran the distance, a little over thirty miles, in five and three-quarter hours, stopping twice for a few minutes to guzzle a basin of rice and swallow some tea. These running men are one of the marvels of Japan. It must be, and is, ultimately ruinous to their health, but in the meantime they trot on and on as unweariedly as horses. Their muscles are iron, their lungs inexhaustible, their tempers angelic. With the exception of the loin cloth they strip naked; a flat straw hat of several feet in diameter is perched on the top of their heads, and on their feet are thick straw sandals. And away they start with us, running hard, shouting, jumping, and laughing with a thirty mile run ahead of them!'

Then, in Kyoto – well, the girls are lovely: 'they are famous in this province for their beauty, and deserve to be' – they are fairer-skinned and prettier than in Yedo, and how marvellously they are dressed! Scarlet obis and petticoats, gowns of fantastic colour and pattern, cuffs and collars stiff with gold thread. And as for Kyoto itself – now he has no doubt about it – 'Kyoto of all towns in Japan is the most attractive'.

How lucky he was to be young, and in Japan, in 1875.

'The opportunity was taken to have the vessel docked', writes Spry, 'for at Yokuska some two thousand Japanese workmen were employed.' He goes on to describe how the shipbuilding industry had been born in the dockyard LEFT, *where* Challenger *lay for a week. From Kobe some of her people took the train to Osaka, and Chief Paymaster Richards preserved the cheerful timetable* RIGHT.

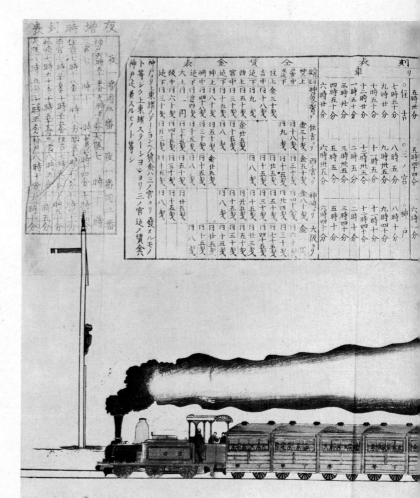

Periphera mirabilis, natural size, drawn from below. 'Few classes of animals appear so ill-suited for life in the deep sea as the medusae, with their soft gelatinous water bodies', wrote Professor Haeckel in the Report. 'There are however some species of the class which descend to great depths'. The medusa (or jellyfish) ABOVE was taken from 1,000 fathoms.

17 *Honolulu and the goddess Pele*

In a very happy interlude sociology and anthropology – so liberally interpreted as to make them acceptable to tourists – had compensated both officers and 'philosophers' for the dreariness of their long voyage from the Admiralty Islands; but now, on June 16th, *Challenger* put to sea again, from Yokohama, for resumption of her proper purpose and a passage to the Sandwich Islands. Again it was a long passage, for not until July 27th was the island of Molokai sighted ahead, Oahu on the starboard bow; and the labour of those weeks cannot be ignored when so many pages have recorded the idle activities of life ashore.

The holiday period had been earned, and psychologically was undoubtedly valuable; but the purpose of the voyage was still incomplete, and the immediate object was 'to run a section across the Pacific on the 35th parallel of north latitude as far east as the meridian of Hawaii': a course which, if continued, would have led the ship in approximately a straight line from Yokohama to San Francisco. No time was wasted, and early in the morning of the 17th the depth was sounded, the sea's temperature was taken, and the trawl put out. The trawling was successful, and in the great quantity of mud brought up were several large pieces of pumice, a hard block of the sea's bottom more than a foot in diameter, some plant fragments, and a surprising number of deep-sea animals. There were nineteen fishes, about a hundred invertebrates, and most of them were of species new to science. Among the most remarkable were four specimens of *Monocaulus*, which defies translation into the common tongue: *Monocaulus* is one of the *Hydroida*, and even the great Oxford

213

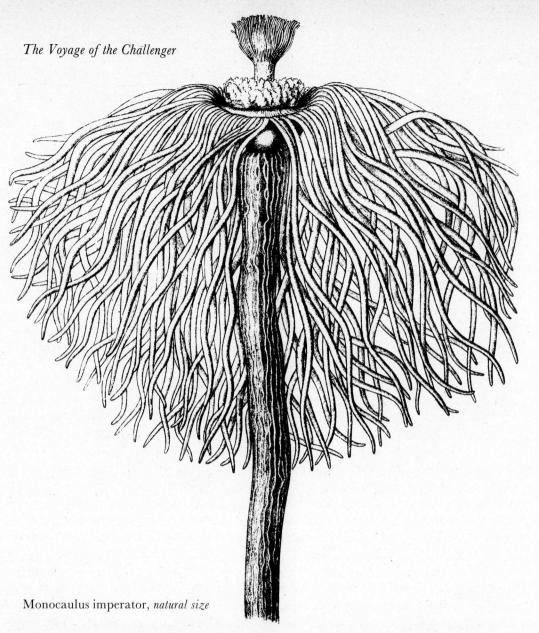

Monocaulus imperator, *natural size*

Dictionary (thirteen volumes of it) can only define *Hydroida* as 'one of the two forms of zooids occurring in Hydrozoa, resembling *Hydra* in structure, but typically asexual'.

One of the four captives, however, earned special mention: 'Among the results of the *Challenger* dredgings must be recorded the discovery of a gigantic Tubularian, which was dredged in the North Pacific from depths of 1,875 and 2,900 fathoms. It is referable to the genus *Monocaulus*, a near ally of *Corymorpha*. One of the specimens whose dimensions were noted by Professor Wyville Thomson and Mr Moseley immediately after its capture was found to measure nine inches from tip to tip of the extended tentacles, which form the proximal tentacular circlet; while its stem rose from its point of attachment to a height of seven feet four inches. This great Tubularian affords indeed an example of a hydroid attaining dimensions far exceeding the maximum which would have hitherto been thought possible in hydroid life – 'a character to which the vast depth whence it was obtained gives additional significance.'

For a week after leaving Japan there were fresh southerly and south-westerly winds, and occasionally, in thick weather, a drizzle of rain. Then light and variable winds, and again clouded skies. In the near neighbourhood of Japan there was a great depression in the sea's bottom, and a depth of nearly 4,000 fathoms was recorded. (Farther north the American ship *Tuscarora* found depths of 4,600 fathoms.) Westwards the bottom gradually rose, and near the Sandwich Islands the gradient became steeper. The temperature on the bottom was remarkably uniform, with a mean of 35°F, while the surface temperature varied from 74°F to 64°F, until, approaching Honolulu, it rose to 78°F.

Such discovery was of scientific value, but cannot have contributed anything of general interest to alleviate what the sailors continued to call 'drudging'. The cruise of the *Challenger* was purposive, patient, and laborious; and the labour was sometimes aggravated by unavoidable accident. On passage to the Sandwich Islands were eleven trawlings and two dredgings: four times the line parted and the trawls with a great length of line were lost, and after the outstanding capture of *Monocaulus* the trawlings were no better than 'fairly successful and productive'. Perhaps the only time when, for the sailors – for Campbell and Swire and young men of their sort – there was any lively interest occurred five days after leaving Japan. The surface temperature dropped sharply, and the ship passed through patches of water coloured red and white. 'The red colour was due to immense numbers of Copepods (*Calanus propinquus*) and Hyperids, the contents of the tow-nets resembling very much those taken in the cold waters south of Kerguelen and the Crozets. There were also in the tow-nets immense numbers of dead pale white Copepods, a species different from the red ones, and the white coloured patches of water appeared to be due to the presence of these. There were in the tow-nets many other dead animals besides the Copepods, and it seems probable that immense numbers of animals belonging to the warm currents had been killed by the streams of cold water flowing southward and breaking into the warm waters of the Japan Stream.' That the hidden drama of oceanic life could colour the surface of the sea was surely beyond anticipation.

Before their discovery by Captain Cook in 1778 the history of the Sandwich Islands is obscure; or, more plainly, unknown. James Cook, than whom few men command more honour, was received by the natives with astonishment and delight, and a year later was murdered by them. He named the islands after the man who, at that time, was the First Lord of the Admiralty. John Montagu, fourth Earl of Sandwich was a notorious gambler, and on one occasion – or perhaps often – was said to have sat at a card-table for twenty-four hours with no more refreshment than a slice of cold roast beef between two pieces of toast. That useful invention is his only memorial, for as First Lord he was both incompetent and dishonest. Cook, though a seaman of consummate genius, was perhaps not a very good judge of the clever people who contrived to live ashore.

Towards the end of the eighteenth century the islands were surveyed by that modest and careful navigator, Captain George Vancouver – who had served under Cook – and their king, Kamehameha, a man of outstanding ability, offered to cede them to Britain: an offer that seems not to have been seriously considered, though in 1824 the reigning king and queen paid a visit to England, where both died of measles. Throughout the nineteenth century the missionaries of different churches competed for the right of instructing natives in the Christian faith, and spiritual colonization was assisted or hindered by such influence as was exercised, without enthusiasm, by British, American, or French interests. In 1875 the widowed Queen Emma was rejected in favour of King Kalakaua: she, a member of the Anglican Communion, was the candidate favoured by British residents, but Kalakaua had American backing, and American influence was growing. It culminated in annexation of the islands by President McKinley's government in 1898, and the name given them by Captain Cook was forgotten. They became the United States territory of Hawaii.

First sight of them woke no enthusiasm: 'The islands of Oahu and Molokai are most remarkable for the extremely barren aspect which they present as viewed from the sea on their leeward sides. In this respect they differ from all other Pacific Islands which were visited during the voyage of the *Challenger*; trees and shrubs do not form a conspicuous feature in the view, but the hill-slopes are covered with a scanty clothing of grass and low herbage, which in the summer season is yellow and parched. . . . There is little more show of vegetation in the general appearance of the islands, as seen from seawards, than is to be seen on the bleak Marion Island in the Southern Ocean.' Honolulu, on the south coast of Oahu, was important as the only really safe harbour in the group, but the little town was unimpressive. It lay inconspicuously on flat land close to the shore, its streets met at right angles, and whether broad or narrow were hot, dusty, and lined by very irregular rows of houses, most of them wooden shanties or general stores. There was one large shop that displayed Chinese and Japanese 'curiosities', and in two photographers' shops large specimens of coral, imported from the Marquesas, and native implements were on sale to passengers of of the mail steamers that called; unfortunately for its purchasers the coral was not the Precious Coral (*Corallium rubrum*) that they supposed it to be, and the native implements were spurious. In Honolulu the tourist market had already been discovered.

There were, however, east of town, an hotel and houses of a better sort in whose gardens imported tropical plants, shrubs, and trees grew prettily, maintained by constant irrigation. Thirty years before not a tree was to be seen along the coast, and the gardens were still an artificial oasis in a desert roughened by outcrop of volcanic rock, where the only conspicuous vegetation was a prickly pear imported from America that had found a congenial soil and multiplied exceedingly. The guava,

A Tahitian girl, taken by the official photographer on board Challenger. '*The feminine garment is a shapeless nightgown. It is not a pretty dress at all*'. *Lord George Campbell.*

also brought in from America, had spread as rapidly – but not, apparently, on the barren plain near Honolulu – and in places formed thickets so dense that half-wild cattle, sheltering in them, could only with difficulty be driven out. 'The whole town of Honolulu', says the Report, 'has a thoroughly American aspect. Americans are supplanting the rapidly decreasing native population; American plants are, as has been said, covering the ground, and American birds have been introduced and bid fair to spread and oust the native fauna, which has no single land bird in common with any other Polynesian island group. The only vigorous opponents of the Americans in the struggle for existence seem to be the Chinese.'

A few miles from Honolulu Campbell discovered the beach at Waikiki, which he calls 'Oahu's Brighton'; and thought little of it. 'A very thin grove of gaunt, rheumatic-looking coco-palms, their lean stems much bent and their crowns much dilapidated by the prevailing wind; under the cocos, on a plain of burnt-up grass diversified by marsh, wherein grows a tall reed-grass, is a scattering of cottages and low trees, a native church, a soft sandy beach, blue sea and surf, where bathe the heated Honolulans, and all overblown by a constant trade-wind from the hills in rear. I cannot say I thought it a cheerful spot. I attempted one day to ride to the left of the town, but soon gave it up; it made one shudder – a hard white road running over a tract of barren, red, disintegrated lava, scattered over with lava blocks and boulders, and that most ugly and dismal thing, a species of cactus, growing thickly over it.'

Campbell, however, takes a kindlier view of Oahu than Moseley. He appreciates the great variety of fruit that could be bought 'alligator-pears, strawberries, marsh and water melons, figs, small pineapples, great green oranges, rose apples – a curious fruit, smells like a rose, and tastes just as one would imagine the most sweet-scented rose ought to taste – delicious bananas and mangoes'. He saw ex-Queen Emma driving a pony-carriage and pair, and thought her in good health despite the loss of a throne. He hires a horse and enjoys riding; he meets – with his customary good luck – a great number of friendly, hospitable, and amusing people; there is a landscape more agreeable than the beach in a steep-walled valley behind the town 'where the hills rise to 4,000 feet and waterfalls shine bright as silver, small ravines hide bathing pools, tropic birds soar high among the lofty peaks', and 'at its narrow head, six miles behind and some thousand feet above the town, you suddenly stand on the brink of a precipice, and a startlingly beautiful view lies beneath'. No one reading Moseley's account could find in it any promise of the popular and populous, brilliant and thriving holiday resort that American enterprise was to create in Honolulu and Waikiki; but in Campbell's letters the germ is visible. And five miles west of Honolulu there was a long, branching inlet of the sea called Pearl Lochs; that, too, was to become more widely known under the slightly different name of Pearl Harbor.

What first evoked in Moseley a positive and memorable pleasure was the visit to *Challenger* of King Kalakaua. The ship's officers, as was to be expected, wore full-dress uniform, but Kalakaua arrived in a black frock-coat, white waistcoat, and straw hat,

A small red carpet was produced and rolled out for King Kalakaua when he came aboard Challenger *with his staff. The young man holding out his sword is the king's son and heir.*

which to Moseley seemed more appropriate for a visit inspired by scientific purpose; and to his great delight 'the king took the liveliest interest in the special work of the *Challenger*, and was almost the only distinguished visitor of the many to whom I had exhibited microscopical objects during our voyage, who recognized the well-known anchors in the skin of the Holothurian *Synapta*, and named them at first glance'. That requires explanation, and a brief return to the New Hebrides where on a coral reef Moseley 'saw for the first time one of the huge *Synaptas*, which are abundant among the East Indian islands and at the Philippines. The animal was a yard long and two inches in diameter, and looked like an ugly brown and black snake. The instant I touched one I knew what it was, for I felt the anchor-shaped hooks in its skin cling to my hand.' Those anchor-shaped hooks got much attention, and in popular reports of the voyage *Synapta* was given a new name: it was called 'the Admiralty worm', and its capture was supposed to be the most wonderful of deep-sea discoveries.

High praise to King Kalakaua, and then to the musicians of Oahu: 'There is a most excellent musical band at Honolulu, composed almost entirely of Hawaiians, and numbering twenty or thirty performers, who execute complicated European music with accuracy and most pleasing effect'. 'The Hawaiians', says Moseley, 'seem to be ahead of some of our own colonists in the matter of music, and have a better band than existed at the time of our visit to New South Wales, even in Sydney'. Perhaps more lasting, however, was the pleasure he derived from a visit to the north-east side of the island, where at Waimanalo he was able to collect a series of native skulls from a deserted burial-place. 'The burials are amongst dunes of calcareous sand, and the bones are exposed by the shifting of the sands by the wind. . . . I know of no place where so abundant material is ready at hand for a study of the skeletal peculiarities of a savage race, by examination of a long series of crania and skeletons as here.' According to Campbell, Moseley was not the only one to leave Oahu with a collection of skulls. The other 'philosophers' also wanted souvenirs, and who shall blame them? The Kanakas of Hawaii were already a dying or disappearing race; their relationship to other Pacific peoples was unknown; and in their bleached, abandoned bones there might even be evidence of their singularity.

In 1778 Captain Cook estimated the population of the islands at 300,000, but seemingly the Hawaiians had no defence against the diseases of civilization and the invasion of their more industrious neighbours. They were good-looking and friendly, they were indolent and gay, and they went down like ninepins before measles and small-pox and tuberculosis, before Chinese and Japanese and the various European peoples who came in by way of the United States. They died untimely, or carelessly married immigrants of any sort, and about a generation ago, when the total popu-lation was well over half a million, it was estimated that the remnant Hawaiians, or part-Hawaiians, numbered not many more than 50,000.

Moseley was more interested in their past than in their future, in their origin and ancient gods than in the impact upon them of the modern world. Their favourite gods, he decided, had not been the Sun and Moon and the Oceanic deities whom they shared with other Polynesians, but the Goddess Pele and her attendants, the off-spring of the enormous and still active volcanoes that dominated their landscape. It was much to be regretted that, under the influence of missionaries of one sort or another, the Hawaiians had been persuaded to identify their old deities with the Devil of Holy Writ; and even more deplorable that the missionaries had compelled them to destroy the images of their gods.

One of the ornaments that the natives still wore was a curiously shaped pendant that looked rather like a very open fish-hook, without a barb and with a hole bored through the shank. It was usually cut from the tooth of a sperm whale, and both men and women wore it hung from the neck on a string of plaited human hair. The significance of the strange shape of the ornament had not previously been realized, but drawings remained – many in poor condition – of the old gods or their images, and from comparison and study of them Moseley deduced that the hook on a necklace was the symbol of the head of a god.

In an account of the Sandwich Islands by William Ellis, published in London in

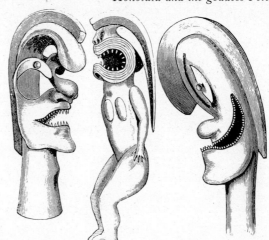

Dr Moseley illustrated his theory about the crescent ornaments of Hawaii with this picture of carved 'gods'. The one on the left is from Cook's A Voyage to the Pacific Ocean, *the others are copied from Ellis's narrative of the Sandwich Islands.*

1827, he found a drawing that showed gods of an almost human sort, and with them were wooden posts topped with a substantial crescent. The gods were all shown with wide-open mouths, that gave their faces a crescentic shape, and it seemed probable that a crescent on a pole was a conventional or symbolic representation of a god's head. Some of the images with well-marked human features wore crowns, possibly made of feathers; and some of the poles, topped only by a crescent, showed a similar crown on that. In one of the plates, moreover, that illustrated an account of Captain Cook's third voyage, Cook was to be seen seated obligingly at the base of a wooden idol while preparation was made to placate or worship it by the sacrifice of a pig; and the post-like idol had a wide, crescent-shaped opening for a mouth.

In Moseley's *Notes by a Naturalist* there are two illustrations that show gods or images and gods' heads: they seem to substantiate his theory, and he has Cook's evidence that the wearing of the fish-hook ornament was general in his time. He goes farther, indeed, and his *Notes* present two drawings of New Zealand carvings of Maori heads in wood, immensely stylized, that also exhibit an extraordinary exaggeration of the mouth. He quotes his friend, Mr A. W. Franks, FRS, whose opinion was that 'as regards the special development of art, and forms of implements in use amongst the New Zealanders, that people are nearly allied to the Hawaiians. . . . The stone adzes of the New Zealanders are of the same form as those of the Hawaiians, and both differ, for example, from those of Tahiti.' That implies a bold speculation: so bold, perhaps, as to defy proof and rebuff dissent. His explanation of the fish-hook ornament is truly ingenious, and it is surprising that his ingenuity did not recognize the significance of the local belief that Pele lived in a volcano which opened its mouth to talk in thunder. If the ornament symbolized the gaping head of a god, surely the god was the volcano or its spirit?

On August 11th the ship left Honolulu for Hilo Bay in Hawaii Island, to let the naturalists visit the volcano of Kilauea. There was a stiff head wind, and even with steam to help the fore-and-aft canvas that was set, the passage was a slow one. But

The falls of Waianuenne, near Hilo.

Hawaii had a more rewarding appearance than Oahu. The distant, enormous volcano of Mauna Loa was nearly 14,000 feet high, but its vivid green sides rose so gradually that the mountain seemed without menace. Closer to the Bay, and almost as high, was the rugged blue crest of Mauna Kea, said to be extinct. Tall cliffs rose abruptly from the sea, water from the heights fell over them in narrow, white cascades, and above a surf-beaten beach houses stood among green lawns. It was a clear, hot morning when they landed, and by early afternoon Campbell and one of the naturalists – he seems more likely to have been Moseley than Murray, but he is identified only by an initial – were mounted and on their way, with a guide, to the long ridge of Kilauea. A larger party was to follow, but they had chosen to make an early start. They made less progress than they expected, however, for M's horse moved only at a fast canter or a very slow walk, and to Campbell's annoyance M preferred the latter.

They rode across rough grass into a broad belt of thickly undergrown, luxuriant forest; over rocky, rutted ground to mile after mile of 'satin rock' – a gritty, black-brown lava – devoid of life; more grass, and thin woods bordered with dead and

RIGHT: *cascade of solidified lava from the crater of Kilauea.*

blistered trees; and were sorely disappointed by a half-way house where they had expected to find some comfort. The half-way house stood on muddy ground; it was only a poor grass hut whose projecting roof sheltered a young woman ironing night-gowns, an older woman nursing a naked baby, the master of the house, and some children. They ordered a fowl to be cooked, and a dog was sent off to catch it.

It was dark when they rode on again – but the darkness was lighted by an almost full moon in a cloudless, windless sky – and presently from the heights of Mauna Loa, far to their right, rose a great column of flame-in-smoke. The ground was rough, their pace slow, the air was chill and damp. On either side of the track the bush was thinning, then disappeared. They were on grass again, and on their left lay a vast depression confined, as it seemed, by blackness. They rode close to the edge, and moonlight was reflected from a gleaming bed of lava; but only when they saw, below them, two glowing patches of light and smoke did they realise they were looking down into the crater of Kilauea. From the ground rose a white vapour, to which moonlight gave the appearance of frost, and then for their comfort – it was long past midnight – the solid shape of an hotel became visible

At half-past six Campbell was wakened by the arrival of Wyville Thomson and his party, who had been nearly seventeen hours on the road, having dawdled at the half-way house and at another hut farther on, 'where they appear to have made a number of small girls get out of bed and dance a *hula hula*'. Campbell and M returned to their sofas, but rose at half-past ten – the late arrivals, on the floor, were still fast asleep – bathed themselves in a tub of 'very warm, whisky-coloured water', and enjoyed 'an excellent breakfast of beef-steak, fresh milk, butter, bread, treacle, coffee, tea, etc'.

The hotel was a simple structure of grass roof and walls on a light wooden frame, put together without nails, but as there were beds for twelve people – in addition to sofas and the floor – it afforded comfort as well as shelter, and all admitted that it was remarkable indeed to find such luxury thirty rough miles from Hilo, 4,000 feet above the sea, on the brink of an active volcano and a plain constantly shaken by earthquakes.

The other visitors – those who had arrived early enough to be given beds – were already down in the crater, but the *Challenger*'s people waited until afternoon. Then, climbing down a precipitous slope, they stepped on to 'the black bed of lava which lies there just as it flowed out at different periods from the molten lakes in the southern part of the crater. It is a tumbled, jammed, hummocky sea of hideous blackness – earth's vomit – lying there in great bouldery masses; smooth, slippery, and shiny as

RIGHT: *minerals from the South Pacific Nos. 5, 9, 10, 11 and 13 are manganese nodules, No. 11 containing a shark's tooth, and No. 8 is a microscopic detail of manganese. Nos. 1, 3 and 12 show philipsite crystals and Nos. 2, 4, 6 and 7 are of volcanic origin, dredged from the sea's bottom.*

OVERLEAF: *an eruption within the crater of Kilauea. 'A surf of liquid lava melted in the bowels of the earth; of the indescribably fiery colour of molten metal'. Campbell*

224

1.

2.

3.

4.

5.

6.

7.

8.

9.

10.

11.

12.

13.

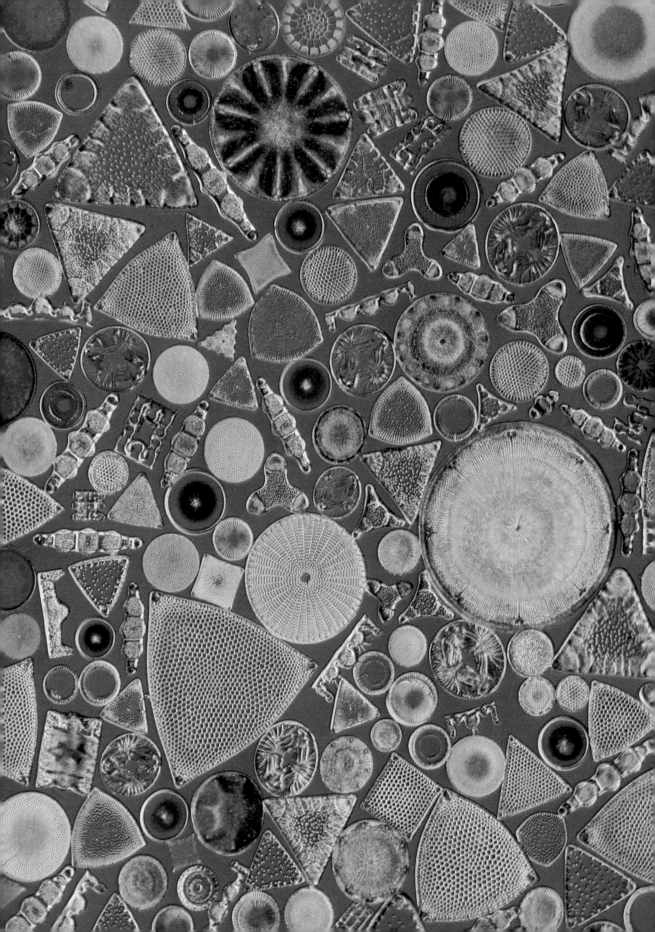

black ice would be; in fan-shaped streams, deeply and closely wrinkled; in flat sheets, disintegrating into small, sharp, needly chips which cut the naked feet of our guide-girl; in hawser-like coils of wire-rope, fathoms long, as if made and laid out by human hands; and everywhere split open and cracked by pressure from beneath. Here and there more recent lava has oozed up and flowed over in rounded streams of black-lead colour, sometimes filling up cracks, or lying on the surface in strange shapes of dragons, birds' heads, roly-poly puddings. And up these cracks – some of which are quite small, while others yawn broadly and deeply – hot air comes blasting with fiery heat, making the soles of our boots very palpably hot, and everything quiver that one looks at. Several hundred yards from where we stepped on to the lava bed we have again to descend a little to the lowest bed of all.'

Under high cliffs two lakes of molten lava lay ahead, and 'a miniature Vesuvius spouting liquid lava'. But the general surface of the lakes was still, 'of a shiny, white-grey colour, cut across by zigzag and curving lines of a vivid pink, and only round the edges – on the shore, as it were – was the lava visibly molten and in heavy motion; the forces beneath, seemingly, forcing themselves out only along the sides of the lakes, and there huge fountainous waves of liquid lava were playing, with ever-varying height and strength, surging and dashing high against the cliffs, and breaking in showers of heavy spray.

'When first we arrived the sun was quenching the glare from the volcanic cauldrons, and five or six of these wave-fountains of a dulled crimson colour were separately playing on the opposite side of the lake. Gradually as the sun goes down and sinks behind the high terminal wall of the crater, and darkness deepens, the glow of the molten lava becomes whiter and more awfully intense; the cliffs illumined luridly; the smoke – blue-white in the moonlight as it issues from the vents in the slope to windward – all crimsoned as it slowly drifts over; the surface of the lake darker, and the lines which run through it of a fiery red. Along the whole length of the shore opposite to which we stand these billows of liquid lava were playing furiously, sometimes separating, leaving dark gaps between them, and then again all uniting, a broad belt of tumbling, heaving, crimson, molten lava.... There was no fire and very little smoke, simply molten lava in violent agitation, accompanied by a hissing, swishing, and clashing, a dull throb and rush of escaping gases.'

They spent three or four days in the grass-walled hotel, they rode over the hills, and, fascinated by the crater, returned to it by night – the scene was more impressive than in daylight – and yet again the following day. Moseley describes, more closely than Campbell, the curious phenomenon called 'Pele's hair': 'The waves [of lava] dashed against the cliffs, threw their spray high into the air above them, and the wind carried part of this spray over the edge of the cliffs, so as to fall on the hard lava platform above.

'The spray masses, cooling as they fell, formed in their track the threads known as

Pele's hair, like fine-spun green glass. Many of the threads could be picked up, each with the small mass of hardened lava still attached. . . . Pele's hair, thus formed, drifts away with the wind and hangs in felted masses about the rocks, and the birds sometimes gather it, and make their nests entirely of it.'

As if for contrast with the crater of Kilauea, Campbell and some others, on their last day ashore, watched a mild exhibition of the sport for which Hawaii was to become famous throughout the world. They first approached three plump and amiable girls who misunderstood their request, but obligingly led them to a bathing place – 'a high leap from a projecting platform into a deep narrow creek' – and there, removing the Mother Hubbards that they wore in obedience to the missionaries, emerged in pink underclothes and jumped into blue water. 'It was very pretty, but not what we wanted.' So the girls found two men whose surf-boards were conveniently leaning against a tree, and though the waves were not running very high Campbell and his friends saw a demonstration – primitive, perhaps, by modern standards – of surf-riding.

'There is a true story', he writes, 'of a native whose hut, while he was within, was swept out to sea by an earthquake-wave; he wrenched off a plank and came in surf-riding on the top of the returning wave, some fifty feet in height, and was thrown uninjured on the land. What a glorious thing to do and survive!'

18 Thirty days to Tahiti

The transit of Venus – its passage across the disk of the sun – occurs only four times in 243 years. There were passages in 1874 and 1769, and in December of the year before *Challenger*'s arrival a party of English astronomers watched the transit from Hawaii. Now the ship was bound for Tahiti, where Cook's *Endeavour* had carried Sir Joseph Banks and other scientists to observe the previous transit in June, 1769.

The scientists spent another month at sea – almost throughout the passage the ship was close-hauled, the north-east trade was squally, the south-east steady, but fine weather brought a flat calm – and before reaching Tahiti their number was reduced by the death of a young man of remarkable ability and brilliant promise. Rudolf von Willemoes Suhm, a native of Schleswig-Holstein, had spent the summer of 1872 with a Danish expedition to the Faroes; returning to Leith, he met Wyville Thomson, who invited him to join his staff. He was well qualified. He had studied in Bonn and Göttingen, and a doctor's degree certified academic approval of his natural gifts as a zoologist. He had welcomed the opportunity to pursue knowledge in far-off islands and unknown seas, and during the voyage he had worked with tireless enthusiasm. But he fell ill with erysipelas, and dying within a few days was buried under 2,700 fathoms of salt water. He was only twenty-eight.

The voyage was lengthened, not only by head winds and lack of wind, but by very careful temperature soundings – when the thermometers went overboard the temperature of the water was noted at every ten fathoms down to 200 fathoms, then at every 100 to 1,500 fathoms – and by much trawling or dredging. 'Infinitely

LEFT: *Rudolf von Willimoes Suhm.* RIGHT: *the harbour of Papeete, capital of Tahiti.*

wearisome,' says Campbell, but the Report, with some complacency, declares that 'the deposits between Honolulu and Tahiti presented many points of interest'. To the layman the sharpest point of interest may be what, to him, will be the improbable discovery that the bed of the Pacific was littered with pieces of manganese. 'Over a peck of heavy, very compact oval nodules was obtained from 2,750 fathoms on September 11th. The largest were four inches in diameter and two inches thick, the upper surface was smooth while the under one was rough and irregular. . . . Along with the nodules were sixteen sharks' teeth of considerable size, and eight earbones of cetaceans.' And on September 16th, 'from 2,350 fathoms the trawl brought up more than half a ton of manganese nodules which filled two small casks. The great majority were small and nearly round, resembling a number of marbles with a mean diameter of three-quarters of an inch. . . . Among the nodules were counted 250 sharks' teeth.' The detritus, it may seem of a marine dentist's workshop, encased forever in protective manganese.

Deep-sea animals were less numerous: Holothurians and a new starfish, sponges, annelids, echinoderms, and shrimps. All were counted, measured, classified, and preserved, and at last on September 18th, Eimeo Island was seen ahead, and Tahiti on the port bow. Tahiti, the pearl of the Pacific: one is prepared for ecstatic description of its scenery, for envious comment on the indolence of friendly, handsome natives, but what one first reads in Moseley's *Notes* is a typically insular, spendidly Victorian exclamation of innate superiority and pretended surprise at the spectacle presented by a French shooting party. 'One of the first sights I saw on landing was a party of Frenchmen starting off into the mountains to shoot wild pigs. One of them was laden with long French loaves. Another led a dejected-looking mongrel dog by a large rope tied round its neck, and a third had his body encircled by the usual huge horn, without the assistance of which a Frenchman cannot go out shooting even partridges at home.'

232

Campbell is equally scathing, and quite as complacent. 'The whole history', he writes, 'of the manner in which the French came to occupy this island is irritable and lamentable. Although we may have occupied countries in a high-handed manner as regards the natives, still we invariably have something to show for it besides the mere advantages of a naval station, whereas here the French have nothing to show worthy the name of a European power, and this not because they don't try, but because they do try and fail, which, in two words, is the history of all their colonial attempts. There is no liberty of conscience, no doing anything in Tahiti without the feeling that you are being watched.' It is probable that Campbell formed other opinions before he left Tahiti, but the French may indeed have had cause for wariness. Their presence was still resented, and they compared unfavourably with the British because the British, who at one time were invited to assume protection of the islands, had declined the offer and thereby escaped criticism; while the French, taking advantage of a pretended insult to their missionaries, had, in or about 1840, assumed control without regard for local feeling.

During the fortnight spent at Tahiti, Swire was kept hard at work, under Murray's direction, on a survey of the coral reef that guarded Papeete harbour; but found leisure to tell a sad, delightful, Dido-and-Aeneas tale of an earlier voyager and a forgotten Queen of the islands. It was in 1767 that Captain Samuel Wallis, of HMS *Dolphin*, went ashore to be received with loud hostility. So hotly were he and his landing party pelted with stones that he had to return on board and use his 'great guns' pretty freely. But the bombardment did not last long. Peace was established, and friendship quickly followed. *Dolphin*'s voyage had been long, Wallis and some of his officers were ill – exhausted, presumably, or poisoned by the Navy's abominable rations – and when the Queen discovered their condition she had them brought ashore, installed them in her palace, and nursed them with her own hands. They recovered their health, and they had to go back to sea. But by then the Queen was in love with Wallis. In tears and despair she begged him to stay. She knew no English words, but her gestures were eloquent, her eyes had no need of grammar. Wallis himself – though there was only one answer he could give her – admitted the emotion he felt. 'About 10 o'clock', he wrote, 'we were got without the reef, and a fresh breeze springing up, our Indian friends, and particularly the Queen, once more bade us farewell with such tenderness of affection and grief, as filled both my heart and my eyes.'

Such was the spell of Tahiti, but Swire, though not unaware of it, was protected by a programme of daily toil. From a segment of the off-shore reef, 1,120 yards long, he in one of the ship's boats had to take a series of soundings, running at right angles to the reef and extending seawards, at intervals of 200 yards, to a depth of 180 fathoms; the soundings to be then continued, from the ship under steam, to a depth of 680 fathoms. To a distance of about 150 fathoms from the reef the downward slope was gradual, and to a depth of 35 fathoms the coral grew in luxuriant abundance and wild irregularity; but in deeper, farther water – it deepened suddenly – the bottom was a coral sand 'with volcanic minerals and pelagic shells'. It was Murray's belief that the reefs had been built from the shore seawards, and the lagoons within were formed by the solvent action of sea-water on the inner, dead parts of the reef. To the masses of living coral on the outer slope food was brought by oceanic currents, and these processes – growth on the seaward side, decay and dissolution on the inner slope – could account for the conformation of the Tahiti reefs without recourse to Darwin's theory that there had been subsidence of the sea's bottom. So Murray maintained, and later investigation in the Solomon Islands appeared to confirm his opinion.

Moseley worked closely on corals, and was fascinated by what he discovered. Much of what he wrote is minutely academic, but it may be possible to say something, in general terms and the common tongue, of his Mushroom Coral, his *Millepora*, and his *Errina*. The Mushroom was common, but he had to search for a long time before he found a mass of the nurse-stocks 'from which the disk-shaped free corals are thrown off as buds'. On the nurse-stock – a mushroom-like stem – a small, cup-shaped coral is formed; as it grows, the mouth of the cup expands, the disk grows broader; a line of separation forms in the stem, and the opened bud falls off. Then a new bud starts from the centre of the scar left on the stem, and the process is repeated.

Much more complicated are the stony *Millepora*. Their hard part is porous; fine, tortuous canals run through it in full communication with each other, and on its surface are open pores of two sizes. In the canals is a network of living tissue made up of branching, communicating tubes which permit free circulation from one part of the coral to another. In the open surface-pores live polyps of two kinds: a large pore is inhabited by a short, stout polyp with a mouth and a stomach; a small pore by a slender polyp with numerous tentacles but neither mouth nor stomach. The slender polyp is called a *Dactylozooid*, the stout polyp a *Gastrozooid*; and the function of the

234

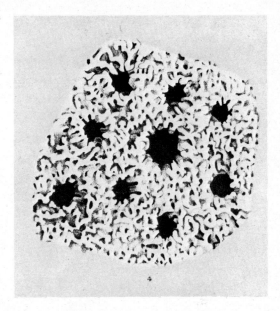

The drawing ABOVE LEFT *shows* Errina labiata, *natural size. The other pictures illustrate* Millepora nodosa. ABOVE RIGHT: *the surface of the external skeleton* × *80.* BELOW: *Fig. 1: a short stumpy Gastrozooid surrounded by five Dactylozooids, all extended. In Fig. 2, both forms are retracted below the surface, the Dactylozooid at the left. Fig. 3 shows this in plan from above; Fig. 4, the structure from below.*

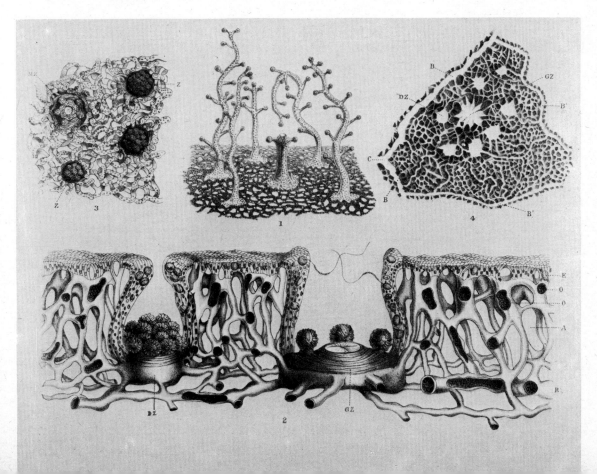

Dactylozooid is to catch food for the colony, and deliver it to the *Gastrozooids* which are able to swallow and digest it.

The *Millepora* believe in division of labour, and the genus *Errina* has also evolved a sexual *apartheid*. As in the *Millepora*, two kinds of polyp, with and without a mouth, live in *Errina*, and each colony is either male or female. There are, then, members of the colony that do nothing but catch food, and other members whose function is to eat and digest it. The latter, having thoroughly digested their food, supply blood – the product of digestion – to the whole colony by means of a common circulation system; and the remaining members, which neither catch food nor eat it, produce eggs and larvae to maintain the survival of *Errina* by punctual reproduction. The indefatigable Moseley examined other corals, of even more elaborate structure, but three examples are probably enough to demonstrate the ingenuity of these animals.

The invisibly busy lagoon also reflects the hills, and for scenery Campbell can usually be relied on. Faced with a Tahitian sunset he does indeed pretend a little diffidence, but boldly sets out to conquer it: 'How the sun setting behind Eimeo in a brilliant soft saffron sky, splashed with small golden and mauve-coloured clouds, threw boldly forward in a clear-cut, opaque purple mass, that fantastically pinnacled island, near the summit of whose highest peak there glittered star-like a speck of light, the sky seen through a hole in the mountain; how in the sea, smooth as a mirror within the reef, and here and there to seaward blue-ruffled by a cat's-paw, away to the horizon was reflected the saffron hue from above; how against purple Eimeo a coco-crowned islet in the harbour appeared dark olive-green, a gem set in the yellow water; how the sunlight left the vivid green shore of palm-fringed Tahiti and stole upward till only the highest ridges and precipice were illuminated with strange pink and violet tints springing straight from the depths of dark blue shadow; how from the loftiest crag there floated a long streamer cloud; then how as the sun sank lower and lower the saffron of the sky paled to the turquoise blue of a tropical twilight, the cloud-banner melted and vanished, and the whole colouring deepened and went out in the sudden darkness of a moonless night! Who would describe it?' he asks. And having described it very prettily, exclaims 'Not I for one'.

Compared with some of the islands they had seen Tahiti, of course, was a civilized place – 'Here one never sees a wild-looking, half-nude girl rushing out of a hut to stare' – and it was both unexpected and disappointing to find the little town of Papeete so crowded with people and yet not civilized enough. There were French soldiers and sailors in the streets, black-cassocked priests, brightly clad Tahitian women – better dressed than Hawaiians – many grog-shops, and in general a rather unkempt appearance. Everyone was friendly and cheerful, on Saturday night *Challenger*'s band played in the square, and on Sunday morning high mass was celebrated on the upper deck of a large French transport which – after dropping a batch of convicts in New Caledonia – had arrived with a relief of troops. But Tahiti,

LEFT: *drawings of the stony coral* Desmophyllum ingens.

Taloo Bay. Eimeo.

The first part of Tahiti sighted by Challenger *was the island of Eimeo, with its 'singular zig-zag outline, precipitous crags, mysterious gorges.'*

said Moseley, 'was wretchedly supplied with provisions. The guava bush has over-run all the lower country and covered it with scrub; hence there is scarcely any pasturage. Cattle are procured from the Sandwich Islands, and it depends on the kind of weather that the sailing-ships which bring them meet with, whether they are worth eating or not when they arrive. We bought for the use of our mess at Papeete the most miserable specimens of sheep that I have ever seen. They had come from Easter Island.' Then, more agreeably, he adds an anthropological note: 'One of the greatest treats to the natives is tea and bread-and-butter. A Chinaman keeps a restaurant to which Tahitian girls are taken by their lovers in order to consume these luxuries.'

On the hills Moseley was less fortunate than on coral reefs. There were mountain-crests that rose to 7,000 feet or more, and he wanted to collect plants from their higher slopes. He set off with Lieutenant Channer, F. Pearcy – 'our excellent bird-skinner and factotum' – and some native guides. All went well on the first day, and they made camp at the head of the Fataua valley, at a height of about 1,600 feet, in a grove of 'Fei', or wild plantains: a banana-like fruit that differed from bananas in not hanging down, but standing up from its parent stem. It was easy to cook: you

Spry made an excursion to Point Venus, site of Captain Cook's observation in 1769. 'The scenery was exceedingly pretty', he says, and notes the Tamarind tree on the left planted by Captain Cook.

lit a fire, and threw in a bunch of 'Fei'. When the skin was black and charred, you peeled it off with a pointed stick, and the yellow, floury interior was 'most excellent eating, like a mealy potato'. According to Moseley it was 'one of the very few plants which, growing spontaneously and in abundance, affords a really good and sufficient source of food to man. Hardly any improvement could be wished for in the fruits by cultivation'.

But there were rats in the mountains, and wild pig. The rats climbed the trees and ate the ripe plantains, the pigs fed on fallen fruit. 'It is strange', says Moseley, 'that the pig should run wild and thrive, under such widely different conditions as it does, and should be able to exist equally well on wild plantains in warm Tahiti, and on penguins and petrels in the chilly Crozets'. And there is the cheerless comment: 'In this power of adaptation it approaches man'.

It was, by then, raining heavily. The guides built a small hut of sticks and plantain leaves. The botanists had brought no blankets, and the night was cold. In the morning they climbed to a steep, narrow ridge, 3,000 feet high. Beyond the ridge the slope was so precipitous that they had to use ropes. They went down through a forest of tree fern, giant fern, and bird's nest fern. They camped at the head of the

239

Punaru valley, where they suffered from both cold and mosquitoes. They tried to cross another high ridge, but the guides lost their way, and in darkness they put up a very small hut which covered the sleepers' bodies but not their legs; and again it was raining heavily. In the morning two other guides were found, and they started up a steep-sided spur of Orofena, the highest of Tahiti's mountains. Again they needed ropes, and the crest of the spur was barely a yard wide, but thickly growing bushes mitigated giddiness. They climbed to 4,000 feet, and came to an unscalable precipice. The newly recruited guides had also lost their way, but Moseley maintains a noble silence about them. Like a true scientist he noted and classified what was to be seen under the precipice – a thick growth of the fern *Gleichenia dichotoma*, a whortleberry *(Vaccinium)*, a tree with a large yellow flower, the burrows of a petrel, probably *Procellaria rostrata* – and said no more.

Campbell fared much better. With Wild, the artist, he hired a trap, two horses, and a young native driver. Their destination was Papeuriri, a village thirty-five miles from Papeete. The road followed the coast, and was decorated by tropical fruit and flowers in extravagant variety: bread-fruit and oranges, mangos, limes, and papayas – to make tough meat tender, said their driver, wrap it in the big leaves of a papaya tree – add banyans, candle-nuts, hibiscus, and a bright blue sea on the other side; the scenery was sufficient even for travellers jaded by Pacific beauty, but did not blind them to the ravages of guavas that had spread like evil weeds. 'The rabbit of vegetation,' says Campbell with a memory of Argyll and its pests. Bread-fruit, on its native ground, grew to a great size, and they drove through a pretty village, where those handsome trees shaded a smooth sward, and beside well-built houses grew roses and oleanders.

(It was to gather a cargo of young bread-fruit trees, and take them to the West Indies, that the much maligned Lieutenant Bligh, of HMS *Bounty*, went to Tahiti in 1787. To do what he had been ordered to do, he had to stay there for five

240

months, and during that time most of the ship's complement found it agreeable to live with the friendly women of the island. Bligh was a hot-tempered man, but considerate of his crew. It was not his brutality that provoked their notorious mutiny, but the mischief-making Fletcher Christian and a glum comparison of life afloat with the bliss they had left behind them. Bligh was set adrift in an open boat, and eighteen men decided to go with him. Ahead of them lay a voyage of 3,600 miles to Timor; that they did not know, of course, but one cannot believe that eighteen good seamen would, of their own free will, choose danger and the company of a man who in any way resembled the sadist of popular repute.)

At an inn kept by a Frenchman, Campbell and Wild stopped to change horses, and drove on into ever more spectacular country. Green mountains on their left, and on their right the sea, smooth as a mirror within protective reefs. A long avenue of plantains, then the melancholy of an abandoned plantation, and they reached the house of the local chief, called Teré, to whom they had been recommended. There they enjoyed a resounding drama. It was a drama of words only – there was no action – but the Tahitians, like the Maoris of New Zealand, excelled in debate because they had, in addition to sonorous voices, the orator's gift of imagery and a fluency that did not falter. With Teré on his verandah were three men of less importance, and on the grass before them sat a large audience. Teré, for a start, read from a thick book. Then someone in the crowd stood up and spoke, and was answered from the verandah. The debate continued, but there was nothing unduly formal or unnaturally stiff about the performance. Women and children, dogs and chickens went to and fro; an occasional pig intruded. The orators still trod their certain paths of speech with flawless, unhurried grace and dignity. There was a popular clown who raised laughter, but eloquence returned and gravity and close attention ruled the argument. Then, when all had said what they had to say, they quietly dispersed.

Teré's house was handsomely furnished, and when Campbell and Wild sat down to dine – on soup and fowl and fish, and big fresh-water crayfish – a choir of about twenty men, women, and girls began to sing part-songs on the lawn where there had been debate, and made rushing, rollicking melodies – uniting, diverging, and rejoining – against a background of sombre sound that reminded Campbell, to his great pleasure, of a piper's drones. He had been so provident as to bring some rum with him, and with rum's encouragement the bubbling, rippling songs went on and on, till the singers began to dance, when Teré broke the party up. Campbell, before returning to Papeete, may have regretted his strictures on French rule, and admitted that it was not entirely repressive.

The ship's band learned some native tunes, and won much applause. The Governor gave a dance, and the band played on his verandah. '*Beaucoup de tapage*', said his little daughter with evident approval, and old Queen Pomaré – neither young nor pretty but full of life – was equally delighted. She had several daughters or grand-daughters who inherited her vivacity, but were saved the unhappiness that befell the royal lady whom Captain Wallis knew, by a weakness more painful than love: taken for a short voyage outside the protective reef, they were very sea-sick.

Tahiti had maintained its reputation for gaiety, and when *Challenger* steamed out of Papeete harbour the band played the national air which, unlike any other national anthem, went to a jig-tune.

Tahitian Girl
Front.

Tahitian Girl
Profile

19 The castaways of Juan Fernandez

'The voyage to Juan Fernandez occupied six weeks, as we had the bad fortune to be becalmed for twelve days on the passage. It was with the liveliest interest that we approached the scene of Alexander Selkirk's life of seclusion and hardship. . . .'

It was *Robinson Crusoe*, says Moseley, that first gave him a desire to go to sea, and Darwin's *Journal* settled the matter. That Selkirk's 'life of solitude and hardship' was the inspiration of Defoe's story is generally known; less familiar is the fact that Captain Woodes Rogers, the privateer who rescued Selkirk, had described him in detail, and written an account of his experiences, in a book called *Cruising Voyage round the World*, which Defoe must have read. It was first published in 1712, and a second edition appeared in 1719, the year when Crusoe became a national figure. There was a library aboard *Challenger*, which probably included a copy of Rogers's *Voyage*, for the 'philosophers' reveal a quite unexpected interest in the island of Juan Fernandez. It had had, indeed, a curious history; it had sheltered many castaways or maroons, who seem to have found in it a natural habitat – almost as natural as Heard Island for Sea Elephants – and that, perhaps, is why the magisterial Report gives it as many pages as it devoted to corals in the chapter on Tahiti.

If a copy of the *Voyage* was available, the 'philosophers' would all have found time to read it, for their forty days at sea were not entirely occupied by sieving and identifying the contents of the busy trawl. Patient and periodic sounding gave anticipated results, but trawling, though it suffered only one accident, when a trawl and 1,600 fathoms of line were lost, captured few 'animals'. It did, however, discover the same sort of litter as had been found somewhere south of Hawaii; it brought up an astonishing number of sharks' teeth, bones of cetaceans, and manganese nodules. On October 6th – three days after leaving Papeete – more than two bushels of nodules were found at a depth of 2,385 fathoms. They were of two kinds, 'the one round with a concentric arrangement of layers, the other large slabs containing in the centre a volcanic tufa. There would appear to have been at this locality an old sea bottom of red clay, in which round manganese nodules had been formed, and then at a later date a fall of volcanic ashes, covering the bottom in some places to a depth of two inches.' Among the nodules were 116 sharks' teeth – the largest of which resembled many fossil specimens – and nine pieces of bone from the middle or inner ear of dolphins.

On October 14th there was a haul of 1,500 sharks' teeth, forty-two cetacean ear-drums, and two bushels of manganese nodules that looked like marbles; on the 16th 340 sharks' teeth, a bushel of nodules, and 132 fragments of the inner or middle ear of various cetaceans; on the 23rd more of the same, including three large tympanic bones of between three and four inches; and on November 11th a manganese nodule as big as a hen's egg. Were the nodules of cosmic origin? Had they entered the sea as incandescent particles thrown off by meteorites in their passage through the atmosphere? The arguments, for and against, are too complex and too long for easy summary, and the strange litter of the ocean's bed – cosmic dust on a sharks' necropolis – must be left behind as the high cliffs of Juan Fernandez rise ahead.

The island, thirteen miles long, lies 360 miles west of Valparaiso. It was in dull, stormy weather that the ship approached, and under driving cloud there was a gloomy grandeur in the view. The next morning, however, was calm and sunny, and the island wore a different aspect. Now there was general admiration of its beauty. Dark basaltic cliffs contrasted with the brightness of a rich herbage, and the ground rose sharply to peaks of fantastic appearance, 3,000 feet high; from *Challenger*'s

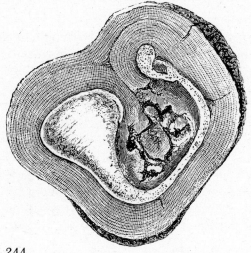

Cross-section of a manganese nodule formed around the ear bone of a cetacean, Mesoplodon, *dredged from 2,600 fathoms.*

244

Challenger in Cumberland Bay

anchorage in Cumberland Bay they were dominated by a precipitous mass called *El Yunque*, the Anvil.

To Moseley's great pleasure there were, among the twenty-four different ferns that grew on the island, no less than four species peculiar to it, while one, *Thyrsopteris elegans*, was of a genus occurring only there, and was doubly unique in that no other genus of ferns was confined to one, small, isolated locality. Below 700 feet there were no trees – all had been cut for fuel – but Moseley and a guide walked through a thicket of the gigantic, rhubarb-like *Gunnera chilensis* that grew almost as tall as small trees: the stalks were seven feet high, the huge leaves were umbrellas above them. There were wild white strawberries on the lower slopes, as yet unripe – it was spring in Juan Fernandez – and a tree called Winter's Bark, a magnolia, was flowering in resplendent white, bignonias in dark blue. Wild peaches were common and appeared to be spreading, as were wild turnips; and there were luxuriant thistles.

Hovering over bush and tree, humming-birds were everywhere. There were two species, one peculiar to the island, the other, of the same genus, common also in Chile. The plumage of the local bird was remarkably different in male and female, the female being green while the male was chocolate-coloured with an iridescent golden-brown patch on the head. Pigeons, said to be imported, fed in flocks on the

Crusoe's cabbage Gunnera chilensis

hill-side. Fish and large rock-lobsters were abundant, and easily caught; and the flesh of wild goats, pastured on good grass, was 'most excellent eating'. At Selkirk's Monument, at a height of 1,800 feet above the sea, with a view of the sea on both sides of the island, Moseley sat and thought happily that within a dozen miles of isolated land, most of it visible, could be found birds, land-shells, trees, and ferns that occurred nowhere else in the universe.

The first of the goats – perhaps the distant ancestors of the meat that Moseley ate with relish – were imported by Juan Fernandez himself, a Spanish navigator who discovered the island in 1563, and gave it his own name. He obtained a grant of his discovery, brought in goats and pigs, but grew tired of isolation and returned to the mainland. By 1680 the goats had so multiplied that a buccaneer called Sharp, putting in to refit, was able to kill and salt a hundred over and above as much fresh meat as his crew wanted. He was surprised by three Spanish ships of war, hurriedly recalled his men, slipped his cable, and put to sea. A Mosquito Indian called William was accidentally left behind and four years later was rescued by Cook, another buccaneer, in whose ship were several men who had served with Sharp. One of these, also a Mosquito – from Nicaragua, that is – went ashore, and saw William come down to the beach. They met most affectionately, and Cook's men killed and took aboard goats, fur seals, elephant seals, and fish, as well as wild vegetables.

In 1687 five men, buccaneers, voluntarily remained on the island: their captain,

246

Edward Davis, was so generous as to give them a canoe, arms, ammunition, various tools, and a negro attendant for each of them. They remained until 1690, when the English ship *Welfare* took them off. In February, 1704, that strangely gifted, unfortunate man, William Dampier – buccaneer, navigator, hydrographer, and an admirable writer – arrived with two ships, licensed privateers, the second one commanded by a Captain Stradling, who quarrelled so grievously with his crew that forty-two deserted. Dampier was able to pacify and reconcile all but five of them. They remained on the island, and in October of the same year Stradling returned and found two survivors; the others had apparently been captured by the French.

On his second visit Stradling quarrelled with his sailing-master, Alexander Selkirk, who demanded to be put ashore, preferring to be left on a desert island rather than remain under the command of a captain who was intolerable. Stradling, in the circumstances, behaved well, and let Selkirk take with him his clothes, bedding, a firelock, one pound of gunpowder, a hatchet, cooking utensils, some tobacco, and his books. Then, before the ship sailed, Selkirk changed his mind, and asked permission to come aboard again. Stradling refused, and Selkirk was left on Juan Fernandez until February, 1709, when Captain Woodes Rogers in the ship *Duke* called at the island and found him there. With Woodes Rogers, serving as sailing-master, was Dampier; and in consort with them was the ship *Duchess*, commanded by another literary sea-captain, Edward Cook. Rogers and Cook both wrote accounts of their voyage, and of Selkirk's strong endurance and extraordinary survival; but there seems no doubt that Defoe got his material for *Robinson Crusoe* from Rogers, whose description of Selkirk is Crusoe in the looking glass. He saw:

> a man clothed in goat-skins, who seemed wilder than the original owners of his apparel. His name was Alexander Selkirk, a Scotsman, who had lived alone on the island for four years and four months. . . . He had with him his clothes and bedding, with a firelock and some powder and bullets, some tobacco, a knife, a kettle, a bible, with some other books, and his mathematical implements. He diverted himself and provided for his sustenance as well as he could; but had much ado to bear up against melancholy for the first eight months, and was sore distressed at being left alone in such a desolate place. He built himself two huts thatched with long grass and lined with goat skins. . . . He employed himself in reading, praying and singing psalms, so that he said he was a better Christian during his solitude than he had ever been before . . . When his clothes were worn out, he made himself a coat and cap of goat-skins, which he stitched together with thongs of the same, cut out with his knife, using a nail by way of a needle or awl. . . . At his first coming on board, he had so much forgotten his language, for want of use, that we could scarcely understand him, as he seemed to speak his words by halves.

That passage is quoted in the sturdily authoritarian *Cambridge History of English Literature*, and it is interesting to read, on a neighbouring page, the suggestion that Rogers, as a writer, may have been given some help by his sailing-master: of buccaneers the most incongruously gifted, one of the most unfortunate of men, Dampier gained nothing from all his arduous and terrible adventures but a small literary fame of brief duration, that is now quite forgotten.

Juan Fernandez continued to attract visitors. George Shelvocke lost his ship *Speedwell* there in 1718. His crew of seventy-one all saved themselves, and built huts which they roofed with the skins of elephant seals and fur seals. The goats outwitted them – they had very little powder and shot – but someone unknown, on an unrecorded occasion, had brought in a couple of cats, and cats were now numerous: Shelvocke's men found them a pleasant addition to a diet of seal-meat, wild turnips, and 'cabbage palm'. From the remains of their wrecked ship they built a schooner of about twenty tons burden, and forty-seven of them put to sea. They captured a better ship near Pisco, in Peru, and transferred to her; they did not return to Juan Fernandez to rescue the eleven Englishmen and thirteen Indians they had left behind.

Most famous of all who found solace in Cumberland Bay was Commodore Anson who arrived in 1741 after a voyage of appalling hazard and fearful hardship. In his flagship *Centurion* he had sailed from Spithead with a squadron of six, ill-found, poorly provisioned vessels; in tempestuous weather he rounded the Horn, where two of them were lost; on a desolate island off southern Chile he lost another, the *Wager*, one of whose young officers was the poet Byron's grandfather, 'Foul-weather Jack', who survived; and reached Juan Fernandez with a crew so reduced by death or crippled by scurvy that a watch could muster no more than ten or a dozen men. He remained on the island from June till September, and cured scurvy with its abundant vegetables. The remaining three of his original squadron also came limping in, and in due course *Centurion* led them off to war with Spain, for which they had been commissioned. They took the town of Paita in Peru, but the smaller ships were now quite unseaworthy, more of his men had died or been killed, and when Anson turned westwards, across the breadth of the Pacific, all who survived were in the flagship. Then, off Espiritu Santo in the New Hebrides, *Centurion* took the Manila galleon *Nuestra Señora de Covadonga* and Anson – or, more accurately, his government – was rewarded. The galleon, on passage from Mexico to the Philippines, carried a million and a half dollars: equivalent, perhaps, to a contemporary £500,000.

Some time later the Spaniards established a settlement and built a fort on Juan Fernandez. In 1751 the first settlement was overwhelmed by a tidal wave following an earthquake, but the Spaniards built again, on higher ground, and maintained a garrison until the revolutionary wars in South America compelled withdrawal in 1814. Then the Chilean government sent convicts there, but after another earthquake in 1835 the convict settlement was abandoned, and when *Challenger* arrived the island was rented by a man who employed forty or fifty people to hunt fur seals.

It would be an exaggeration to pretend that Juan Fernandez had given *Challenger*'s scientists an opportunity to study a controlled experiment in man's adaptability, but

RIGHT: Pantathera avenacea *collected by Moseley on Juan Fernandez.*

10

Scorpaena thomsonii

for a little while its history had certainly diverted their attention from those less highly organized creatures who lived in the globigerina ooze of the sea's bottom.

The voyage was resumed, but again the weather was hostile, and it took four days to cover the three hundred and sixty miles to Valparaiso. But they were not wasted, for when the trawl was put out, in 2,225 fathoms, it brought up fifty specimens of deep-sea animals, among which were fifteen new species, five belonging to genera first discovered by the *Challenger*'s naturalists. Valparaiso itself gave less pleasure. The Andes, that on a map appeared to be so near the coast, were almost invisible, and 'how Valparaiso came to be called the Vale of Paradise I cannot well understand', says Moseley. 'The surrounding country has a most barren and inhospitable appearance. Not a tree is to be seen anywhere from the anchorage in the harbour.' As a port-of-call, however, it was immensely useful. Supplies of every description were plentiful, and from November 19th till December 11th the crew were kept busy. New sails were bent, there was much repairing and refitting to meet the shock of the heavy seas that might still be encountered. And while the sailors were at work the scientists went off to Santiago and the nearer slopes of the Andes.

Santiago differed from Valparaiso in the most agreeable fashion. 'Santiago', says Campbell, 'is the Paris of all towns in the Republic bordering the South Pacific. It is built at the foot of the mountains, on a great agricultural plain running along the base of the Cordillera with hill ranges between it and the sea. Fine hotels, clubs, and

Chilean peasants, dressed 'in the European style' LEFT. *Not all the people of Chile lead an easy life. Moseley brought back the picture* RIGHT *of a Patagonian peasant in Santiago.*

cafés; houses enclosing a *patio* bright with flowers, fountains, and coloured pavements; every window barred with handsome iron work; tramways along the streets; fine cathedrals and churches; good horses and somewhat too flashy carriages; a theatre and newly built opera house, a gem of its kind; beautiful women, whether attired in Parisian fashion or as Chilean peasants; a visibly wealthy population in manners and dress; a town full of luxury and dissipation and scandal; of life, riches, and gaiety; very expensive, hospitable, and enjoyable in every way.'

There will, unfortunately, be no further opportunity to quote that engaging young man, Lord George Campbell; and how pleasant to quote him, for the last time, in so typical a vein. He and A. F. Balfour left the ship on promotion to Lieutenant and travelled overland to the river Plate – an adventurous journey, but of no scientific interest – and from Montevideo sailed home in the comfort of the mail steamer *Britannia*. This narrative would have been a duller piece of writing without the constant enthusiasm of his letters, and after his departure *Challenger* may have been a quieter ship.

251

ABOVE: *the brittle-stars* Ophiocreas carnosus *and* Ophiocreas oedipus.

RIGHT: *a little larger than natural size, the tooth of an extinct shark* Carcharodon megalodon, *still sharp enough to cut through leather with its serrated edge. It has been in the British Museum for the last hundred years, at the bottom of the Pacific Ocean for the previous ten million.*

20 The firths of Patagonia

Without the help of a chart it will be impossible to follow *Challenger*'s course from the Pacific into the Atlantic. To begin with, a prevailing southerly wind compelled a beat far to the westward until, somewhere south of latitude 40°, it was possible to turn on a slant leading to the Gulf of Peñas that makes a ragged hole in Patagonia's coast-line. There the ship entered a series of tortuous long firths that took her through sheltered waters – sheltered, that is, from oceanic violence, but not from occasional fierce downdrafts of wind from the high hills – into the Straits of Magellan, and so to the stormy, sheep-nibbled Falkland Islands.

On the westward passage Juan Fernandez was sighted again, the depths were sounded – how tiresome must temperature soundings have been – and three times the trawl was launched. Though the wind remained contrary the weather was fine, the sea calm, and the trawling was productive though not especially memorable. It confirmed previous observation and prompted a carefully phrased opinion that on the blue mud near continental coasts the trawl was likely to make a larger capture than 'on other kinds of deposit far removed from continents'. To the lay mind that seems a probability which few would doubt, and complementary to it is a suggestion that animals taken in oceanic trawling may be more 'abnormal' than those brought up from a similar depth close to the land. Of that there is no conclusive proof, but 'there are indications that such is the case'.

LEFT: Phalacrocorax imperialis *and,* afloat, P. albiventris, *cormorants from the Falkland Islands.*

255

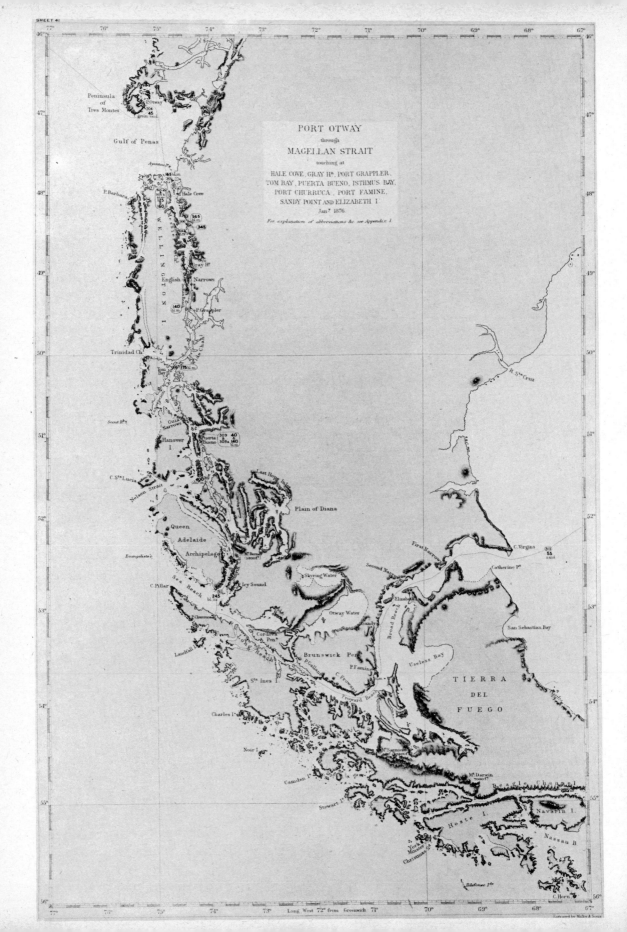

SHEET 41

PORT OTWAY
through
MAGELLAN STRAIT
touching at
HALE COVE, GRAY H.ᵈ, PORT GRAPPLER,
TOM BAY, PUERTA BUENO, ISTHMUS BAY,
PORT CHURRUCA, PORT FAMINE,
SANDY POINT AND ELIZABETH I.
Janʸ 1876.

For explanation of abbreviations &c see Appendix I.

Peninsula
of
Tres Montes

Gulf of Penas

P. Barbara

Hale Cove

Gray Hᵈ

English Narrows

P. Grappler

WELLINGTON I.

Trinidad Ch.

Scout R.ᵏˢ

Guia Narrows

Hanover I.

Puerta Bueno

C. Sta Lucia

Nelson Strait

Queen

Adelaide

Archipelago

Evangelists

Sea Reach

C. Pillar

Icy Sound

Churruca

Landfall I.

Cordova Penᵃ

Sta Ines

Charles I.

Noir I.

Camden I.

Stewart I.

Last Hope Inlet

Plain of Diana

Skyring Water

Otway Water

Sandy

Brunswick Penᵃ

P. Gallant

P. Froward

Froward Reach

M. Sarmiento

M. Darwin

Hoste I.

York Minster S.

Christmas S.

Ildefonso Iˢ

First Narrow

Second Narrow

Elizabeth I.

Broad Reach

P. Famine

Useless Bay

R. Sta Cruz

C. Virgins

Catherine P.

San Sebastian Bay

TIERRA
DEL
FUEGO

Beagle Channel

Navarin I.

Nassau B.

C. Horn

Long. West 72° from Greenwich

Engraved by Malby & Sons

On the morning of December 31st, twenty days after leaving Valparaiso, the commanding headland of Tres Montes, on the peninsula north of the Gulf of Peñas, was visible through a coastal haze. The sky was clouded, there was a drizzling rain, but the weather brightened after passing the headland, and the menacing grandeur of an iron-bound coast was revealed. It was here – somewhere in the Gulf – that HMS *Wager*, of Anson's squadron, was wrecked. A small party landed at Port Otway, on the inner shore of the peninsula, but stayed only a short time and brought away nothing of more durable memory than a bucket of good mussels. The Captain and Wyville Thomson entertained officers and naturalists at a New Year's Eve party, and at midnight sixteen bells announced the end of 1875.

At five a.m. on January 1st the ship left Port Otway and steamed across the Gulf of Peñas towards the Messier Channel, the entrance to the inner Straits that lead narrowly, between empty islands and an almost empty mainland, to the Magellan Straits. Through vacant, uncountable centuries implacable glaciers, fed by perpetual snow, had carved those tortuous channels and high-pitched landscapes of remarkable beauty. The scenery, in some of its aspects, was reminiscent of Norway; or, more accurately, suggested a magnified Norway whose major fjords were continuous: branches ran off or into them, but a long, purposive channel led steadily to the south between mountain-sides which, in the Messier Strait, were covered from crest to sea-level with forests of small trees. The trees leaned over the shore, over mussel-beds growing on the rocks; in the Straits a multitude of fur seals gambolled like porpoises; and here and there the distant mountain-tops were capped with snow or shining glaciers.

The ship anchored for the night in Hale Cove, a small, sheltered bay between steep hills, and some of her complement went ashore to shoot a few oyster-catchers, cormorants, and geese. That set a pattern for the inland voyage: the straits were too narrow and tortuous for navigation by night, and on shore there was usually something to be shot. Nowadays it may be difficult to find a good reason for shooting cormorants and oyster-catchers, but Patagonia, a hundred years ago, bore little resemblance to our contemporary world, and rules of behaviour have always been subject to time, place, and transient judgement. 'Oecology' was already a word – it seems to have been born in 1873, its parent being the German naturalist, Ernst Heinrich Haeckel – but it was a long, long way from recognition as something which, in an over-crowded, over-industrialized world, would eventually be deemed important. On *Challenger*'s decks it was necessary to let both sailors and naturalists relieve the boredom of a voyage which, though its importance could not be doubted, suffered from isolation and the laborious repetition of exercises that – even to those interested in their results – must have acquired, after three years, an oppressive monotony. A few cormorants and oyster-catchers were a small price to pay for the maintenance of a healthy interest in life: a sailor's or a naturalist's life, that is.

LEFT: *the passage of* Challenger *from Port Otway through the Straits of Magellan to the Atlantic.*

View near Gray Harbour. Mr Wild's drawing, before his escapade with the fire.

Then from Hale Cove to Gray Harbour – more glaciers gleaming on the heights – and though broken ice in the pale green water chilled the air, it was still picnic weather, and round every bend of the channel – its smooth water mirrored the hills – the scene changed and another Patagonian picture was displayed for admiration. Gray Harbour was reached before sunset – there were no inhabitants – and the ship lay for another day. Here there was better sport – Moseley reports duck, snipe, and wood-cock, as well as geese – and on a large lake those who preferred a fishing-rod caught 'plenty of small fish having the general appearance of a trout'. For the botanist with his less lethal vasculum there were ferns in abundance, and for simpler pleasure mussels on the beach. The ship's company had been landed to wash their clothes, but they gathered mussels as well, and mussel-boiling set the hills ablaze.

Like picnic-parties everywhere, the sailors lighted fires to cook their catch, and some were careless. The grass was dry, the pale bleached moss was dry, and so was the tangled undergrowth on the thickly wooded hills. There was a breeze blowing up the valley, and before darkness fell there was fire on both sides. Smoke filled the air, the flames were still spreading, and the unhappy Mr Wild – the artist who doubled as secretary to Wyville Thomson – saw little hope of escaping them.

He had landed on the beach opposite the ship, and climbed up through the forest to a bare hill-top where he walked until he found the view he wanted. He sat down to draw it, and had almost finished when he was alarmed by the ominous, rising sound of a fire in the trees below him. Between him and the ship the woods were burning, and from several directions flames were dancing uphill before the breeze. He saw what appeared to be an opening – a path to the beach – and over rough ground and fallen timber hurried down, with fire roaring on either side, till it occurred to him that he might be safer on the bare hill above the wood. He retreated, and found marshy ground where he lay exhausted, and looked at a wall of fire halted by the swamp. Then the wind shifted, he tried again to find his way to the shore, and crossed a stream on a fallen tree. But again he had to retreat, and from the heights saw a boat leave the ship.

At six o'clock – dinner-time aboard ship – he was reported missing. No one had seen him for several hours, and the hills were on fire. Search-parties were mustered and put ashore. Bugles were blown, rifles fired, to attract his attention, and Wild was saved. Lieutenant Bethell brought him off, and all hands cheered the rescue. In spite of exhaustion Wild was sufficiently composed to admire the blazing forest and trees, like flaming torches, that reflected their image in the water. Poor Wild! He drew busily, painted some charming pictures, and wrote a short, dullish account of the voyage that is quite devoid of excitement except on the pages that tell the tale of his adventure at Gray Harbour.

In the morning the fire was still burning – the nearer ground charred and melancholy with bare, black stumps – and the ship did not leave until half-past ten: a few miles to the south were the English Narrows, an exceptionally difficult part of the strait in which *Challenger*, having waited for slack water, had to twist and turn to find a way through; at its narrowest the channel was only four hundred yards across, and in the middle was a small island.

Now the land showed bolder contours, higher hills, and the air grew cold. Angry squalls blew down deep gorges, and the howling of the wind seemed a warning of what lay ahead. There was, however, a good, well-sheltered anchorage at Port Grappler, and in the harbour lay another ship. She was a derelict German steamer called *Karnach*, bound from Valparaiso to Hamburg, which had struck a sunken rock and put into Port Grappler badly holed. Her cargo was valuable – she was laden with silver ore, copper, hides, and sugar – and in possession of her were four Englishmen of obscure background. They were said to be part of the crew of a Chilean steamer, but how they had acquired *Karnach* was not discovered. They were aware of her value, however, and refused all offers of assistance from *Challenger*. At Port Grappler there was continuous rain, but the drenched and dismal land offered temptation to those who still had cartridges for their scatter-guns, and a few more ducks and geese were carried aboard.

There was a delusive promise of better weather in the morning, with a fresh breeze from the south, and more open water in Wide Channel. In Tom Bay, the anticipated harbour, was a confusion of islets, and with the weather again worsening the ship had to up-anchor, anchor again, and lie to her anchors with steam up. A survey of the Bay had been intended, but the darkness of low skies prevented it, and the main event of a stormy day or two at Tom Bay was the killing of a Steamer Duck. That curious creature, found only in or near Tierra del Fuego and the Falkland Islands, is as much like a penguin as a duck, and rushes through the water at great speed and in a cloud of spray, using its wings, which are incapable of flight, as furious paddles. The first expedition, in *Challenger*'s steam pinnace, was unrewarded but returned with a

259

Aphritis gobio, *a shore fish from the Straits of Magellan.*

tale that the duck had steamed faster than the pinnace's top speed of ten knots. Another attempt, in abominable weather, was more successful, and as well as a Steamer Duck in fine plumage, seven geese and two woodcock were shot, and three goslings captured alive.

South of Wide Channel the mountains are broken by intrusive, broad fjords, as if the carving glaciers had run wild, and again it was intended to make careful surveys of potential harbours on the way. But again intention was denied by heavy rain and overcast, low skies. Puerto Bueno was the next anchorage, which lived up to its name. The weather improved, the bay was pretty and sprinkled with small islands whose charm was magnified by the gaunt hills above them. Fishing-rods and guns were again deployed, but sport was poor, and a lurid thunderstorm brought it to an end.

Ten days had now elapsed since *Challenger* entered the Messier Channel, and though it was midsummer in those high, southern latitudes the snow-bound hills continued to show a very wintry landscape. Isthmus Bay was the ship's proximate anchorage, and whoever has followed her course will see that she has steamed south of Wellington Island, Hanover Island – between them and the mainland of Patagonia – and is approaching a confusion of fjords, peninsulas, and islands, from which a south-going channel runs to Sea Reach, the main Pacific entrance, sign-posted by Cape Pillar, to the Straits of Magellan. Isthmus Bay gave good shelter, and the following morning *Challenger* passed Queen Adelaide's Land – Patagonia on the port side pouring cascades of bright water down formidable chasms – and crossed Sea Reach to find harbour in the land-locked bay of Port Churruca, surrounded by woods so thickly entangled – so deeply cut by crevasses filled with bright blue ice – that even the

Challenger *steaming around Cape Froward.*

hardiest guns were defeated. Only the botanists – a second day was spent at Port Churruca – got any reward for exertion.

A strong gale was blowing when *Challenger* continued her passage, with steam up and double-reefed topsails, and by mid-afternoon she was off Cape Froward, geographically distinguished as the southernmost corner of the South American continent, and memorable as the place – or approximately the place – where Joshua Slocum defeated the savages of Tierra del Fuego.

Captain Slocum was the first man to sail alone round the world. He put to sea from Boston in July, 1895, and reached the Straits of Magellan in February of the following year. He had a rough, dangerous passage to the Pacific, and after sailing out past Cape Pillar was driven south, by furious gales, almost as far as Cape Horn. He survived a tempestuous battering in what was called the Milky Way – where the sea boiled between sunken reefs – and was scholar enough to quote Darwin who, having seen it from the *Beagle*'s deck, wrote 'Any landsman, seeing the Milky Way, would have nightmares for a week'. He might have added 'or seamen' says Slocum; who again found his way, through gale-driven, shoal-broken seas, into the Magellan Straits somewhere to the south of Cape Froward.

On his first passage he had been warned of the hostility he might expect from the murderous, predatory natives of Tierra del Fuego, and for protection against them Captain Pedro Samblich – a friendly Austrian 'of large experience', says Slocum – had given him the curious present of a bag of carpet-tacks. When Slocum, having re-entered the Straits at Froward Reach, saw that natives were near at hand – in their canoes they appeared to be stalking him – he loaded his guns, scattered carpet-tacks on his deck, and went to bed. He was awakened, a few hours later, by angry shouting

Challenger *in the Straits of Magellan.*

that turned suddenly to screams of pain and dismay, and came up from his cabin in time to fire a round or two at the bare-footed, rapidly retreating pirates who had tried to make capture of him and his boat. Now Slocum and his book, *Sailing Alone around the World,* have countless admirers, and there has been much debate about this story; for Slocum, though manifestly a truthful man – his narrative is matter-of-fact, convincing in detail, down to sea-level if not to earth – has stirred a good deal of incredulity with a tale that seems bizarre to people who, perhaps, have little knowledge of the now extinct natives of Tierra del Fuego, and have never walked, bare-footed, on a deck lavishly sprinkled with tin-tacks. The natives were invested with an almost legendary menace; they were said to reach a height of well over six feet, and to be so indifferent to Cape Horn weather as to walk abroad almost naked; but they were certainly unacquainted with the painful impact of tin-tacks. When, moreover, one reads again the story of Slocum's phenomenal achievement it seems improbable that he felt any need to decorate it; and it is better to believe that he was able to complete his circumnavigation by a judicious use of Captain Samblich's unexpected gift.

To the great disappointment of Moseley, and others aboard *Challenger,* they saw little of the dreaded natives except a small, pathetic party of two girls and a boy who slept huddled together for warmth. The wind off Cape Froward blew bitterly cold, and smoke fled streaming from three fires on the shore; against a background of smoke and rain a few figures were dimly visible, but Moseley came no closer to the wild tribes who had accommodated themselves to the fearful inclemency of their savage island, and did not long survive the more lethal impact of civilization.

Froward Reach was blown white by williewaws from the dark gorges of the hills above it, and round the corner, as *Challenger* turned north, she found an anchorage at Port Famine: a dismal name that recollected the fate of a hapless Spanish colony.

Those who landed returned with a depressing description of the surrounding country as one vast bog, but the harbour was sheltered and the trawl captured – as well as starfish and seaweed of a limited scientific interest – a great haul of big prawns.

The morning broke bright and calm, and the ship, still steaming northward, dropped anchor at Punta Arenas, or Sandy Point, the site of a small Chilean colony that was expected to rear cattle – there was good grazing – and mine a bituminous coal. Moseley has nothing to say about it, except that there were no Patagonians to be seen, and his narrative goes quickly on to Elizabeth Island, which seemingly owed its name to the patriotism of Sir Francis Drake. Elizabeth Island, treeless but growing good grass, was the breeding-place of large numbers of wild geese (*Chloephaga patagonicha*). 'The geese are very abundant', says Moseley, 'and a wild-goose chase in Elizabeth Island is a very different matter from one at home. When I had shot nine geese I found that I had no light task before me in carrying them to the boat at the

Two Fuegian girls and a boy. Few Fuegians ever had to face a camera, and soon after Challenger's *visit there were none to photograph.*

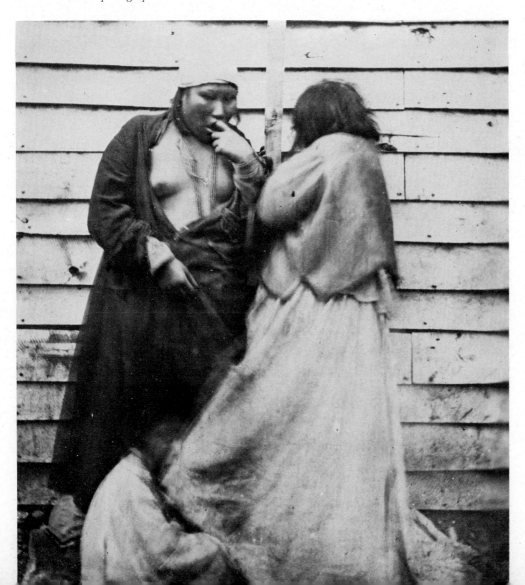

end of the island, over the soft and yielding soil.' He adds a little, rather vague speculation about the history and pre-history of the island: 'Elizabeth Island is fringed
with kitchen middens of large extent, which are full of vast quantities of bones of the
Sea Lion (*Otaria jubata*). Mr Murray excavated some of these mounds, and found
some stone arrow-heads and stone fishing-net sinkers. The island was inhabited at
the time of the early Dutch voyages. Besides the middens there are plenty of small,
shallow, circular excavations with the thrown-out earth heaped around, which
mark the site of Fuegian huts. The human debris is evidently of all ages.' And then,
with the ingenuousness which is so large a part of his charm, he concludes his notes
on Elizabeth Island with the admission that 'the young wild geese, whilst still covered
with black down, run among the grass with astonishing quickness, and are as difficult
to shoot as rabbits'.

On the morning of January 20th, with the advantage of a flood tide beneath her
and a strong breeze behind, *Challenger* sailed swiftly through the notorious Narrows
of the Straits, past a low-lying uninteresting landscape, and came into the Atlantic at
Cape Virgins. She had been lucky in her passage from the Pacific. Slocum is not the
only witness to the difficulty of navigation in Magellan's Straits, and it is interesting
to read, in Hakluyt's *Voyages*, his account of Drake's prodigious enterprise of breach-
ing the farther ocean which Spain then dominated.

> The 21. day (of August) we entered The Streight, which we found to have many turnings,
> and as it were shuttings up, as if there were no passage at all, by meanes whereof we had the
> wind often against us, so that some of the fleete recovering a Cape or point of land, others
> should be forced to turne backe again, and to come to an anchor where they could.
>
> In this streight there be many faire harbors, with store of fresh water, but yet they lacke
> their best commoditie: for the water is there of such depth, that no man shal find ground
> to anchor in, except it bee in some narrow river or corner, or betweene some rocks, so that
> if any extreme blasts or contrary winds do come (whereunto the place is much subject) it
> carieth with it no small danger.
>
> The land on both sides is very huge and mountainous, the lower mountains whereof,
> although they be monstrous and wonderfull to looke upon for their height, yet there are
> others which in height exceed them in a strange maner, reaching themselves above their
> fellowes so high, that betweene them did appeare three regions of cloudes.
>
> These mountaines are covered with snow: at both the Southerly and Easterly partes of
> the streight there are Islands, among which the sea hath his indraught into the streights,
> even as it hath in the main entrance of the freat.
>
> This straight is extreme cold, with frost and snow continually; the trees seeme to stoope
> with the burden of the weather, and yet are greene continually, and many good and sweete
> herbes doe very plentifully grow and increase under them.

Drake was not only the first Englishman to circumnavigate the globe, but the
first Englishman to feed a diminished crew on Steamer Ducks: 'The 24. of August we
arrived at an Island in the streights, where we found great store of foule which could
not fly, of the bignesse of geese, whereof we killed in lesse than one day 3,000 and
victualled ourselves throughly therewith.'

21 From the Falklands to Spithead

As the ship rounded Cape Virgins into the Atlantic, she was not far from the scene of an extraordinary episode in Drake's circumnavigation. In a good harbour called Port St Julian, three days' sail north of the Cape, he had had to enquire into the conduct of Thomas Doughtie, lately in command of a prize-ship. Doughtie was found guilty, partly by his own confession, of intended mutiny and condemned to death. Drake spoke of his great affection for Doughtie, who asked if he might be given Holy Communion. Drake joined him, drank from the cup, and Doughtie 'having embraced our Generall and taken his leave of all the companie, with prayer for the Queenes majestie and our realme, in quiet sort laid his head to the blocke, where he ended his life'. There shows the high temper, the dedicated mind, and ruthless splendour of England in her Elizabethan florescence; and in the comparable period of Victorian expansion there was evidence, in *Challenger* herself, of a dominating spirit that deserves profound respect. It was a sense of duty, rather than a taste for glory, that moved Victoria's Britain, and though the course of duty often coincided with the course of political or economic advantage, the element of duty cannot be disparaged; and in *Challenger*'s continuing voyage, across the familiar waters of the Atlantic, the dictation of duty is starkly apparent. Dredging and sounding – the tedious process of sounding to take the sea's temperature at intervals of twenty or a hundred fathoms – went steadily on, as steadily as when the first thermometers were lowered more than three years before; and almost until Finisterre was seen ahead, that laborious exercise was punctually conducted.

From Cape Virgins she reached the Falklands in three days, and Moseley's comment on them is less than enthusiastic. 'The Falklands,' he writes, 'are a treeless expanse of moorland and bog, and bare and barren rock. Though it was summer, and the islands are in about a corresponding latitude to London, a bitterly cold hailstorm pelted in my face as I was rowed to the shore. The islands are occupied as sheep and cattle runs, and since sheep are found to pay best, they are supplanting the cattle. The mutton is most excellent, but the supply is so far in excess of the small demand, that the Falkland Island Company has a large boiling-down establishment, where their sheep are boiled down for tallow.'

With Lieutenant Channer he rode some sixty miles across the main island 'on which the town of Stanley is situate', and found a population of Scots. 'At every ten miles or so a shepherd's cottage was met with. Usually the shepherd was a Scotchman in the employ of the Falkland Company. Otherwise the entire route was uninhabited. Some of the shepherds are married. They seem well off and were very hospitable. These Scotchmen have almost entirely supplanted the "gauchos" from the mainland, who did all the cattle work at the time of Darwin's visit to the islands. They come out from home entirely unaccustomed to riding, but very soon become most expert with the lasso and bolas, and can ride and break-in the wildest horses.'

Moseley was more interested in the horses than in the shepherds, and they seem to have deserved his interest; by his account they had established a degree of independence within a marked social relationship. Each of the Company's shepherds had eight riding-horses and a pack animal. The horses ran free, but stayed together in a troop which included an old broken-down mare with splayed and overgrown hooves. Though most of the gauchos had gone, some of their language remained, and the old mare was called a *chapina*, the troop a *tropija*, and the *tropija* never deserted the *chapina*. 'A man,' says Moseley, 'after riding thirty or forty miles and about to change horses, merely takes the saddle off, gives the animal's back a rub with his fingers to set the hair free where the saddle-cloth pressed, and lets the horse go. The horse never fails to return to its *tropija* and feeding-ground. We changed horses several times on the route, since we were the guests of the Company and were treated most hospitably. We always simply turned our tired horses loose to find their own way back.'

Small boys and 'some Dipterous insects with rudimentary wings' also aroused his interest. There was a species of gnat (*Tipulidae*) of a like sort to *Diptera*, incapable of flight, found at Kerguelen's Land; and a fly that seemed to be of the same genus as one of the Kerguelen flies which hitherto had been found nowhere else but there and on Marion Island. Some connection between the flora of the Falklands and of Kerguelen's Land had long since been demonstrated, and clearly it was of importance to consider the possibility of other association.

The boys attracted his attention by their ingenuity in inventing a small bolas with which to catch geese. In Brazil, in the early months of the voyage, Moseley had seen *vaqueiros* using the bolas to bring down cattle: it consisted of three heavy balls of stone or iron on thongs of raw hide brought together in a single knot; and a lighter one,

The principal town on the Falkland Islands, Stanley, 'which, in dismal weather', writes Spry, 'we all concurred in regarding as one of the most wretched settlements we had seen for a long time, all the houses . . . appearing most dreary'. Later, more cheerfully, he added that after fourteen days they 'imparted a little gaiety to the colonists, with dances and dinner parties'.

with only two balls, was used to capture ostriches. In the Falklands a miniature bolas had been contrived with the knuckle-bones of cattle as the larger balls, and a lesser bone as the ball which the thrower holds in his hand. The boys 'use the bone bolas for catching wild geese, creeping up to a flock and throwing the bolas at the birds on the wing as they rise. They generally succeed in thus entangling them, and bringing them to the ground, and their mothers always send out their boys when they want a goose.'

There was a tragic incident to mar the ship's stay at these islands whose bleak weather and dismal aspect were mollified, for the sailors, by the abundance of fish that were caught, of geese that were killed, of good mutton at threepence a pound, and of draught ale and porter at threepence a glass. It was, perhaps, threepenny porter that contributed to the death of a sailor called Bush, for when coming off from the shore, late at night in the steam pinnace, he fell overboard. The pinnace was close to the ship, but rain fell so heavily, and so fierce were the constant squalls of wind, that the two men in the bows of the boat saw nothing. On board, however, Lieutenant Carpenter heard the splash – perhaps a despairing shout – and diving from the gangway swam to the man's rescue in a bitterly cold sea. Bush had gone down, but Carpenter found him, pulled him to the surface, and someone in the pinnace pushed out an oar towards them. They were picked up, both exhausted, and Bush, despite long effort by the ship's surgeons to keep him alive, died within a few hours. Lieutenant Carpenter, who had joined the ship at Hong Kong, recovered and lived to be awarded the Albert Medal.

'On March 27th the solitary island of Ascension was in sight.'

The ship sailed for Montevideo, and the cumulative effect of three years at sea – three years of constant service to a microscope, of recurrent activity as an interested tourist – is clearly evident in Moseley's *Notes*. Early in 1873 he had written at great length about all he had seen and heard in Brazil, but in February, 1876, he has nothing at all to say of Uruguay, though in Uruguay 1875 had been 'the terrible year' that concluded a long and miserable period of revolt, internecine battle, and economic distress. Even in Montevideo's English Club the fine marble staircase was pock-marked by bullets – seven men having lately been shot on the stairs – but neither of Montevideo nor of Buenos Aires, only twelve hours away by steamer, has Moseley anything to report. The scientist was still on duty, but the tourist had retired exhausted.

Ten days of unpleasant weather were spent at Montevideo – the ship lay two miles from the shore and strong northerly winds and heavy seas made it difficult to land – and on February 25th she put to sea and headed north-east for the lonely island of Ascension. On March 13th *Challenger* crossed the course of her outward voyage, between Bahia and the Cape of Good Hope, and so completed her circum-navigation of the globe; and fourteen days later Ascension was sighted. An island with a climate notoriously dry, Ascension, at the time of the ship's arrival, was lashed

268

by tropical rain, and its inhabitants, though previously short of water, complained bitterly about the damage done by the downpour. The island had been uninhabited until 1815 when the British, with Napoleon isolated on St Helena, some seven hundred miles to the south-east, thought it prudent to occupy Ascension. Until 1922 it remained within the Admiralty's control, and people born there, deemed to have been born at sea, were registered in the parish of Wapping. It was maintained as a coaling depot when *Challenger* called, but there was no harbour and ships had to anchor offshore. From their decks the view was not inviting: a typical volcanic island, it rose to a height of nearly 3,000 feet, and its lofty, rugged tableland towered above naked rock, cindery hills, and plains of lava.

Its most notable amenity was turtles, and turtlemeat was known as 'island beef'. Close to the dockyard was a turtle pond that accommodated a hundred of them, and a sandy beach was enclosed for the convenience of their females, who dug deep holes in which to lay their leather-shelled eggs that were a little smaller than a billiards ball. In buckets of sea-water the young turtles were often kept as pets by the seamen stationed on the island. Turtlemeat was served twice a week as rations to the garrison.

Moseley, always fascinated by crabs, was pleased to find land crabs that swarmed 'all over this barren and parched volcanic islet. They climb up to the very top of Green Mountain, and the larger ones steal the young rabbits from their holes and devour them. They all go down to the sea in the breeding season.'

There was, too, bird-life of some interest: 'In holes on the sides of the cliff, burrowed in the accumulated guano, nest two kinds of Tropic Birds (*Phaethon aethereus* and *P. flavirostris*). In bracket-like nests, as at St Paul's Rocks, fixed against the lower parts of the cliffs, breeds a species of Noddy (*Anous*), and together with these birds a beautiful snow-white Tern with black eyes (*Gygis candida*), called by the seamen the White Noddy, to distinguish it from the Black Noddy.

'The summit of the rock is flat, and the plateau is covered with guano, in hollows on which nest the Booby (*Sula leucogaster*) and a Gannet (*S. piscatrix*), and the Frigate Bird (*Tachypetes aquila*). The throat of the Frigate Bird hangs in the form of a sort of pouch in front. This pouch is bare of feathers and coloured a bright vermilion, looking as if rubbed over with some bright red powder. The bird is thus very handsome.'

Ascension had briefly given food and shelter to William Dampier, the buccaneer of whom a memory had been revived at Juan Fernandez. In 1701 he was on his way home from a Pacific voyage – he had explored some part of the coasts of Australia and New Guinea – when, off Ascension, his ship foundered. For five weeks Dampier and his crew lived on turtles and goats, until they were rescued by two returning East Indiamen. Dampier's ill luck continued, and his next misfortune was to be court-martialled for cruelty to his lieutenant. He does not seem to have been punished, for a little while later he was in command of two privateers, bound for the South Seas and more disappointment.

At five a.m. on April 3rd *Challenger* sailed for England. The wind was light and variable, there was damp, oppressive heat off the coast of Africa, but work continued – three dredgings, four soundings, eight serial temperature-readings – and on the 18th the ship anchored off Porto Grande, St Vincent, in the Cape Verde Islands. There she lay till the 26th, while the steam pinnace went off to dredge in shallow water. The last chapter of the voyage was tediously prolonged, for soon after leaving the tropics the wind hung persistently in the north, and on May 20th, when the coast of Spain was sighted, it was necessary to put into Vigo for coal. There was no further difficulty: some squalls off Finisterre, fair weather in the Bay, and the bright light on Ushant pointed to Eddystone and the Start, Portland Bill and the Needles; and before darkness on the 24th *Challenger* anchored at Spithead.

'The objects of the Expedition have been fully and faithfully carried out', wrote Wyville Thomson. 'We always kept in view that to explore the conditions of the deep sea was the primary object of our mission, and throughout the voyage we took every possible opportunity of making a deep-sea observation. Between our departure from Sheerness on December 7th, 1872, and our arrival at Spithead on May 24th, 1876, we traversed a distance of 68, 890 nautical miles, and at intervals as nearly uniform as possible we established 362 observing stations.'

The voyage had not been accomplished without casualties – casualties had to be expected on a voyage of that duration – and when the crew were paid off at Chatham 144 remained of the 243 who had embarked. Only seven had died: twenty-six had been invalided out of the service or left ashore in hospital; and five had gone with Captain Nares on his expedition to the Arctic. Most of the casualties were due to desertion, and newly opened gold-fields in Australia, diamond-mines in South Africa, were largely to blame. Sixty-one men had vanished in pursuit of riches.

RIGHT: *Carefully labelled,* The Challenger Collection *of marine specimens and deep sea deposits is housed in twenty cabinets at the British Museum (Natural History).*

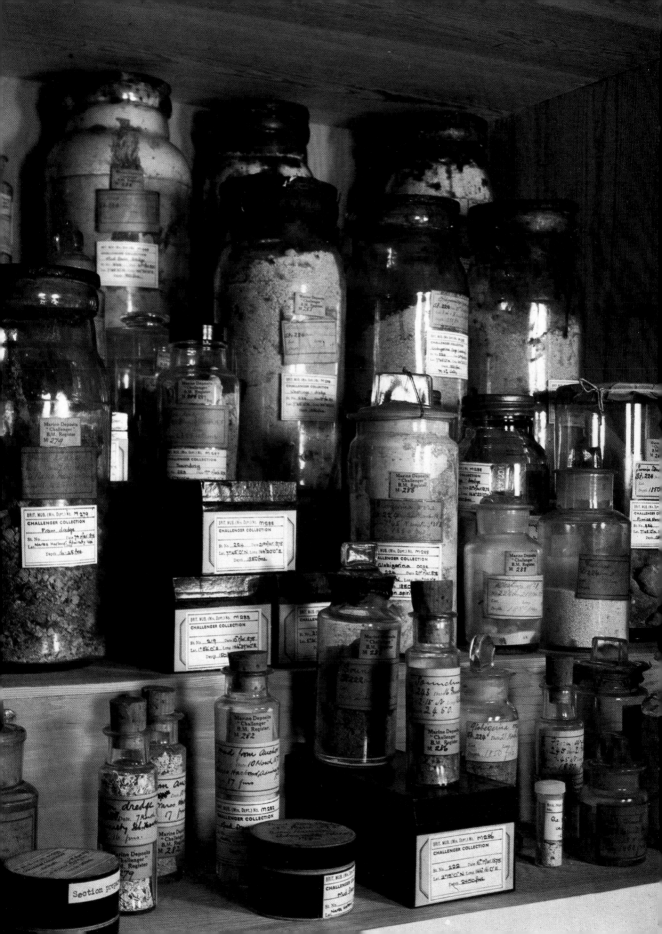

Postscript:

Achievements of the voyage

The voyage had been successful, but the work of the expedition had only begun, and to complete it the sea-borne naturalists – the explorers of the depths, the collectors who had filled storehouses and many laboratories with their discoveries – would have to recruit a great company of auxiliaries, specialists learned in their own subject, to write in detail *On the Procellariidae*, *On the Hydroida*, *On the Copepoda*, on *Meteorological Observations*, and scores of other topics. (In an appendix to the first volume of the final Report there are several pages that catalogue the names of almost a hundred scholars who contributed to it.) And even when that work was done, there would still be the ponderous task of publishing it. Fifty large volumes, each measuring about thirteen inches by ten and thick as a family bible, would be required to hold the cargo of knowledge that *Challenger* had brought home, and in the event – by accident or unforeseen difficulty – the greater part of that last labour would be shouldered by John Murray. Some notes on what he did to preserve the cargo, and make it available to scientists throughout the world, will conclude this postcript.

Mention must also be made of the several books, written by members of the expedition, which have been used in putting together the present narrative. Foremost among them is Wyville Thomson's account, published in 1877 in two handsome volumes, well illustrated, and entitled *Voyage of the Challenger, Atlantic I and II*. It dealt only with what was seen and captured in the Atlantic, in the early and concluding months of the voyage, but at the beginning of Volume I, and the end of

LEFT: *Sir John Murray, a portrait by Sir George Reid, 1913.*

Volume II, there are clear and useful statements of the drill or routine of oceanic search, and of what, in Thomson's first assessment, had been achieved when *Challenger* returned to Spithead.

Thomson says again that on a voyage of nearly 69,000 nautical miles 362 observing stations had been established, and 'at each of these stations the following observations were made, so far as circumstances would permit. The position of the stations having been ascertained:

1   The exact depth was determined.

2   A sample of the bottom averaging from one oz to one lb in weight was recovered by means of the sounding instrument, which was provided with a tube and disengaging weights.

3   A sample of the bottom water was procured for physical and chemical examination.

4   The bottom temperature was determined by a registering thermometer.

5   At most stations a fair sample of the bottom fauna was procured by means of the dredge or trawl.

6   At most stations the fauna of the surface and of intermediate depths was examined by the use of the tow-net variously adjusted.

7   At most stations a series of temperature observations were made at different depths from the surface to the bottom.

8   At many stations samples of sea-water were obtained from different depths.

9   In all cases atmospheric and other meteorological conditions were carefully observed and noted.

10 The direction and rate of the surface current was determined.

11 At a few stations an attempt was made to ascertain the direction and rate of movement of the water at different depths.

He goes on to say: 'The somewhat critical experiment of associating a party of civilians, holding to a certain extent an independent position, with the naval staff of a man-of-war, has for once been successful. Captain Nares and Captain Thomson both fully recognized that the expedition was intended for scientific purposes. . . . All the naval officers, without exception, assisted the civilians in every way in their power, and in the most friendly spirit; if I wished anything done I had only to consider who was the man, naval or civilian, who was likely to do it best; and the consequence has been that with the entire sanction of Captain Nares and Captain Thomson, the parties sent to camp out or detailed for any special service have always been mixed, to the great advantage I believe of all concerned.' And when the voyage was still young, and the ship put in to Lisbon, he makes the genial note that 'there are many things in Lisbon to interest 'philosophers' as our naval friends call us – not I fear from the proper feeling of respect, but rather with good-natured indulgence – because we are fond of talking vaguely about "evolution", and otherwise holding on to loose ropes; and because our education has been sadly neglected in the matter of

'A good portly man, i' faith, and a corpulent; of a cheerful look, a pleasing eye, and a most noble carriage; and, as I think, his age some fifty, or, by'r lady, inclining to three-score; and now I remember me, his name is . . . .' (*Henry IV, 1st Part, Act I, Scene 4*).

Charles Wyville Thomson, caricatured and characterized by Herbert Swire.

cringles and toggles and grummets, and other implements by means of which England holds her place among the nations'.

Then, towards the end of Volume II, he records his tentative judgement that 'The first general survey of the deep-sea collections, undertaken with a knowledge of the circumstances under which the specimens were procured, justify us, I believe, in arriving at the following general conclusions:

1 Animal life is present on the bottom of the ocean at all depths.

2 Animal life is not nearly so abundant at extreme, as it is at more moderate depths; but, as well-developed members of all the marine invertebrate classes occur at all depths, this appears to depend more upon certain causes affecting the composition of the bottom deposits, and of the bottom water involving the supply of oxygen, and of carbonate of lime, phosphate of lime, and other materials necessary for their development, than upon any of the conditions immediately connected with depth.

3 There is every reason to believe that the fauna of deep water is confined principally to two belts, one at and near the surface, and the other on and near the bottom; leaving an intermediate zone in which the larger animal forms, vertebrate and invertebrate, are nearly or entirely absent.

4 Although all the principal marine invertebrate groups are represented in the abyssal fauna, the relative proportion in which they occur is peculiar. Thus Mollusca in all their classes, Brachyurous Crustacea, and Annelida, are on the whole scarce; while Echinodermata and Porifera greatly preponderate.

5 Depths beyond 500 fathoms are inhabited throughout the world by a fauna which presents generally the same features throughout; deep-sea genera have usually a cosmopolitan extension, while species are either universally distributed, or, if they differ in remote localities, they are markedly representative; that is to say, they bear to one another a close genetic relation.

6 The abyssal fauna is certainly more nearly related than the fauna of shallower water to the fauna of the tertiary and secondary periods, although this relation is not so close as we were at first inclined to expect, and only a comparatively small number of types supposed to have become extinct have yet been discovered.

7 The most characteristic abyssal forms, and those which are most nearly related to extinct types, seem to occur in greatest abundance and of largest size in the southern ocean; and the general character of the fauna of the Atlantic and of the Pacific gives the impression that the migration of species has taken place in a northerly direction, that is to say, in a direction corresponding with the movement of the cold under-current.

8 The general character of the abyssal fauna resembles most that of the shallower water of high northern and southern latitudes, no doubt because the conditions of temperature, on which the distribution of animals mainly depends, are nearly similiar.

Wyville Thomson's preface to the two volumes opens with the assertion that they 'consist chiefly of an abstract of the less technical portions of my own journal'; but one does not go very far before discovering that his notion of what was 'less technical'

Before and after the leap.

A respectable old party.

rarely coincides with a layman's opinion. Typical of his writing – always clear, sometimes vivid, but too often assuming that what he knew was known to all – is part of a description of Tristan da Cunha: 'While the party on hand were struggling among the tussocks and penguins, and gaining an experience of the vigour of spontaneous life, animal and vegetable, which they are not likely soon to forget, the ship took a cruise round the island to enable the surveyors to put in the coast line; and in the afternoon the hauls of the dredge were taken in 100 and 150 fathoms. A large quantity of things were procured of all groups, the most prominent a fine species of *Primnoa*, many highly coloured *Gorgoniae*, and a very elegant *Mopsea* or some closely allied form. *Lophohelia prolifera* or a very similar species was abundant, associated with an *Amphihelia* and a fine *Coenocyathus*. Hydroids and sponges were in considerable number tangled in masses with calcareous and horny Bryozoa. There were a few star-fishes, and a very few Mollusca. The whole assemblage resembled a good deal the produce of a haul in shallow water off the Mediterranean coast of Morocco.

'On the following day we crossed over, sounding and dredging on our way, to within a mile and a half of the west shore of the Island of Tristan. A haul in 1,000 fathoms gave us somewhat to our surprise some most typical samples of the common *Echinus flemingii*, along with *Ophiomusium lymani* and *Rhizocrinus*. We dredged a second time as we was nearing Tristan at 550 fathoms, and took one or two specimens of a species of *Antedon*, some corals the same as those off Nightingale Island, and a quantity of Bryozoa. In the evening we set all plain sail, and with a favouring breeze from the north-west, proceeded on our voyage towards the Cape.'

Without considerable reservation, Wyville Thomson's narrative cannot be recommended for general reading; but Moseley's *Notes* unequivocally can because Moseley, who was as dedicated a naturalist as Thomson, also had a perpetually inquisitive mind that looked for more. Of the naval officers who wrote accounts of their voyage, Campbell was an invaluable contributor to this narrative, for his letters are filled with a bubbling enthusiasm that often rises to brisk and vivid description; and Herbert Swire, a very capable young officer, succeeded in writing a sensible book which, most pleasantly illustrated, can now be bought for an extravagant price. Wild, the artist, wrote a mediocre account, redeemed by some charming pictures, and W. J. J. Spry, an Engineer Sub-Lieutenant, published, in repeated editions, a detailed, conscientious story whose remarkable popularity is difficult to explain except on the assumption that in the 1870s a large number of people were hungry for information, and willing to pay for it though it was conveyed, for the most part, in the flattest of guide-book prose.

There is, on page 281, a bibliography of these narratives, and no more need be said of them here. He who was initially chosen as editor of the Report – the official, fifty-volume Report – was Sir Charles Wyville Thomson, who died in March, 1882. He had drafted the first volume, but his professional work and increasing ill-health had prevented him from preparing a manuscript for the press. His death necessitated the appointment of a new editor, and the Government of the day nominated John Murray. Accepting responsibility, Murray consulted his former colleagues in the *Challenger*, as to the proper course to adopt, and it was finally decided that the first volume of the Narrative of the Cruise should be undertaken jointly, and 'should embrace as far as possible a general account of the Scientific Results of the Expedition'. That volume – which, in fact, became two volumes, associated as Parts I and II – was published by Her Majesty's Stationery Office, in 1885, and its authors were named as Staff-Commander T. H. Tizard, RN, Professor H. N. Moseley, FRS, Mr J. Y. Buchanan, MA, and Mr John Murray, PhD, Members of the Expedition.

Now must be told something of the circumstances which brought about Murray's conclusive importance in ensuring publication of the Report in the amplitude that was finally achieved; and some quotations from several monographs published after his death, in a motor-car accident in 1914, may, as succinctly as possible, contribute a final page to a tale of unexampled scientific interest. Murray, it should be noted, at no time sought publicity for himself. He permitted only the barest mention of his own part in the affairs of the voyage. He deprecated all personal detail, and forbade his family to keep letters. He used to say it was a man's work that counted, not his private opinions.

'Sir John was never a man who could appreciate or tolerate the red tape of Government Offices, and hence, when in time the Treasury turned restive, he spent his own money bringing out the volumes of the Report. He liked to have a hundred per cent of his own way, and very often got it; if not, he would, as a rule, withdraw from the enterprise. . . . Later in his career he became comparatively rich, and some of these riches he spent in promoting the subject to which he had devoted his life.' (*Sir John Murray, A Great Oceanographer* by A. E. Shipley.)

'One episode in Murray's life furnishes a good example of the unexpected practical benefits that may result from the pursuit of pure science. While cruising in the regions adjacent to the island of Java, the nets of the *Challenger* collected some bits of phosphate. A careful examination of these objects convinced Murray that they must have been formed on land. Subsequent search for their origin, under Murray's auspices, led to the discovery of the phosphate deposits of Christmas Island. The island was annexed to Great Britain, and a company under Murray's presidency developed a highly prosperous mine. Some years before his death the company had already paid in royalties, for the protection of the English flag, more than the entire cost of the *Challenger* expedition.' (*Sir John Murray,* by G. R. Agassiz.)

'In 1895 the Challenger Report was completed. It discussed with full detail of text and illustrations the currents, temperatures, depths and constituents of the oceans, the topography of the sea bottom, the geology and biology of its covering and the animal life of the abyssal waters. The report consisted of fifty large, royal quarto volumes of which seven were written largely or entirely by Murray. The last two of the series were his own summary of the scientific results in which he described the completed work as "the greatest advance in the knowledge of our planet since the celebrated geographical discoveries of the fifteenth and sixteenth centuries".

'The authors of the reports, many of whom had spent years on the work, received nothing more than a copy of the publication or a small honorarium to cover their expenses. In further appreciation it was resolved that a Challenger medal be struck. The Treasury refused to pay for it and John Murray had the medal designed and executed at his own expense and himself sent replicas to those who had shared in the expedition or in the preparation of the Report. He himself was honoured by the Royal Society when he was admitted Fellow in 1896. Official commendation by the Government was deferred until 1898, when the Queen conferred on John Murray the rank of KCB in recognition of his outstanding contributions to science. (*Sir John Murray, A Chronic Student* by W. N. Boog Watson).

It should be noted, finally, that Murray's introductory notes to the first double volume of the Report are dated from the Challenger Office, 32 Queen Street, Edinburgh, on March 6th, 1885. Edinburgh University, the Royal Societies of London and Edinburgh, and the Royal Navy can all claim credit for *Challenger's* momentous voyage, but he who ultimately gave to the world her great scientific cargo was Sir John Murray.

The Challenger *medal, actual size, made of silver. This side commemorates the voyage, the verso the work of the scientists who helped to produce the* Report.

Bibliography

The Report of the Scientific Results of the Exploring Voyage of HMS Challenger during the years 1873–1876 50 Vols. London, Edinburgh and Dublin, 1885–95. (Buchanan, J. Y., Moseley, H. N., Murray, J., Tizard, T. H., *Narrative of the Voyage*, contained in Volume One, parts 1 and 2.)

Boog-Watson, W. N., *Sir John Murray, a Chronic Student*. University of Edinburgh Journal, Autumn 1967.

Campbell, Lord George, *Log-Letters from The Challenger*. London 1877.

Moseley, H. N., *Notes by a Naturalist on HMS Challenger*. London 1880.

Spry, W. J. J., *The Cruise of HMS Challenger*. London 1877.

Swire, Herbert, *The Voyage of the Challenger*. Two volumes, limited edition, London 1937.

Wild, J. J., *At Anchor*. London 1878.

Wyville Thomson, Sir C., *Voyage of the Challenger, The Atlantic*. Two volumes, London 1877.

Where *The Report* is quoted below amongst the sources, this refers to *The Report of the Scientific Results of the Exploring Voyage of* HMS *Challenger during the years 1873–1876*, 50 Volumes, 1885–95.

Title page: HMS *Challenger* in Dock in Bermuda. From Prof. Moseley's Albums, Dept of Zoology, Univ. of Oxford.

10 Robert Jameson. The Mansell Collection.

11 HMS *Challenger* shortening sail. From *The Report*, Narrative part 2.

13 Professor Edward Forbes. Daguerrotype. Scottish National Portrait Gallery.

14 LEFT: Professor Charles Wyville Thomson. From a special edition of *The Cruise of* HMS *Challenger* by W. J. J. Spry. RIGHT: Dr W. B. Carpenter. Both from the Mansell Collection.

15 Captain G. S. Nares. Ronan Picture Library.

16 Chemical laboratory on board HMS *Challenger*. The Mansell Collection.

17 John Murray. From Prof. Moseley's Albums, Dept of Zoology, Univ. of Oxford.

18 Officers and Professor Wyville Thomson aboard HMS *Challenger*. From Prof. Moseley's Albums, Department of Zoology, University of Oxford.

19 LEFT: J. J. Wild. Self-portrait from *At Anchor*. *Photo: Michael Holford*. RIGHT: W. J. J. Spry. The Mansell Collection.

20 Prof. H. N. Moseley. Alphabet and Image.

21 H. N. Moseley's cabin aboard HMS *Challenger*. Watercolour by H. N. Moseley from Prof. Moseley's Albums, Department of Zoology, University of Oxford.

22 HMS *Challenger*. An engraving from the Illustrated London News, 1872.

23 Shipping in the Tagus, Lisbon. From *The Cruise of* HMS *Challenger* by W. J. J. Spry. *Photo: Michael Holford*.

29 *Umbellula thomsoni*. Drawing from *The Report*, Narrative part 1.

30 LEFT: The dredge. RIGHT: The current drag and marker buoy. Both from Ronan Picture Library.

31 The beam trawl under repair. From *The Report*, Narrative part 1.

32 HMS *Challenger* at St. Thomas. From Prof. Moseley's Albums, Department of Zoology, University of Oxford.

33 Negroes at St Thomas. Cartoon by Lt Channer from R. R. A. Richards' Journal, Archives of the Royal Geographical Society. *Photo: Derrick Witty*.

34 Prof. Wyville Thomson and Dr Suhm at Bermuda. The Mansell Collection.

35 Dr Moseley at Bermuda. The Mansell Collection.

36 Woman wearing shawl with hood at Horta. From *Notes by a Naturalist on board* HMS *Challenger* by H. N. Moseley.

37 Porto Praya, Cape Verde Islands. From *Voyage de la Corvette L'Astrolabe*. National Maritime Museum, Greenwich.

38 Sailors with a shark. From *The Report*, Narrative part 1. *Photo: Michael Holford*.

39 Nest of a Noddy at St Paul's Rocks. From *Notes by a Naturalist on board* HMS *Challenger* by H. N. Moseley.

40 St Paul's Rocks from the East. Illustrated London News.

41 HMS *Challenger* made fast to St Paul's Rocks. Illustrated London News.

42 Convict fisherman, Fernando Noronha. Cartoon by Lt Channer from R. R. A. Richards' Journal, Archives of the Royal Geographical Society. *Photo: Derrick Witty*.

43 The Peak of Fernando Noronha, sketched from the deck of HMS *Challenger*. From *The Report*, Narrative part 1. *Photo: Michael Holford*.

44 Ships at anchor, Bahia. The Challenger Collection. British Museum (Natural History).

45 *Bathypterois longipes*. From *The Report*, Narrative part 1. *Photo: Michael Holford*.

46 Cricket Match at Campo Grande, San Salvador (Bahia) Brazil. From '*At Anchor*' by J. J. Wild. *Photo: Michael Holford*.

47 *Ipnops murrayi*. From *The Report*, Narrative part 1. *Photo: Michael Holford*.

48 Peter Green, head-man of Tristan da Cunha. The Mansell Collection.

49 Tristan da Cunha. From *The Cruise of* HMS *Challenger* by W. J. J. Spry. *Photo: Michael Holford*.

50 Tristan da Cunha. From *The Report*, Narrative part 1. *Photo: Michael Holford*.

51 Housebuilding at Tristan da Cunha. From *The Report*, Narrative part 1.

52 Rock Hopper penguins. Sketch by H. N. Moseley. From Prof. Moseley's Albums. Dept of Zoology, Univ. of Oxford.

55 Scientist kicking penguins. From *The Report*, Narrative part 1. *Photo: Michael Holford*.

56 Penguins' high street. From *The Report*, Narrative part 1. *Photo: Michael Holford*.

57 Nightingale Island from the south. From *The Report*, Narrative part 1. *Photo: Michael Holford*.

58 Party of sailors from HMS *Challenger* with the brothers Stoltenkoff. From Prof. Moseley's Albums, Department of Zoology, University of Oxford.

59 Table Mountain, Cape of Good Hope. From *The Cruise of* HMS *Challenger* by W. J. J. Spry. *Photo: Michael Holford*.

60 Signboard at Farmer Peck's. From R. R. A. Richards' Journal, Archives of the Royal Geographical Society. *Photo: Derrick Witty*.

61 *Scotoplanes globosa*. From *The Report*, Narrative part 1. *Photo: Alphabet and Image*.

63 *Lithocoronis challengeri*. From *The Report*, Narrative part 1. *Photo: Michael Holford*.

64 *Peripatus capensis*. From *The Report*, Narrative part 1. *Photo: Michael Holford*.

65 *Salenia hastigera*. From *The Report*, Narrative part 1. *Photo: Michael Holford*.

68 Radiolaria. From *The Report on the Radiolaria*. *Photo: Alphabet and Image*.

69 LEFT: *Discoaster brouweri* Tan. Calcareous organisms, now extinct, probably related to the coccoliths. The species illustrated is from the Lower Pliocene (zone N.19, about 5 million years ago). It was isolated from an Indian Ocean core, collected from a depth of 3,660 metres. BM Specimen No. 1968,0,240. Magnification: × 4,680.
RIGHT: *Globigerinoides sacculifera* (Brady). The photograph shows the structural details of the final chamber of a common planktonic species of foraminifera. The pores and the primary and secondary spines are clearly visible. From a vertical plankton tow, 125–0 metres, Indian Ocean. BM Specimen No. 1970,0,64. Magnification: × 1000. Both stereoscan photographs taken by H. A. Buckley, British Museum (Natural History).

Index